T0301644

The Dynamics of Economic Growth

The Dynamics of Economic Growth

Policy Insights from Comparative Analyses in Asia

Vu Minh Khuong

National University of Singapore

Edward Elgar
Cheltenham, UK • Northampton, MA, USA

Published by
Edward Elgar Publishing Limited
The Lypiatts
15 Lansdown Road
Cheltenham
Glos GL50 2JA
UK

Edward Elgar Publishing, Inc.
William Pratt House
9 Dewey Court
Northampton
Massachusetts 01060
USA

A catalogue record for this book
is available from the British Library

Library of Congress Control Number: 2013944947

This book is available electronically in the ElgarOnline.com
Economics Subject Collection, E-ISBN 978 0 85793 964 7

ISBN 978 0 85793 963 0

Typeset by Servis Filmsetting Ltd, Stockport, Cheshire
Printed and bound in Great Britain by T.J. International Ltd, Padstow

Contents

Foreword

The emergence of Asia from the underdevelopment that persisted until the middle of the last century is the great economic achievement of our time. This has created a new model for economic growth built on globalization and the patient accumulation of human and non-human capital. Economic commentators, especially those outside Asia, have been reluctant to recognize the new paradigm for economic growth that originated in Asia, since this would acknowledge the failure of Western ideas that still greatly predominate in the literature on economic growth and development.

A common task facing Asian economies has been to overcome the legacies of failed policies that have arisen from very diverse histories. This has required strong and sustained leadership in both authoritarian and democratic settings. The new Asian growth paradigm places a premium on skillful management by public and private authorities. The performance of the leading countries in developing this paradigm – Japan, then the Asian Tigers, and China and now India – has changed the course of economic development in Asia and around the world.

Vu Minh Khuong's book is the first attempt to bring all the tools of quantitative economics to bear on the Asian growth model. Through his own research, Vu has overcome the lack of key empirical data that has stymied previous efforts to quantify the characteristic features of Asian economies. Existing systems of national accounts were developed for stabilization of advanced economies through monetary and fiscal policies. Building on the contributions of Lawrence Lau and Alwyn Young, the pioneers of quantitative research on the Asian economies, Vu has dispelled the mysteries that have surrounded the debate over Asian growth for the past several decades.

Vu documents the characteristic features of Asian growth – surprise, speed, and scale. Asian growth continues to *surprise* economists schooled in the experience of the industrialized economies of Western Europe and North America. How did the extremely poor countries develop the strategies that have led them to surpass the advanced economies held up as models by economists outside Asia? The *speed* of Asian growth is unprecedented and cannot be explained by any simple tweaking of standard models of economic growth. The sheer *scale* of China and India at first appears to be a barrier to growth and then re-emerges as an advantage in the crucial process of replication of existing technologies that predominates in economic development.

Vu continues by identifying the common elements in successful strategies for Asian economic growth. These begin with opening the economy to imports and exports to benefit from the comparative advantages through increased trade. The second step is to create a business environment that is favorable to saving and investment, including foreign direct investment. The final and most challenging task for a successful growth strategy is to mobilize labor resources and initiate the long and arduous process of accumulating human capital through education and experience.

Asia has turned its relative backwardness into a source of numerous advantages. At the outset of development, entrenched interests are few and relatively feeble, so that a small cadre of determined leaders can change the direction of economic policy. The opening of Asian economies to trade and foreign investment has had sufficient impact to overcome inertia and build up momentum. Later in the development process, the task of political leadership is to maintain high incremental returns from investment against the forces that could generate sharply diminishing returns. Far-sighted strategies for human capital accumulation are crucial in maintaining the steady rise in levels of technical sophistication and managerial complexity that sustains economic growth.

Japan, the United States, and other industrialized countries will remain far in advance of China and India in terms of per capita GDP, but the experience of Japan and the four Asian Tigers tells us the advanced economies can emerge outside Europe and North America. It is only a matter of time until these developments spread to China, India, and the other major countries of Developing Asia, but this will be measured in decades rather than years. There is now an opportunity to accelerate the process of adjustment to the New World Economic Order in Japan, Europe, and the United States. This will require rethinking approaches to business, the economy, and the political system.

We also need new economic tools to deal with the issues that arise in understanding the Asian model. The growth strategy of many advanced economies emphasizes innovation, which has been quite satisfactory for the past decade, but neglects investment in human and non-human capital, which continues to fall. For example, given the pre-eminence of Japan in many areas of information technology, it is surprising that Japan continues to lag in applications of IT equipment and software. This reflects the long-term policy of protecting the sectors where these applications have been most profitable outside Japan, namely, trade and services.

A thorough renovation of our national accounts is now underway and similar revisions of our statistical systems are taking place around the world, especially in Asia. The World KLEMS Initiative is a worldwide effort to supply the 'missing half' of the national accounts by providing data on supplies of capital (K), labor (L), energy (E), materials (M), and services (S). This is supported by leading statistical agencies and research organizations throughout Asia and around the world. We will be learning much more about economic growth as we come to terms with the Asian model described in Vu Minh Khuong's prescient book.

Dale W. Jorgenson
Samuel W. Morris University Professor
Department of Economics, Harvard University
Cambridge, Massachusetts
May 12, 2013

Preface

Asia is an exciting example of the rapid transformation of a poor and backward region into a region of prosperity and modernization. Sixty years ago, when Asia was burdened by wars, ideological struggles, and severe poverty, no one could imagine its current development success, which is characterized by prevailing peace, openness, and remarkable economic achievements. Although it remains difficult to predict what Asia will look like in sixty years, it is possible to propose a scenario in which the lower-income countries in the region will follow the development model that has brought many countries to remarkable successes. If this scenario materializes, Asia's prospects will be brilliant. There will be hundreds of cities like Singapore across Asia, from China to India, from Indonesia to Pakistan, and from Vietnam to Bangladesh. In this imaginative picture, although it is not perfect, Singapore can be used as a symbol of Asia's future prospect because it has the three prominent features that character- ize the development trends of the world in the twenty-first century. The first feature is embracement of globalization. Singapore is a global city that is highly international in culture and deep in economic integration with the region and the world. Second, Singapore's development is sus- tainable because of its good governance based on the excellent combina- tion between the effectiveness of government and the efficiency of market forces. Third, Singapore has developed a robust learning capability that fosters learning through four typical channels of organizational learning: competency acquisition, experimentation, benchmarking against the best models, and continuous improvement.

In offering this prediction of the future of Asia in the next sixty years, one should consider the prospects of both struggling countries and suc- cessful nations. For struggling countries, it is worth recalling the remark that was offered sixty years ago by Arthur Lewis, an economics Nobel lau- reate and a leading economist in the field of economic development, with respect to the crucial role of national leadership and aspiration:

> It is possible for a nation to take a new turn if it is fortunate enough to have the right leadership at the right time [. . .] All nations have opportunities which they may grasp if only they can summon up the courage and the will. (Lewis, 1955, p. 418)

With regard to successful nations, one should appreciate the saying by Mencius more than 2000 years ago: 'We survive in adversity and perish in ease and comfort.' This coincides with the observation of Victor Hugo, one of the greatest French writers of the nineteenth century: 'Adversity makes men, and prosperity makes monsters.' The statements as such indicate that currently successful countries will also be confronting formidable challenges that may pose obstacles to their prosperity in the next sixty years. Therefore, it is essential for policy makers in all countries, regardless of how successful or struggling today, to be most thoughtful, knowledgeable, and devoted in carrying out their duty to create the future of their nations.

Economic development is a profound transformational process that requires many decades to bear its true fruits. Economic growth and governance quality are important indicators that can be used to capture the progress in the economic development process. As a transformational process, the development of a nation is driven by two forces: emotion and enlightenment. Emotion is shaped by aspiration, anxiety, and a sense of responsibility that a country's leadership can summon for the nation. Enlightenment is ensured by an open mindset that is free of dogmatism, an eagerness to learn, and a strong outward orientation to understand the world better. Emotion and enlightenment are akin to the two wings of a bird. A nation can be as mighty as an eagle in its economic development if it is strong in both wings: emotion and enlightenment. However, in reality, most countries are weak in at least one wing, frequently in the enlightenment wing. The absence of enlightenment can cost a nation dearly, especially when its emotion is strong. The cases of pre-reform China, pre-reform Vietnam, and North Korea can serve as vivid examples.

Asia is not only a great story of economic development, but also a convincing model of the belief that lower-income countries can learn a great deal to accelerate their catching-up endeavors. Asia is not only a valuable case derived from the past but also an exciting example of how nations blaze their own paths into the future. It is important to study Asia's development experiences both because it provides valuable insights and because the region is a major force that is shaping the future of the world economy.

This book is written with the motivation of providing essential insights into economic development in Asia and its growth model. The book provides a comprehensive and in-depth examination of economic growth in Developing Asia during the last two decades (1990–2010). With the insights from this investigation, the book sketches a strategic policy framework for the development strategies that successful Asian economies have adopted to realize remarkable achievements in their economic catch-up endeavors. The book will be a helpful resource for policy makers in developing countries, especially in Asia, and for students and researchers who want to develop true comprehension of the nature and dynamics of economic development in the region.

In writing this book, I am deeply grateful to Professor Dale Jorgenson for his extremely valuable advice and support. Every chapter of this book has a deep imprint of his enlightening comments and suggestions. I am much indebted to Dean Kishore Mahbubani of the Lee Kuan Yew School of Public Policy (LKYSPP), National University of Singapore, for his indispensable advice and encouragement of my work on this book project. His vision of the future of Asia and the mission of the LKYSPP in transforming the region toward prosperity is indeed a great source of motivation in writing this book.

I would like to express my deep gratitude to John Ross, who has worked closely with me on this book since its conception. John's thoughtful comments and generous support undoubtedly contributed much to sharpening the focus and presentation of the book. I owe much gratitude to Mun Ho for his rigor and sharpness in reviewing the manuscript, which helped me to improve significantly the clarity and effectiveness of the book. I am thankful to Koji Nomura for his valuable exchange of ideas and data when I worked on this book.

I acknowledge with deep gratitude the valuable encouragement and support of Frank Gollop, Lawrence Lau, Dwight Perkins, Barbara Fraumeni, Justin Yifu Lin, Edward Robinson, T.N. Srinivasan, Marcel Timmer, Bart van Ark, and David Weil. I have learned a great deal from their works on economic growth and development in Asia.

I am very much thankful to Nguyen Chi Hieu for his outstanding research assistance. His contribution to this book involved not only his tireless efforts and solid analytical skills but also his deep passion for assisting in enhancing the value of this book. I would also like to thank Alvin L. Diaz for his valuable research assistance at various stages of this project.

I would also want to take this opportunity to express my deep appreciation for the excellent support that the LKYSPP has provided for my research. My research for this book is supported by my Academic Research Fund, provided by LKYSPP. I also want to acknowledge the support that Asian Competitiveness Institute (ACI) provided to me when I worked on this book. I am indebted to all friends and colleagues at LKYSPP who have given me so much help and support. Among them, I would particularly like to express my special thanks to Kenneth Paul Tan, Kanti Prasad Bajpai, Astrid Tuminez, Suzaina Abdul Kadir, Elizabeth Ong, Agnes Tan Swee Tin, May Phoi May Kong, Jeannie Straussman, Jason Yuen Wee Jing, and Cassandra Lee Wan Jing.

Throughout any endeavors I have undertaken, my family is always the main source of my energy and commitment. My parents, my wife, and my son always share my deep aspiration to witness Asia and the world prospering in peace, partnership, and enlightenment. I am deeply grateful to my wife for her unconditional support and earnest encouragement throughout my hard work on this book project.

Abbreviations

ADB	Asian Development Bank
ALP	Average Labor Productivity
ANRC	Average Net Ranks Changed
APO	Asian Productivity Organization
CAGR	Compound Annual Growth Rate
FDI	Foreign Direct Investment
GDP	Gross Domestic Product
GFCF	Gross Fixed Capital Formation
ICP	International Comparison Program
ICT	Information and Communication Technology
IMF	International Monetary Fund
NB	Net Balance
OECD	Organisation for Economic Co-operation and Development
PPP	Purchasing Power Parity
ROW	Rest of World
TED	Conference Board's Total Economy Database
TFP	Total Factor Productivity
UN	United Nations
UNCTAD	United Nations Conference on Trade and Development
UNDP	United Nations Development Programme
WB	World Bank
WDI	World Development Indicators
WTO	World Trade Organization

1. Introduction

Economic growth has rightly attracted major attention from economists and policy makers. It is vital from the point of view of human welfare, and challenging intellectually, to attempt to answer basic questions related to the past, present, and future performance of nations in economic development: Why are some countries rich while others are poor? What factors have enabled some poor countries to achieve miraculous success in catching up with rich countries? Is the disparity in per capita income between rich and poor countries decreasing? Addressing these questions requires rigorous theories and robust empirical studies. In these efforts, one needs not only well-established concepts but also in-depth knowledge of prominent development stories, not only knowledge of development patterns in the past events but also the current dynamics that are shaping the trends in the world's future economic growth.

Of these questions, none is more important than what has produced remarkable economic growth in Asia. In a single lifetime, countries have been lifted from rural underdevelopment to the living standards of developed economies. According to World Bank (2013), if China can complete this process in the next 20–30 years, the number of people living in high-income economies would more than double.[1] If India could achieve the same, then for the first time in modern human history, the majority of the world's population would enjoy high-income living standards, with all the immense benefits in human welfare that would follow from this. The Asian Development Bank's *Asia 2050* report, published in 2011, described a bold vision and a convincing prediction that if trends of the past three decades continue, in 2050 Asia will become a prosperous region with an average annual income of $45,800 in purchasing power parity (PPP) terms. This far exceeds the predicted annual income of $37,300 for the world average (ADB, 2011). This is remarkable because the current income levels of most countries in the region, especially the most populous countries, are still well below the world average.[2]

---

[1]   The 'China 2030' report jointly prepared by the World Bank and the Development Research Center of the Government of China sets forth a vision of China becoming a modern, harmonious, and creative high-income society by 2030.
[2]   In 2010, the income level relative to the world average was 67 per cent for China and 30 per cent for India (see Table 1.1).

1.1   THE ASIAN ECONOMIC GROWTH SAGA

Asia is a remarkable story of economic growth and catching up. The story began with the astonishing transformation of Japan since the Meiji Restoration reforms in the late nineteenth century and the country's revival from defeat and poverty to its position as the world's second largest economic power only a few decades after the end of World War II. The Asian success has gone beyond a story to become a model of development as the four Asian Tiger economies—South Korea, Taiwan, Hong Kong, and Singapore—have made 'miraculous' achievements in economic catch-up since the 1960s. The remarkable growth recorded by China and India, the two Asian economic giants in recent decades, have even led to theorizations such as those of a coming 'Asian century'. The prominent features of the Asian success on economic development can be described in three words that begin with the letter 's': surprise, speed, and scale. These developments have reversed what was, until rather recently, a quite different conventional wisdom.

1.1.1   Surprise

Asia's economic growth story has surprised the world in several ways. First, the region's unprecedented economic success had been for a prolonged period an unthinkable accomplishment. The socio-political infrastructure of the Asian countries was considered an insurmountable obstacle in building prosperous modern societies. For example, the first Western visitors to Japan in the nineteenth century had the following impression of the country:

> Wealthy we do not think it will ever become: the advantages conferred by Nature . . . and the love of indolence and pleasure of the people themselves forbid it . . . In this part of the world principles, established and recognized in the West, appear to lose whatever virtue and vitality they originally possessed and to tend fatally towards weediness and corruption.[3]

Weber (1930) and Parsons (1937) offered hypotheses for why Chinese culture inhibited the rise of capitalism. The authors argued that this Confucianism-influenced society lacked the three critical factors for capitalism: rationality, individualism, and self-motivation to compete and win to attain goals.[4]

At the same time, Hubertus van Mook, Acting Governor-General of the

---

[3]   Quoted in Easterly (1995, p. 279).
[4]   See Tai (1989) for in-depth discussions on this topic.

Dutch East Indies (which included South Asia and Southeast Asia) during 1942–1948, was concerned about the cultural resistance of Southeast Asia to modernization and development. He asserted:

> The age-long influence of the West . . . failed, with only few exceptions, to instill its economic activity and enterprise into the minds and habits of these peoples. The Western apparatus of finance, commerce, and production remained an alien, undigested and indigestible element in Southeast Asia [. . .]. The solidarity, the public spirit, and the economic energy that were necessary for a vigorous resurgence were lacking.[5]

With regard to India, Lucas (1988, p. 5), puzzled by the country's meager growth of 1.4 per cent during the period 1960–1980, posed the following questions:

> Is there some action a government of India could take that would lead the Indian economy to grow like Indonesia's or Egypt's? If so, what exactly? If not, what is it about the 'nature of India' that makes it so?[6]

Given the aforementioned views about Asia's readiness for modernization, many scholars and observers were shocked or skeptical as a few countries in the region embarked on their catching-up endeavors. Paul Romer, a leading theorist on economic growth, commented on the skeptical reactions to the early stage of the phenomenal performance of the East Asian economies:

> When Japan grew at this pace, commentators said it was a special case propelled by postwar recovery. When the four East Asian tigers (Hong Kong (China), Taiwan (China), Singapore, and Korea) matched it, skeptics said it was only possible because they were so small. When China surpassed them, people said it was only because China was so big. (World Bank, 2008, p. 20)

In fact, the first World Bank mission to Korea in the early 1960s criticized the country's development program because its growth objective for 1962–1966 far exceeded its potential and because its export growth target, the mission argued, was inconceivable.[7] Similarly, Rosenstein-Rodan (1961) produced a forecast that represented the thinking of mainstream economists in the 1960s, projecting that Argentina's per capita income would be

---

[5] Quoted in Easterly (1995, p. 278).

[6] The economic reforms initiated in India in the early 1990s have changed the situation. The country's GDP growth accelerated to 7.4 per cent during the period 2000–2010; this rate was more than 2 percentage points higher than the rates that were attained by Indonesia and Egypt during the same period.

[7] See Easterly (1995, pp. 278–279). This criticism turned out to be incorrect.

twice as high as that of Singapore by 1976 and that Colombia's per capita income would be significantly larger than that of Hong Kong.[8]

Furthermore, economic growth in the rapidly growing Asian economies did not proceed according to orthodox principles generally held at that time. The growth in these countries was heavily driven by government intervention (except in Hong Kong), which fostered capital accumulation. Meanwhile, the countries' total factor productivity (TFP) growth was relatively low. Kim and Lau (1994) and Young (1995) examined the growth of South Korea, Taiwan, Hong Kong, and Singapore and found that their unprecedented growth was not supported by robust TFP growth. This finding raised suspicion regarding the technical progress in these economies and the sustainability of the East Asia economic growth model. As Fogel (2011) noted, the success of the newly industrialized Asian economies was not convincing even in the early 1990s because there was a strong belief that the high growth rates of these economies were flukes that could not persist. For example, Krugman (1994) expressed his pessimistic view of the East Asian development model by comparing the growth in these economies with that of the Soviet Union, which achieved outstanding growth through rapid input accumulation over a long period of time before its economic stagnation and eventual collapse in 1991. He went on to predict:

> From the perspective of the year 2010, current projections of Asian supremacy extrapolated from recent trends may well look almost as silly as 1960-vintage forecasts of Soviet industrial supremacy did from the perspective of the Brezhnev years. (Krugman, 1994, p. 78)

1.1.2   Speed

The speed of growth achieved by the Asian economies has been admirable. The World Bank's *Growth Report* used a 7 per cent GDP growth rate for a period of 25 years or longer to identify economic growth success stories during the past six decades. As noted in the report, 'growth at 7 per cent a year, sustained for 25 years, was unheard of before the latter half of the 20th century.'[9] Among the thirteen economies that qualified for inclusion in this category, nine are in Asia: China, Hong Kong, Indonesia, Japan, Malaysia, South Korea, Singapore, Taiwan, and Thailand. In addition,

---

[8]   See Hicks (1989, p. 21) for further examples. It is worth noting that Singapore and Hong Kong not only vastly outperformed Argentina and Colombia during the forecast period but also sustained their outstanding performance in the following decades. In 2010, Singapore's per capita income was nearly 4 times higher than that of Argentina, and Hong Kong's per capita income was 5 times higher than that of Colombia (Source: WDI).

[9]   World Bank (2008, p. 2).

the report indicated that it expected India and Vietnam to join this group in the near future.

Moreover, of the Asian economies identified in the World Bank's *Growth Report*, many notably exceeded the thresholds for inclusion by achieving GDP growth rates that were higher than 7 per cent and sustained for 30 years or longer. According to this report, GDP growth during the period 1965–1995 was 8.7 per cent for Singapore, 8.4 per cent for Taiwan, 8.0 per cent for South Korea, 7.6 per cent for Thailand, and 7.1 per cent for Hong Kong. China achieved an even superior performance, recording a GDP growth rate exceeding 10 per cent in the recent 30-year period, 1990–2010.[10]

1.1.3   Scale

The emergence of China and India as high-performing economies during the past few decades has remarkably boosted the rise of Asia. A 7 per cent growth rate is now enjoyed by billions of people rather than merely a few dozen millions. Developing Asia has now become the major engine driving the growth of the world economy, accounting for 46 per cent of the world's economic growth during the 20-year period 1990–2010. Moreover, this contribution increased from approximately 35 per cent during the first decade of that period (1990–2000) to more than 54 per cent during the second decade (2000–2010).[11] The projections for the next 10 years indicate that developing Asia is expected to increase its share of the world GDP (measured in purchasing power parity) from 28 per cent in 2010 to 36.8 per cent in 2020 and is expected to surpass the G7 in this regard in 2018 (Jorgenson and Vu, 2011).

The rapid growth of Asia and the scale of its rise have generated profound changes in the world economy. Bosworth and Collins (2008) concluded that the emergence of China and India as major forces in the global economy is one of the most significant economic developments of the past quarter-century.

1.2   THE NEED FOR BETTER UNDERSTANDING ECONOMIC GROWTH IN ASIA

As Asia's success has become a convincing case, questions remain concerning whether its development model is replicable and how it should be

[10]   Author's calculation (data from the World Development Indicators online dataset).
[11]   Details are presented in Chapter 3 of this book.

replicated. The outstanding performance of China and India in the past two decades, which emulated many of the most important features of the East Asian miracle depicted by the World Bank and other scholars in the early 1990s,[12] provides a clear answer that the East Asian growth model is replicable. The model is applicable not only to small and mid-sized economies but also to very large countries, not only in the past but also at present, not only in East Asia but also in South Asia.

Some scholars even believe that the remarkable performance of China since its launch of reforms can be replicated elsewhere. Justin Yifu Lin, a leading expert on economic growth in China and developing economies and a former Chief Economist of the World Bank, expressed his view:

> Some may think that the performance of a country as unique as China, with more than 1.3 billion people, cannot be replicated. I disagree. Every developing country can have similar opportunities to sustain rapid growth for several decades and reduce poverty dramatically if it exploits the benefits of backwardness, imports technology from advanced countries, and upgrades its industries. (Lin, 2011)

As the success of Asia becomes more convincing and persuasive, especially to policy makers, the need for better understanding of Asia's economic growth model is greater than ever before. The challenge in meeting this need today, however, lies not in coming up with a few generic lessons, which are all known to be fundamental to growth, but in getting policy makers to embrace them with true understanding, critical reflection, and deep commitment.

In learning from a successful country, focusing merely on studying its actual practices concerning organizational structures, policy initiatives, and projects is not enough. A learning country may fail in replicating these practices because its local context and development conditions may be greatly different. The learning efforts, therefore, should start with a true appreciation of the root causes of the country's success and follow with a deep understanding of the country's development strategies that have enabled it to achieve sustained rapid economic growth.

It is astonishing that the root causes of the major reforms that have led many Asian economies to success have been identical. They all rely on the two central factors that drive a profound transformational process: emotion and enlightenment of the nation, especially its leadership. In the context of this discussion, emotion is associated with aspiration, anxiety, and a deep sense of responsibility toward the future of a nation.

---

[12] See Appendix 1.1 for a summary of the key features of the East Asian miracle and their lessons learned.

Enlightenment is characterized by an open mindset that is free of dogmatism, an outward orientation, and an eagerness to learn from successful nations. The experiences of Japan during the Meiji Restoration period, South Korea under Park Chung-Hee, Singapore under Lee Kuan Yew, and China under Deng Xiaoping, as elaborated in Appendix 1.1, provide illuminating examples.

Furthermore, the features of the development strategies adopted by the successful Asian economies in their early stages of development were rather similar. Their strategies all shared three strategic directions: exploiting the 'backwardness' advantage[13] through embracing global opportunities for accessibility to markets, technologies, and learning; upgrading their absorptive capability through promoting human capital formation, building innovation capacity, and strengthening national learning capabilities; and creating favorable conditions for investment, structural change, and efficiency improvements.

1.3   ABOUT THIS BOOK

This book seeks to help policy makers and researchers experience a fresh perspective and deeper reflections on the Asia growth model, which a rich body of literature has studied extensively and discussed in the last two decades or so. For this purpose, this book conducts a comprehensive examination of the economic performance and growth patterns of developing Asian economies during the two-decade period of 1990–2010. With the insights drawn from this investigation, the book sketches out a strategic policy framework that seeks to help policy makers from developing countries to speed up their countries' economic growth endeavors.

The book examines the economic performance and growth patterns of 16 Asian economies, which are divided into four subgroups. They are the two economic giants—China and India; the four Asian Tiger economies—Hong Kong, Singapore, South Korea, and Taiwan (hereinafter referred to as Tigers-4); six other Southeast Asian countries—Cambodia, Indonesia, Malaysia, the Philippines, Thailand, and Vietnam (ASEAN-6); and four other South Asian countries—Bangladesh, Nepal, Pakistan, and Sri Lanka (SAC-4). These 16 economies were chosen based on two criteria: (1) they belong to three major geographic areas of interest: Northeast

[13]   Gerschenkron (1962) identified 'backwardness' as an advantage of lower-income countries that allows them to benefit from the technologies, methods of production, and management techniques that have been developed by advanced countries.

Table 1.1   A snapshot of Developing Asia in 2010: population, GDP, and income level

	Population		GDP (PPP$)		Income Level (World = 100)
	(millions)	Share in World	(billions)	Share in World	
Developing Asia	**3,551.7**	**53.5%**	**20,712.8**	**27.8%**	**52**
China–India					
China	1,337.7	20.1%	10,105.0	13.6%	67
India	1,224.6	18.4%	4,169.0	5.6%	30
Tigers-4					
Hong Kong	7.1	0.1%	333.4	0.4%	421
Singapore	5.1	0.1%	293.4	0.4%	515
South Korea	49.4	0.7%	1,413.8	1.9%	255
Taiwan	23.2	0.3%	824.5	1.1%	317
ASEAN-6					
Cambodia	14.1	0.2%	30.8	0.04%	19
Indonesia	239.9	3.6%	1,032.3	1.4%	38
Malaysia	28.4	0.4%	431.2	0.6%	135
Philippines	93.3	1.4%	367.8	0.5%	35
Thailand	69.1	1.0%	587.5	0.8%	76
Vietnam	86.9	1.3%	276.8	0.4%	28
SAC-4					
Bangladesh	148.7	2.2%	245.1	0.3%	15
Nepal	30.0	0.5%	35.9	0.05%	11
Pakistan	173.6	2.6%	460.9	0.6%	24
Sri Lanka	20.7	0.3%	105.3	0.1%	45
World*	**6,643.1**	**100%**	**74,516.8**	**100%**	**100**

Note: * World includes 177 countries and territories with data available.

Source: WDI; data for Taiwan is from IMF's World Economic Outlook database.

Asia, Southeast Asia, and South Asia; and (2) the data needed for the key analyses presented in this book are available for these countries. This group of 16 economies, referred to hereafter throughout this book as Developing Asia, accounted for more than 50 per cent of the world's population and 28 per cent of the world's GDP in 2010 (Table 1.1). The diversity of this group is prominent. The 16 economies differ vastly in population size and income level. Their populations range from five million (for Singapore) to more than 1 billion (for China and India), and their income levels relative to the world average range from 11 per cent (for Nepal) to 515 per cent (for Singapore).

This book investigates the economic growth of Developing Asia during 1990–2010 in three respects. First, it examines the performance of the group and its individual economies in the global dynamics of catching up and falling behind. Second, it depicts the rise of Developing Asia, which examines the expanding share of the group in the world economy and its increasing contribution to the world's growth as reflected by key economic indicators, including GDP, private consumption, government consumption, fixed investment, exports, and imports. Third, the book employs the growth accounting method to decompose the sources of growth of the 16 Developing Asia economies into the contributions of capital and labor inputs and total factor productivity growth. This thorough and rigorous investigation of economic growth in Developing Asia reveals robust insights into the growth model that has enabled many economies to achieve outstanding success in catching up with higher-income nations. The secret of successful Asian economies lies not in outstanding TFP growth but in sustaining reasonable TFP growth in spite of intensive capital accumulation over extended periods. The book proceeds to propose a strategic policy framework that can enable a low- or middle-income economy to follow the Asia growth model to succeed in its catching-up endeavors. This strategic policy framework consists of a set of policy priorities defined in three strategic directions: (1) exploiting the 'backwardness' advantage, (2) upgrading absorptive capability, and (3) creating favorable conditions for investment, structural change, and efficiency improvements. Examining the experience of China and India—the two giant economies with outstanding economic growth during 1990–2010—the book shows that the two countries have made notable progress in the direction of the proposed strategic policy framework during that same period. At the same time, the progress of China was more substantial than India's, which largely explains the lead of China over India with respect to all the key indicators of economic growth.

This book seeks to help policy makers and students with interests in economic development in Asia truly understand and appreciate the economic growth model behind the success of many Asian economies. For this purpose, the book stands out in three respects: it is accessible to policy makers; it is comprehensive in the information and analysis that it provides; and it is relevant to policy deliberation. As Asia has become an economic hub with transformational impacts on the world economy, reading this book helps one not only better understand the pattern and nature of economic growth in Asia but also gain valuable insights into the dynamics, trends, and forces that are shaping the world economy in the decades to come.

1.4   CHAPTER OUTLINES

This book consists of five chapters. Chapter 2 examines the performance
of the 16 economies in Developing Asia in the global dynamics of catching up and falling behind during the two-decade period of 1990–2010. The
chapter examines the changes in global income rankings[14] of individual
economies over the period 1990–2010 and the two sub-periods 1990–2000
and 2000–2010, to capture the performance of these economies in the
global dynamics of catching up and falling behind. The results show that
Developing Asia was in a strong mode of catching up during 1990–2010
and far outperformed other groups in both the proportion of its economies that made progress in catching up and the average magnitude of their
catching-up progress. Within the group, ten of the 16 economies improved
their global income ranks by ten or more places: China (which moved up
by 31 places), Taiwan (17), Vietnam (16), Cambodia (15), South Korea
(14), Hong Kong (13), Malaysia (11), India (10), Singapore (10), and Sri
Lanka (10). In contrast, the Philippines, with its income rank declining
by one place, was the only country in the group that fell behind during
this period. In addition, during this period, Singapore and Hong Kong
ascended to the league of the world's five wealthiest economies in terms of
per capita income.

Chapter 3 depicts the rise of Developing Asia, examining the performance of the Developing Asia group and its 16 individual economies in
GDP and its key elements, including private consumption, government
consumption, fixed investment, exports and imports. The chapter also
looks deeper into the performance of the group and its individual economies, especially the two giant countries, China and India, with respect to
four detailed measures related to globalization: exports of information
and telecommunication technology (ICT) hardware, exports of manufactures, exports of commercial services, and stock of inward foreign direct
investment (FDI). The following are the most salient findings of the
examination presented in Chapter 3:

- Developing Asia substantially expanded its shares in the world
  economy with respect to all the measures considered. The expansion
  in the world share of the group was lowest in private consumption
  (9.3 percentage points, from 13.2 per cent in 1990 to 22.6 per cent
  in 2010), which was lower than the expansion of its share in world
  GDP (14.9 percentage points, from 13.3 per cent to 28.2 per cent).

---

[14]   The income level of a country for a given year is captured by its per capita GDP measured in purchasing power parity.

The largest expansion of the group's share in the world over the period was in fixed investment (29.1 percentage points, from 16.6 per cent to 45.7 per cent). This suggests that Developing Asia relied heavily on capital accumulation to achieve its outstanding growth during 1990–2010.

- Developing Asia played a major role in driving the world's growth over 1990–2010 in GDP, government consumption, fixed investment, and exports of ICT hardware. In addition, the contribution of the group to the world's growth increased notably between the two sub-periods, 1990–2000 and 2000–2010, in terms of all the measures considered. However, it should be noted that the group of industrialized economies was still a major driver of the world's growth in 1990–2010 in private consumption, exports and imports of goods and services, and inward FDI stock.
- China and India were the leading performers of the Developing Asia group in terms of economic growth in 1990–2010 and in their contributions to the world's growth during this period. China, however, far outpaced India and the other economies in the group in both its rate of growth and the magnitude of its share of the world economy with respect to all the measures considered.
- Both China and India grew faster than the rest of the countries in the group in terms of the key globalization indicators, which include exports of goods and services, exports of ICT hardware, exports of manufactures, exports of commercial services, and inward FDI capital stock. However, the expansion in China's world share with respect to these measures during 1990–2010 was much larger than that of India because relative to India, China grew faster and started with higher bases. For example, both China and India recorded double-digit growth in exports of manufactures during 1990–2010, with an average growth rate of 19.2 per cent for China and 12.7 per cent for India. At the same time, China expanded its world share in this measure over this period by 14.2 percentage points (from 1.9 per cent in 1990 to 16.1 per cent in 2010), while India enlarged its world share by only 1 percentage point (from 0.5 per cent to 1.5 per cent) over the same period. This observation, however, suggests that as India's share in the world economy in 2010 was comparable to that of China in 1990, if India continues its rapid growth, the expansion of its share in the world economy over the next 20 years will be considerable.

Chapter 4 analyses the sources of economic growth in Developing Asia and its individual economies during the period of 1990–2010 and its two sub-periods, 1990–2000 and 2000–2010. This analysis employs the accounting framework for growth in the information age introduced by Jorgenson and his associates.[15] This growth decomposition method, which has been widely accepted as the gold standard for productivity measurement, captures the magnitude of the contributions of various inputs, including investment in ICT assets, to GDP and labor productivity growth.

Among the results presented in Chapter 4, the following stand out:

- Capital accumulation was the largest source of GDP growth over the period of 1990–2010 for most of the 16 Developing Asia economies. Exceptions were observed for only three economies, South Korea, Taiwan, and Sri Lanka, for which TFP growth outweighed capital input in contributing to GDP growth.
- ICT capital was a significant source of GDP and average labor productivity (ALP) growth for all 16 Developing Asia economies. Its contribution to GDP growth over 1990–2010 was notably larger for China, Singapore, Vietnam, Malaysia, India, South Korea, Taiwan, and Pakistan than for the other economies.
- Developing Asia outperformed the group of industrialized economies by 3.2 percentage points and the group of other developing economies by 2.3 percentage points in GDP growth during 1990–2010. Capital accumulation was the key driver of the leads of Developing Asia, accounting for more than 50 per cent of the gaps.
- TFP growth was also an important factor, after capital accumulation, in the lead of Developing Asia in GDP growth over other groups of economies.
- Labor productivity growth, which was largely driven by capital deepening (capital accumulation per worker), played a major role in the lead of Developing Asia over the group of industrialized countries and the group of other developing economies in GDP growth over 1990–2010.
- The major role of capital accumulation in driving economic growth over 1990–2010 was observed not only for Developing Asia but also for the world as a whole and for the groups of industrialized countries and non-Asian developing economies.

Chapter 5 investigates the strategic policy framework that has enabled Developing Asia to achieve outstanding economic growth through rapid

[15] For example, see Jorgenson and Stiroh (1999), Jorgenson (2001), and Jorgenson et al. (2003, 2005).

capital accumulation over extended periods. The chapter argues that the secret of successful Asian economies lies not in achieving high TFP growth but in sustaining reasonable TFP growth in spite of intensive capital accumulation over extended periods. This secret relies on concerted efforts to sustain high marginal product of capital through a strategic policy framework built in three strategic directions: (1) exploiting the backwardness advantage, (2) upgrading absorptive capability, and (3) creating favorable conditions for investment, structural change, and efficiency improvements. It is important to emphasize that the coordination of the government in carrying out these efforts in an effective development strategy plays a crucial role in the success of a nation's catch-up endeavours.

Exploiting the 'backwardness' advantage is initiated with reform efforts that open up the economy, promote trade, attract FDI, and enhance the accessibility of the economy to the world technology frontiers. Among these efforts, promoting exports, importing technologies, and fostering learning play crucial roles.

Upgrading absorptive capability is focused on fostering human capital formation, building innovation capacity, and strengthening national learning capabilities. The fundamental task in fostering human capital formation is to establish a high-quality education system with links to scientific and technological development in the world economy. At the same time, attracting global talent, especially from the national diaspora, is an effective way to fast-track capital formation in the age of globalization. Strengthening national learning capabilities is carried out through the four typical channels of organizational learning: competencies acquisition, experimentation, benchmarking against the best practices, and continuous improvements.

Creating favorable conditions for investment, structural change, and efficiency improvements requires serious reforms that enhance good governance, improve the business environment, and foster structural change. Among the concerted efforts to foster structural change, formulating effective urbanization strategies, promoting industrial upgrading and linkages, and facilitating economic agglomeration are among the top priorities.

Chapter 5 then examines the experience of China and India—the two economies with outstanding economic performance during 1990–2010 in terms of the key dimensions of the strategic policy framework presented above. This examination shows that both China and India made significant progress with respect to almost all the dimensions considered. In addition, China outpaced India considerably in performance with respect to these measures, which to a large degree explains why China achieved a more robust economic performance in comparison to India during 1990–2010. The experiences of China and India during 1990–2010, therefore, support the validity of the strategic policy framework. That is, a lower-income country can foster its catch-up performance by effectively employing the strategic directions and policy priorities adopted by successful Asian countries to formulate and implement its development strategy.

1.5 CONCLUDING REMARKS

Profound transformation, taken place in Asia in the past few decades after its first batch of successful economies, Japan and the four Asian Tiger economies—South Korea, Taiwan, Hong Kong, and Singapore—surprised the world with remarkable catch-up success and unprecedented rapid economic growth driven largely by factor accumulation. Developing Asia has continued this growth model with even more phenomenal success. In particular, China and India—the two giant economies in the group—recorded outstanding growth since their reforms were initiated (in 1978 in China and 1991 in India). The economic growth saga of Asia, which can be described by three words—surprise, speed, and scale—implies that Asia has achieved the impossible, as perceived by conventional wisdom, and forges ahead toward its future with an unprecedented speed and scale of success. In this spirit, one can expect remarkable growth and transformation in the coming decades, not only in China and India but also across Asia—from Indonesia to Pakistan, from the Philippines to Bangladesh, and from Vietnam to Myanmar.

Sustained high economic growth is not a mechanical procedure but a transformational process. The experience of successful Asian countries shows that a nation needs to summon up simultaneously and coherently two driving forces of development—emotion and enlightenment—for a country to wake up and fully exploit its potential in its catch-up endeavors. The stronger a nation is with respect to the two driving forces, emotion and enlightenment, the more successful it is in its catch-up endeavors.

To date, however, at least one of these two driving forces is still absent or weak in most nations. This is why few nations have been able to achieve development comparable to those of successful Asian economies. It should be noted that although emotion plays a crucial role in driving a transformational process, it alone is not sufficient to lead a nation to prosperity. The cases of pre-reform China, pre-reform Vietnam, pre-reform Myanmar, the former Soviet Union, and North Korea can even show that in the absence of enlightenment, a nation with strong emotion may hurt itself in darkness and conflicts.

It is fortunate that enlightenment has become a strong and irreversible trend since the end of the Cold War in the 1990s. The world has entered into an era of great convergence in conceptual thinking for policy formulation and decision-making (Mahbubani, 2013). The changes in China, Vietnam, and other transition economies are among the salient pieces of evidence of this enlightenment trend.

The strategic policy framework proposed in this book, with its robust insights into Asia's economic success and its growth model, seeks to help policy makers in developing countries, especially in Asia, to enhance their enlightenment attribute. The framework lays out three strategic directions for a lower-income country to foster its catch-up endeavors: (1) exploiting the 'backwardness' advantage, (2) upgrading absorptive capability, and (3) creating favorable conditions for investment, structural change, and efficiency improvements.

The prospects that Asia will transform itself into a prosperous region have become brighter and more feasible than ever before. However, the realization of these prospects requires three critical factors: *peace, partnership*, and *productivity*. Peace for Asia, in which territorial disputes and arms races have caused so much anxiety and distrust, should particularly emphasize the development of the culture of peace, which means not only no war but 'zero prospect of war' as the European countries have enjoyed since the end of World War II (Mahbubani, 2008). In efforts to enhance peace and partnership, the leaders of countries in the region, especially those involved in territorial disputes, should heed the advice of Confucius: 'He who acts out of self-interest arouses much resentment.'[16] Only when peace and mutual trust are firmly in place can the region truly deepen the economic integration and business partnerships that are crucial to its prosperous future.

Productivity is associated with the quantity of resources required for a unit of output. Asia and the world will need to achieve substantial improvements in productivity to accommodate and sustain rapid increases in the levels of income and consumption of billions of people living in Asia in the coming decades. With peace, partnership, and productivity, Asia will undoubtedly become a prosperous region in the twenty-first century.

---

[16] Article 4.12, *The Analects of Confucius*, translated by Simon Leys, New York: W.W. Norton & Company, 1997. A popular version of this saying, which is quoted in many books, is 'If one's acts are motivated by only own profit, one will have many enemies.'

APPENDIX 1.1:   EMOTION AND ENLIGHTENMENT AS DRIVING FORCES OF ASIA'S SUCCESS

Emotion and enlightenment play central roles in sparking profound reforms in successful Asian economies and driving them toward prosperity. For a nation, the emotion factor is influenced by its leaders' aspirations, anxieties, and sense of responsibility for the country's future. The enlightenment factor depends on the openness of the leadership's mindset and eagerness to learn. Indeed, the Asian countries that have achieved remarkable catch-up successes embarked on their unprecedented reforms with deep emotion and robust enlightenment. This is evidenced by the experience of Japan during the Meiji reform, South Korea under Park Chung-Hee, Singapore under Lee Kuan Yew, and China under Deng Xiaoping.

Japan During the Meiji Reform

Emotion
Japan's Meiji reform, initiated in the second half of the nineteenth century, was triggered by the looming threat of Western invasion: the country was shocked by the arrival of Commodore Perry's 'black ships' in 1853 and his gunboat diplomacy. The Meiji leaders, who were deeply impressed by the superiority of Western military power and anxious about being dominated by foreign forces, aspired and determined to build a new Japan as a strong nation in the modern world. To strengthen the determination of the entire society to pursue a course of radical modernization, they employed inspiring slogans such as 'Japanese Spirit, Western Knowledge,' 'Civilization, Enlightenment,' and 'Rich Nation, Strong Army.'

Enlightenment
For Japan, the 'Charter Oath of 1868,' which was written by the new Meiji leaders and presented to the people by the newly restored emperor in April 1868, is a clear indication of the Meiji leaders' enlightenment in their efforts to establish the platform for Japan to transform itself profoundly into an advanced nation:

> By this oath we set up as our aim the establishment of the national weal on a broad basis and the framing of a constitution and laws.
>
> 1. Deliberative assemblies shall be widely established and all matters decided by public discussion.
> 2. All classes, high and low, shall unite in vigorously carrying out the administration of affairs of state.

3. The common people, no less than the civil and military officials, shall each be allowed to pursue his own calling so that there may be no discontent.
4. Evil customs of the past shall be broken off and everything based upon the just laws of Nature.
5. Knowledge shall be sought throughout the world to strengthen the foundations of imperial rule. (Tsunoda et al., 1958, p. 644)

In addition, the change of the name of the period of reign of the new emperor to Meiji (enlightened rule) sent a powerful message to the entire society that the country had entered a new era with enlightened leadership.

In its efforts to seek knowledge throughout the world as directed by the Charter Oath, the Meiji government sent more than half of its high-ranking officials to the United States and Europe on a 21-month journey (from December 1871 to September 1873) to search for models and lessons that Japan could learn for its modernization.[17] Kido Takayoshi, who had helped draft up the Charter Oath and was a key member of the mission, emphasized the importance of enlightenment through fostering human capital formation:

> Nothing has more urgency for us than schools. [. . .], unless we establish an unshakable national foundation we will not be able to elevate our country's prestige in a thousand years . . . Our people are no different from the Americans or Europeans of today; it is a matter of education or lack of education. (Jansen, 2000, p. 356)

He also stressed the importance of building good governance. As he noted, those who held office need to 'respect the wishes of the whole nation and serve their country under a deep sense of responsibility, so that even in extraordinary crises they take no arbitrary step contrary to the people's will' and '[for Japan] it is no different from those countries of Europe and America the conduct of whose governments embodies the will of the people' (Jansen, 2000, p. 359). The members of the learning mission were convinced that representative institutions were needed for Japan to build consensus for government actions. Kido Takayoshi, after re-reading time after time the United States Constitution, expressed his belief: 'it is a superb document; we can never allow that spirit change' (Jansen, 2000, p. 339).

As Jansen (2000) asserted, the lessons drawn by the mission had a powerful impact on both institutional building and policy initiatives that enabled Japan to make remarkable accomplishments in its profound transformation and radical modernization.

It is also worth noting that the Meiji leaders made laborious efforts to

---

[17] It is remarkable that the people on these missions had their jobs waiting for them when they returned (Jansen, 2000, p. 355).

enhance the quality of their decisions concerning policy formulation and institutional building. In this process, they vigorously embraced debates and spoke their minds. The design of the Meiji state, as a result, was not rigidly established at the beginning but took shape as it grew (Jansen, 2000, p. 412).

South Korea under Park Chung-Hee

Emotion

When Park Chung-Hee assumed power in South Korea in 1961, the country was in a grave situation, as he remarked:

> The economy was faced with collapse [. . .] The institutional and moral aspects of the society were no better. People fatalistically took poverty and reliance on foreign aid as unavoidable factors of life. Businessmen and industrialists failed to fulfill their important role in economic development. Many corrupt government officials and parvenus worked together to amass illegal fortunes. The market, suffering from its small scale and lack of vigorous competition, did not function normally. The underdeveloped agricultural system was unable to meet the demand for food. (Park, 1971, pp. 104–105)

The conditions were even worse from broader perspectives. The threat of North Korean attack was credible. The country was extremely poor, with per capita income far below 100 USD, and mass famine was a constant threat. Given these circumstances, Park was determined to make extraordinary efforts to turn the situation around:

> I felt, honestly speaking, as if I had been given a pilfered household or a bankrupt firm to manage. Around me I could find little hope or encouragement. The outlook was bleak.
>   However, I had to rise above this pessimism to rehabilitate the household. I had to break, once and for all, the vicious circle of poverty and economic stagnation. Only by curing the abnormal economic structure could we lay the foundation for decent living standards. (Park, 1971, p. 105)

President Park Chung-Hee admired Japan's Meiji Restoration and was inspired by the spirit of the Japanese Meiji revolutionaries. He aspired to transform South Korea into a second Japan: 'I am pushing for the modernization of my country as the modernizing elite of the Meiji Restoration did' (Moon and Jun, 2011, pp. 116–118). He was also inspired by the miraculous revival of West Germany after World War II:

> I intend to witness firsthand the revival of West Germany, a country which has emerged from the ashes of World War II as a prosperous nation that has achieved outstanding economic development. (O, 2009, p. 80)

Park emphasized the moral power in the revival of the nation:

> In human societies, progress and prosperity are achieved only at the cost of sweat, blood and work. If we of this generation do not put forward our most devoted efforts to throw off the yoke of backwardness in this era of tumultuous change, the black clouds of past generations will veil our country, our people and our history forever.[18]

He expressed a deep sense of responsibility and determination:

> All my comrades and I took deep pride in knowing that it was our role to save our country. As most of us had been trained abroad, we felt strongly the need for early modernization of our country [. . .].
>
> We were confident of our organizing ability and felt we could carry out any undertaking with close unity, however difficult it might be. With strong traditionalism and positive popular support, we saw ourselves as standard-bearers to guide the people toward the attainment of their long-cherished hope. (Park, 1971, pp. 99–100)

Enlightenment

Park's government stressed the importance of mobilizing the wisdom and knowledge of scholars in formulating the country's economic development plans. The government used this approach in the preparation of its first Five-Year Economic Development Plan (1961–1965) and considered it a strategic way to enlighten its economic development strategy and stimulate the engagement of the country's scholars in national development endeavors. Park noted:

> [w]e organized a planning committee of college professors and experts with specialized knowledge in many fields. By mobilizing the maximum available expertise for government administration and policy-making, we intended to hold in check the arbitrariness and rashness of the military officers. The establishment of this committee served as a turning point. Korean professors began to show positive interest in the realities of the country and to present policy recommendations on the basis of scientific analyses of the country's situation. (Park, 1971, pp. 107–108)

Park himself was relentless in his learning efforts. He was 'open to new ideas and capable of transforming them into a detailed workable action program,' and 'He studied hard to learn about economic issues and to discover ways to bring about economic development' (Kim and Park, 2011, p. 278). Park was described as a man 'busy studying Japan. He frequently took clippings from Japanese newspapers and read *The History of the*

---

[18]   Presidential inaugural address, Park Chung-Hee, 1963, from Shin (1970, p. 286).

Japanese Economy until midnight. A great portion of Park's modernization policy emerged from the emulation of Japan. He compared South
Korea's economic situation to that of Japan all the time' (Moon and Jun,
2011, p. 120).

Singapore under Lee Kuan Yew

Emotion
Emotion ran high in Singapore, with deep anxiety about the country's
economic survival, after it was cut off from Malaysia in 1965. The small
country, with no natural resources, faced economic difficulties, with an
unemployment rate of 14 per cent and on the rise, and an unfriendly environment in the region.

In this critical situation, Lee Kuan Yew realized that extraordinary
efforts were the only way for Singapore to survive and succeed:

> I concluded an island city-state in Southeast Asia could not be ordinary if it
> was to survive. We had to make extraordinary efforts to become a tightly knit,
> rugged and adaptable people who could do things better and cheaper than our
> neighbors [. . .]. We had to be different. (Lee, 2000, p. 24)

Emotion had a powerful effect on the government officers' devotion and
working attitudes. Lee Kuan Yew remarked, 'I felt strongly that the people's morale and confidence would be decisive in the coming battle for
Singapore's survival' (Lee, 2000, p. 71). For example, the officers of the
Economic Development Board, which is responsible for attracting foreign
direct investment to Singapore, 'worked with inexhaustible energy because
they felt the survival of Singapore depended upon them' (Lee, 2000, p. 78).

Enlightenment
Lee Kuan Yew and his government particularly emphasized the importance of learning and continuous improvement:

> When we started in 1959 we knew little knowledge about how to govern, or how
> to solve economic and social problems. [. . .] We learnt on the job and learnt
> quickly. If there was one formula for our success, it was that we were constantly
> studying how to make things work, or how to make them work better.
> [. . .] I discovered early in office that there were few problems confronting me
> in government which other governments had not met and solved. So I made a
> practice of finding out who else had met the problem we faced, how they had
> tackled it and how successful they had been. Whenever it was to build a new
> airport or to change our teaching methods, I would send a team of officers to
> visit and study those countries that had done it well. I preferred to climb on the
> shoulders of others who had gone before us. (Lee, 2000, pp. 758–759)

A majority of the governance ideas implemented in Singapore were learned and adapted from elsewhere (Neo and Chen, 2007, p. 43). Among the prominent examples of this learning included Changi Airport, the personnel appraisal system, and the concept of garden cities. The decision to shift the international airport from Paya Lebar to Changi and write off S$750 million of investment in the old airport was motivated by the perceived advantage of being located on the coast, like Boston's Logan airport. This advantage allows the airport to minimize noise associated with airplane landings and take-offs. With the new airport at Changi by the sea, the perennial noise problem was effectively solved. In an effort to recruit and promote senior people, Singapore learned from the system developed by Shell, the Anglo-Dutch oil group. The strength of this system is its effective appraisal of a person's 'currently estimated potential' through three qualities: power of analysis, imagination, and a sense of reality. The concept of building a 'garden city' has its origin in the greenery of Phnom Penh, which impressed Lee Kuan Yew when he visited Cambodia in 1962.

China under Deng Xiaoping

Emotion

China's emotion that laid foundation for the launch of its reform in 1978 came from three sources. One was its feeling of centuries-long humiliation due to the domination of the West and the Japanese before the Communist Party of China (CPC) took control of the country in 1949. Another was its realization of the country's severe backwardness and falling further behind advanced countries, after three decades of mismanagement and political turmoil under the leadership of Mao Zedong. The third was China's ambition to become a great power.

In a speech in 1978, Deng Xiaoping stressed the following:

> Profound changes have taken place and new leaps have been made in almost all areas. A whole range of new sciences and technologies is continuously emerging . . . we have lost a lot of time as a result of the sabotage by Lin Biao and the Gang of Four . . . Backwardness must be recognized before it can be changed.[19]

The CPC sparked emotion with a determination to 'advance courageously to make a fundamental change in the backward state of our country so that it becomes a great, modern, socialist power.'[20]

Great ambition is always a key driver behind China's emotion toward

[19] Cited in Naughton (1995, p. 101).
[20] 'Communiqué of the Third Plenary Session of the 11th Central Committee of the Communist Party of China,' adopted on December 22, 1978, Beijing Review, available at http://

reform and development. Deng Xiaoping prodded China to advance faster to catch up with successful Asian economies. In his trip to southern China in January 1992 to rally support for accelerating reforms, he called for the following:

> Now that the peripheral countries and areas have the lead on us in economic development, if we fail to catch up with them or if we advance at a slow pace, the public may have grievances when they make a comparison. Therefore, if an idea can help speed up development, we must not stop it but should try to make development still faster. [. . .] We must seize every opportunity to make the country develop quickly. We have a good opportunity now; if we fail to seize it, it will be gone very soon. Slow development simply means to halt. We must strive really hard to upgrade the economy to a new level every few years.
>
> [. . .] If Guangdong plans to catch up with the four little dragons of Asia within 20 years and wants to speed up its development, it will have to quicken its pace further. Shanghai definitely can go faster. By quickening the pace of development, the situation in the four special economic zones, in the Yangtze Delta, and in China as a whole, will be quite different from what it is at present. [. . .] when I review my work in retrospect, I think one of the great mistakes I committed is that I did not make Shanghai one of the special economic zones at the time when the four existing special economic zones were founded.[21]

Enlightenment

Under Deng Xiaoping, China made strenuous efforts to tap into new ideas and technologies from advanced countries. The CPC's Politburo Decision in 1992 underscored the following:

> The party and country should be bold in absorbing and learning from all the achievement of the civilization of mankind, and in absorbing and learning from the advanced management methods of other countries of the contemporary world, including the developed countries in the West.[22]

In particular, Deng encouraged his people to learn from the example of Singapore and do even better in China:

> Singapore enjoys good social order and is well managed. We should tap their experience and learn how to manage things better than they do today.[23]

www.bjreview.com.cn/special/30yearsofreform/2008-11/29/content_167170.htm, accessed October 10, 2012.

[21] Deng's remarks on his trip to southern China in 1992, cited in Marti (2002, p. 104).

[22] 'Communiqué of the Third Plenary Session of the 11th Central Committee of the Communist Party of China,' adopted on December 22, 1978, Beijing Review, available at   http://www.bjreview.com.cn/special/30yearsofreform/2008-11/29/content_167170.htm, accessed October 10, 2012.

[23] Cited in Thomas (2001, p. 9).

Among China's efforts to learn from Singapore was the appointment in 1985 by the Chinese government of Dr. Goh Keng Swee, Singapore's economic architect, as its economic adviser on coastal development and tourism. On this occasion, the spokesperson of China's Ministry of Foreign Affairs asserted the following:

> In carrying out economic reform and opening to the outside world, we not only will bring the role of Chinese scholars and experts into full place but also hope to receive assistance from foreign scholars and experts and benefit from their views and suggestions.[24]

[24] From'Dr. Goh China's economic adviser,' *Strait Time*, 11 July 1985

2. Developing Asia in the global dynamics of catching up and falling behind

2.1 INTRODUCTION

The 1990–2010 period witnessed profound changes in the world economy. These changes were characterized by the emergence of three driving forces of transformation: globalization, information and communication technology (ICT), and the rise of Asia, led by the outstanding economic performance of China and India. These transformational forces have had palpable effects on economic growth in many economies in the world, especially in developing Asia.

This chapter aims to provide a comprehensive view of the performance of developing Asian economies in the global dynamics of catching up and falling behind on a per capita income level in the past two-decade period. For this purpose, the chapter follows Jorgenson and Vu (2011) in focusing on a sample of 119 of the most significant economies in the world for which key data for economic analysis are available. These 119 economies account for more than 95 per cent of the world's GDP and population. The 119-economy sample can be divided into three sub-samples: (1) the Developing Asia group, which includes the 16 economies that were introduced in Chapter 1. This group represents developing Asia, which is the main focus of this book;[1] (2) the Industrialized Economies group, which includes 24 industrialized economies, as classified by the UN (2002); and (3) the Rest of the World (ROW) group, which includes the remaining economies in the sample.

The Industrialized Economies includes two groups: G7, which includes the seven largest industrialized economies, and Non-G7, which includes

---

[1] As described in Chapter 1, the Developing Asia group can be split into four sub-groups to facilitate this discussion: China–India, which includes the two economic giants, China and India; Tigers-4, which includes Hong Kong, Singapore, South Korea, and Taiwan; ASEAN-6, which includes Cambodia, Indonesia, Malaysia, the Philippines, Thailand, and Vietnam; and SAC-4, which includes Bangladesh, Nepal, Pakistan, and Sri Lanka.

17 non-G7 industrialized economies. The ROW consists of four non-Asia developing groups classified by their geographic location: Latin America, which includes 20 economies from Latin America; Eastern Europe, which includes 21 economies from Eastern Europe and the former Soviet Union; Sub-Saharan Africa, which includes 27 economies from Sub-Saharan Africa; and North Africa and Middle East, which includes 11 economies from this region. The 119-economy sample, therefore, is divided into seven groups: Developing Asia, G7, Non-G7, Latin America, Eastern Europe, Sub-Saharan Africa, and North Africa and Middle East. The 119 economies and seven groups are listed in Table 2.1.

This chapter proceeds as follows. Section 2.2 highlights the ranking of the per capita incomes of the economies. Section 2.3 describes the performance of the seven groups and Section 2.4 describes the performance of individual economies in each of the seven groups in the global dynamics of catching up on per capita income during 1990–2010. Section 2.5 provides a closer look at the performance of the 16 Developing Asia economies by examining the changes in their global per capita income ranks on an annual basis. Section 2.6 summarizes the key results.

2.2 THE PER CAPITA INCOME RANKING EXERCISE

Per capita income, calculated as a country's gross domestic product (GDP) divided by its population, can be used as a simple and effective measure for comparing the levels of development of different countries.[2] Per capita GDP is a good estimate of a country's average standard of living and average productivity, and hence, it is a meaningful indicator of a country's level of development.[3] To ensure the comparability of this measure, per capita GDP must be measured in purchasing power parity (PPP) dollars, which means that a dollar of income in different countries is adjusted to have the same purchasing power (details on the measurement of purchasing power parity are presented in Box 2.1).

---

[2] Another measure of per capita income is gross national product (GNP) divided by population. While GDP is calculated as the value of the total final output of all goods and services produced in a single year within a country's boundaries, GNP is GDP plus income received by residents from abroad minus income generated by nonresidents (Subbotina and Sheram, 2000).

[3] Per capita GDP has been widely used to analyse the economic performance of different countries and the world's income distribution. Among the notable examples of such studies are Madison (1983, 1987, 2001), Jones (1997), Acemoglu and Ventura (2002), and Sala-i-Martin (2006).

Table 2.1   The list of 119 economies by group

Economy	GDP per Capita (2005 PPP$)		Economy	GDP per Capita (2005 PPP$)	
	1990	2010		1990	2010
Developing Asia			New Zealand	18,728	24,923
Bangladesh	747	1,488	Norway	32,117	46,735
Cambodia	683	1,968	Portugal	16,299	21,668
China	1,101	6,816	Spain	19,770	26,934
Hong Kong	23,697	41,714	Sweden	24,567	33,775
India	1,244	3,214	Switzerland	33,417	37,586
Indonesia	2,008	3,880	*Latin America*		
Malaysia	6,607	13,214	Argentina	7,458	14,363
Nepal	709	1,075	Bolivia	3,074	4,350
Pakistan	1,620	2,411	Brazil	7,175	10,056
Philippines	2,552	3,560	Chile	6,585	13,596
Singapore	25,152	51,969	Colombia	6,097	8,488
South Korea	11,383	27,027	Costa Rica	6,239	10,378
Sri Lanka	1,992	4,555	Dominican Republic	3,833	8,387
Taiwan	14,305	33,600	Ecuador	5,414	7,201
Thailand	3,933	7,673	El Salvador	3,672	5,981
Vietnam	905	2,875	Guatemala	3,332	4,292
Seven Largest Industrialized Economies			Honduras	2,658	3,519
(G7)			Jamaica	5,933	6,882
Canada	26,941	35,241	Mexico	9,990	12,441
France	24,306	29,648	Nicaragua	1,886	2,614
Germany	25,881	33,445	Panama	6,073	12,207
Italy	23,775	26,753	Paraguay	4,004	4,647
Japan	26,129	30,573	Peru	4,477	8,555
United Kingdom	23,697	32,220	Trinidad and Tobago	10,820	23,080
United States	31,899	42,338	Uruguay	7,301	12,903
Non-G7 Industrialized Economies			Venezuela	9,574	10,973
(Non-G7)			*Eastern Europe*		
Australia	23,979	34,463	Albania	3,914	7,667
Austria	25,459	35,401	Armenia	2,938	4,900
Belgium	25,096	32,859	Azerbaijan	4,754	8,919
Denmark	25,447	32,499	Belarus	6,434	12,494
Finland	23,143	31,729	Bulgaria	7,536	11,487
Greece	17,318	24,200	Croatia	13,400	16,121
Iceland	25,632	32,843	Czech Republic	16,320	22,564
Ireland	17,606	35,411	Estonia	10,147	16,566
Israel	17,863	26,021	Georgia	6,138	4,551
Luxembourg	42,685	68,901	Hungary	13,120	16,944
Netherlands	26,275	37,004	Kazakhstan	7,089	10,921

Table 2.1 (continued)

Economy	GDP per Capita (2005 PPP$)		Economy	GDP per Capita (2005 PPP$)	
	1990	2010		1990	2010
Kyrgyz Republic	2,505	2,039	Mali	665	955
Latvia	10,090	12,938	Mauritius	6,115	12,284
Lithuania	12,511	15,391	Mozambique	400	845
Poland	8,180	17,350	Namibia	3,987	5,807
Romania	7,858	10,929	Niger	702	653
Russia	12,626	14,183	Nigeria	1,417	2,135
Slovak Republic	12,731	20,151	Senegal	1,478	1,736
Slovenia	16,455	25,001	South Africa	7,975	9,477
Tajikistan	2,961	1,940	Sudan	1,029	2,023
Ukraine	8,063	6,029	Swaziland	3,894	4,754
Sub-Saharan Africa			Tanzania	835	1,254
Benin	1,117	1,424	Togo	917	895
Botswana	6,948	12,463	Uganda	563	1,141
Burkina Faso	681	1,127	*North Africa & Middle East*		
Cameroon	2,082	2,058	Algeria	6,211	7,521
Chad	819	1,229	Egypt	3,237	5,544
Congo, Rep.	3,556	3,808	Iran	6,201	10,680
Côte d'Ivoire	1,911	1,704	Jordan	3,293	5,157
Ethiopia	545	934	Lebanon	5,737	12,619
Gabon	14,944	13,500	Mauritania	1,549	1,744
Ghana	907	1,475	Morocco	2,711	4,297
Guinea	862	978	Syria	2,968	4,741
Kenya	1,421	1,481	Tunisia	4,497	8,566
Madagascar	1,037	869	Turkey	8,088	12,547
Malawi	569	791	Yemen	1,831	2,375

Source: WDI, ADB, Conference Board's Total Economy Database; data for Taiwan (China) is derived from the International Comparison Program (ICP) and ADB's Statistical Database.

This chapter presents a per capita income ranking exercise for the 119-economy sample, using per capita GDP measured in PPP dollars at the 2005 price level, provided by the World Development Indicators (WDI) database.[4] The per capita income rank for an economy in a given year is

[4] Data for Taiwan (China) is derived from information from the International Comparison Program (ICP) and the Asian Development Bank's Statistical Database.

BOX 2.1   MEASURING GDP IN PURCHASING POWER PARITY

GDP can be calculated in three different ways. On the production side, it is the sum of value added in different sectors (agriculture, industry and services), net of duplication. On the income side, it is the total of wages, rents and profits. On the demand side, it is the sum of final expenditures by consumers, investors and the government.

Cross-country comparisons of economic performance require GDP to be measured in terms of a common currency with purchasing power parity (PPP). PPP is defined as the number of currency units required to purchase the amount of goods and services equivalent to what can be bought with one unit of the currency of the base country, for example, the US dollar. Using PPP units as conversion factors helps researchers and analysts gain insights into the relative economic well-being of countries, monitor the incidence of poverty, and assess the relative productivity and investment potential of different countries.

Estimating GDP in PPP units examines the components of GDP from the demand side. In principle, computing PPP units requires two types of data: prices of comparable and representative items and expenditure weights. The number of items constituting the International Comparison Program (ICP) GDP basket may vary from 800 to 2,500. Expenditure weights are compiled at the basic heading level, with basic headings representing the lowest-level component of GDP for which expenditure weights are available. The number of basic headings varies from 155 to 222. The number of individual items (goods and services) constituting a basic heading normally varies from several to 30 or more, depending primarily on price variations associated with the products in the basic heading and its expenditure weight.

The International Comparison Program (ICP)—the world's largest statistical initiative, which is currently hosted by the World Bank—produces internationally comparable price levels, economic aggregates in real terms, and PPP estimates. The latest major ICP report provides estimates of PPPs benchmarked to the year 2005 for GDP, GDP per capita, household consumption, collective government consumption, and capital formation for 146 economies. These estimates are derived from PPPs based upon national surveys that priced nearly 1,000 products and services.

Source: World Bank, the International Comparison Program (ICP).

its order in the list of the 119 economies sorted by per capita income in that year. That is, the richest economy has the 1st place in the ranking, while the poorest has the 119th place.

Over a given period, such as 1990–2010, for example, an economy can be characterized by one of the following three different scenarios with respect to its per capita income ranking:

- Rank improvement: the economy moved up by at least one place in the global ranking. This means the economy made catch-up progress.
- Rank deterioration: the economy declined by at least one place in the global ranking. That is, the economy fell behind in the global dynamics of economic growth.
- Rank stability: the economy stayed at the same place in the global per capita income ranking.

The list of 119 economies, with their per capita income ranks in 1990 and 2010, is presented in Table 2.2.

2.3   THE GLOBAL DYNAMICS OF CATCHING UP AND FALLING BEHIND, 1990–2010: PERFORMANCE BY GROUP

Table 2.3 reports the performance of the seven groups in the global dynamics of catching up and falling behind over the 1990–2010 period. In the overall picture of the world sample, 54 of the 119 economies (45 per cent) improved their places in the global per capita income ranking between 1990 and 2010, while 58 economies (49 per cent) declined in the ranking, and only seven economies (6 per cent) maintained their ranks over this period. The 54 economies that experienced rank improvement, which are referred to here as catching-up economies, moved up by a total of 385 places; while the 58 economies that experienced rank deterioration,

Table 2.2   The change in global income ranks over 1990–2010

Economy	Group	Income Rank		Income Rank Change
		1990	2010	1990–2010
China	Developing Asia	101	70	31
Lebanon	North Africa & Middle-East	64	45	19
Taiwan	Developing Asia	30	13	17
Ireland	Non-G7	24	8	16
Vietnam	Developing Asia	106	90	16
Cambodia	Developing Asia	113	98	15
South Korea	Developing Asia	36	22	14
Chile	Latin America	54	40	14
Hong Kong	Developing Asia	18	5	13
Malaysia	Developing Asia	53	42	11
Panama	Latin America	62	51	11
India	Developing Asia	99	89	10
Singapore	Developing Asia	12	2	10
Sri Lanka	Developing Asia	90	80	10
Argentina	Latin America	48	38	10
Dominican Republic	Latin America	74	64	10
Mauritius	Sub-Saharan Africa	60	50	10
Poland	Eastern Europe	42	33	9
Trinidad and Tobago	Latin America	37	29	8
Belarus	Eastern Europe	55	47	8
Uganda	Sub-Saharan Africa	117	109	8
Bangladesh	Developing Asia	110	103	7
Armenia	Eastern Europe	83	76	7
Thailand	Developing Asia	71	65	6
Peru	Latin America	68	62	6
Albania	Eastern Europe	72	66	6
Azerbaijan	Eastern Europe	66	60	6
Sudan	Sub-Saharan Africa	103	97	6
Tunisia	North Africa & Middle-East	67	61	6
Australia	Non-G7	16	11	5
Uruguay	Latin America	49	44	5
Egypt	North Africa & Middle-East	79	74	5
Indonesia	Developing Asia	89	85	4
Botswana	Sub-Saharan Africa	52	48	4
Burkina Faso	Sub-Saharan Africa	114	110	4
Ethiopia	Sub-Saharan Africa	118	114	4

Table 2.2   (continued)

Economy	Group	Income Rank		Income Rank Change
		1990	2010	1990–2010
Nigeria	Sub-Saharan Africa	98	94	4
El Salvador	Latin America	75	72	3
Estonia	Eastern Europe	38	35	3
Jordan	North Africa & Middle-East	78	75	3
Syria	North Africa & Middle-East	81	78	3
Sweden	Non-G7	14	12	2
Pakistan	Developing Asia	94	92	2
Mali	Sub-Saharan Africa	115	113	2
Mozambique	Sub-Saharan Africa	119	117	2
Iran	North Africa & Middle-East	58	56	2
United Kingdom	G7	19	18	1
Austria	Non-G7	10	9	1
Finland	Non-G7	20	19	1
Nicaragua	Latin America	92	91	1
Slovak Republic	Eastern Europe	33	32	1
Chad	Sub-Saharan Africa	109	108	1
Tanzania	Sub-Saharan Africa	108	107	1
Morocco	North Africa & Middle-East	84	83	1
United States	G7	4	4	0
Luxembourg	Non-G7	1	1	0
Norway	Non-G7	3	3	0
Nepal	Developing Asia	111	111	0
Slovenia	Eastern Europe	26	26	0
Ghana	Sub-Saharan Africa	105	105	0
Yemen	North Africa & Middle-East	93	93	0
Netherlands	Non-G7	6	7	−1
Philippines	Developing Asia	86	87	−1
Costa Rica	Latin America	56	57	−1
Belgium	Non-G7	13	15	−2
Israel	Non-G7	23	25	−2
Spain	Non-G7	21	23	−2
Bolivia	Latin America	80	82	−2
Colombia	Latin America	61	63	−2
Hungary	Eastern Europe	32	34	−2

Table 2.2   (continued)

Economy	Group	Income Rank		Income Rank Change
		1990	2010	1990–2010
Lithuania	Eastern Europe	35	37	−2
Malawi	Sub-Saharan Africa	116	118	−2
Greece	Non-G7	25	28	−3
Portugal	Non-G7	28	31	−3
Ecuador	Latin America	65	68	−3
Honduras	Latin America	85	88	−3
Czech Republic	Eastern Europe	27	30	−3
Namibia	Sub-Saharan Africa	70	73	−3
Turkey	North Africa & Middle-East	43	46	−3
Switzerland	Non-G7	2	6	−4
Kazakhstan	Eastern Europe	51	55	−4
Latvia	Eastern Europe	39	43	−4
Swaziland	Sub-Saharan Africa	73	77	−4
Canada	G7	5	10	−5
New Zealand	Non-G7	22	27	−5
Bulgaria	Eastern Europe	47	52	−5
Croatia	Eastern Europe	31	36	−5
Russia	Eastern Europe	34	39	−5
Guinea	Sub-Saharan Africa	107	112	−5
Senegal	Sub-Saharan Africa	96	101	−5
Mauritania	North Africa & Middle-East	95	100	−5
France	G7	15	21	−6
Germany	G7	8	14	−6
Denmark	Non-G7	11	17	−6
Jamaica	Latin America	63	69	−6
Benin	Sub-Saharan Africa	100	106	−6
Italy	G7	17	24	−7
Iceland	Non-G7	9	16	−7
Guatemala	Latin America	77	84	−7
Cameroon	Sub-Saharan Africa	88	95	−7
Kenya	Sub-Saharan Africa	97	104	−7
Niger	Sub-Saharan Africa	112	119	−7
Brazil	Latin America	50	58	−8
Romania	Eastern Europe	46	54	−8
Mexico	Latin America	40	49	−9
Kyrgyz Republic	Eastern Europe	87	96	−9
Paraguay	Latin America	69	79	−10

Table 2.2   (continued)

Economy	Group	Income Rank		Income Rank Change
		1990	2010	1990–2010
Congo, Rep.	Sub-Saharan Africa	76	86	−10
Algeria	North Africa & Middle-East	57	67	−10
Côte d'Ivoire	Sub-Saharan Africa	91	102	−11
Togo	Sub-Saharan Africa	104	115	−11
Venezuela	Latin America	41	53	−12
Gabon	Sub-Saharan Africa	29	41	−12
Japan	G7	7	20	−13
Madagascar	Sub-Saharan Africa	102	116	−14
South Africa	Sub-Saharan Africa	45	59	−14
Tajikistan	Eastern Europe	82	99	−17
Georgia	Eastern Europe	59	81	−22
Ukraine	Eastern Europe	44	71	−27

Note: The ranking is based on per capita income measured in purchasing power parity (2005 PPP$); the economies are sorted by change in income rank in decreasing order.

Source: Author's calculations.

which are referred to here as falling-behind economies, moved down by the same number of places, 385.[5]

The performance across the seven groups in the global dynamics of catching up and falling behind can be judged based on the following two main indicators: net balance (NB) and average net ranks changed (ANRC). The NB of a group is defined as the proportion of its economies with rank improvement minus the proportion of its economies with rank deterioration. The NB values for the seven groups are shown in column (7) of Table 2.3. A positive NB implies that a majority of the economies in the group of interest were catching up, whereas a negative NB means that a majority of its economies were falling behind. The NB, therefore, can be considered an indicator of the general trend of a group in the global dynamics of catching up and falling behind.

The ANRC of a group is defined as its total net ranks changed, which is calculated as its total number of places moved up minus its total number of places moved down, divided by the total number of economies in the

---

[5] It is possible to prove that the number of places moved up is always equal to the number of placed moved down by all the economies in the world sample.

Table 2.3 The global dynamics of catching up and falling behind, 1990–2010: performance by group

	Number of Economies				Proportion of Economies			Total Number of Ranks Changed		Average Net Ranks Changed	Share in World's Total Number of Ranks Changed	
	Total	Up	Down	Un-changed	Catching-up	Falling-behind	Net Balance	Up	Down		In "Up"	In "Down"
	(1)	(2)	(3)	(4)	(5) = (2)/(1)	(6) = (3)/(1)	(7) = (5)-(6)	(8)	(9)	(10) = [(8)-(9)]/(1)	(11) = (8)/385	(12) = (9)/385
World	**119**	**54**	**58**	**7**	**45%**	**49%**	**-3%**	**385**	**385**	–	**100%**	**100%**
Developing Asia	16	14	1	1	88%	6%	81%	166	1	10.3	43%	0.3%
Industrialized economies	24	6	15	3	25%	63%	-38%	26	72	-1.9	7%	19%
G7	7	1	5	1	14%	71%	-57%	1	37	-5.1	0.3%	10%
Non-G7	17	5	10	2	29%	59%	-29%	25	35	-0.6	6%	9%
Latin America	20	9	11	0	45%	55%	-10%	68	63	0.3	18%	16%
Eastern Europe	21	7	13	1	33%	62%	-29%	40	113	-3.5	10%	29%
Sub-Saharan Africa	27	11	15	1	41%	56%	-15%	46	118	-2.7	12%	31%
North Africa & Middle East	11	7	3	1	64%	27%	36%	39	18	1.9	10%	5%

Note: The ranking is based on per capita income measured in purchasing power parity (2005 PPP$).

Source: Author's calculations.

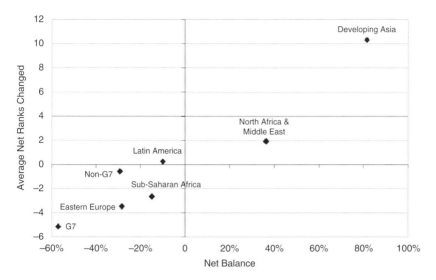

Source: Author's calculations.

Figure 2.1   *The global dynamics of catching up and falling behind,*
1990–2010: Average Net Ranks Changed (ANRC) versus Net
Balance (NB) by group

group. The ANRC values for the seven groups are shown in column (10) of Table 2.3. This indicator captures the average pace of a group's overall movement in the global dynamics of catching up and falling behind. A large positive ANRC implies that the group, in its overall movement, has made notable progress in catching up, whereas a large negative ANRC means that the group, in its overall movement, suffered from a severe decline in its global per capita income ranking.

Figure 2.1 depicts the performance of the seven groups, including Developing Asia, in the global dynamics of catching up and falling behind over the period 1990–2010 with respect to the NB and ANRC indicators. As the figure shows, Developing Asia stood out as the best performer, while G7 was the laggard, with respect to both the NB and ANRC indicators.

Developing Asia recorded an NB of 81 per cent and an ANRC of 10.3, while the values of these indicators were −57 per cent and −5.1, respectively, for G7 (Table 2.3). This indicates that Developing Asia as a group made sizable strides in catching up with more advanced nations during 1990–2010, while the G7 group suffered a notable decline over the same period.

North Africa and Middle East was the second-best performing group after Developing Asia. However, the performance of the former, for which the NB was 36 per cent and the ANRC was 1.9 (Table 2.3), was far behind that of the latter.

Joining the G7 group in the quadrant with negative values of both NB and ANRC were Eastern Europe (NB=−29 per cent; ANRC=−3.5), Non-G7 (NB=−29 per cent; ANRC=−0.6), and Sub-Saharan Africa (NB=−15 per cent; ANRC=−2.7), as shown in Figure 2.1 and Table 2.3. That is, these four groups all exhibited consistent patterns of falling behind.

Latin America was the only group that exhibited mixed patterns of catching up and falling behind. While the group's general trend was one of falling behind, with a moderate negative NB of −10 per cent, its overall movement was characterized by catching up, with a small positive ANRC of 0.3 (Table 2.3). This situation occurs because the falling-behind trend of the group was not severe, while some economies in the group, such as those of Chile, Argentina, and Peru, recorded notable success in catching up, as described in the following section on the performance by economy of each of the seven groups.

Although the number of economies differs among the seven groups, ranging from seven economies for the G7 to 27 economies for Sub-Saharan Africa, the share of each group in the world's total number of places changed in a given direction during 1990–2010 provides some meaningful information. With respect to the catching-up movement, Developing Asia accounted for 43 per cent of the world's total number of places moved up, while this share was only 18 per cent for Latin America, 12 per cent for Sub-Saharan Africa, 10 per cent for North Africa and Middle East and Eastern Europe, 6 per cent for the Non-G7 countries, and 0.3 per cent for the G7 countries. This means that Developing Asia was the major contributor to the global dynamics of catching up during 1990–2010.

On the other hand, the share of Developing Asia in the world's total number of places moved down was only 0.3 per cent, while this share was 31 per cent for Sub-Saharan Africa, 29 per cent for Eastern Europe, 16 per cent for Latin America, 10 per cent for G7, 9 per cent for Non-G7, and 5 per cent for North Africa and Middle East. This indicates that Developing Asia economies were not significantly affected by the global shake-up in per capita income ranking during 1990–2010.

2.4   THE GLOBAL DYNAMICS OF CATCHING UP AND FALLING BEHIND, 1990–2010: PERFORMANCE BY ECONOMY

This section presents the performance of individual economies in each of the seven groups in the global dynamics of catching up and falling behind over the 1990–2010 period. The seven figures from 2.2A to 2.2G illustrate the performance of individual economies of the seven groups: Developing Asia (Figure 2.2A); G7 (Figure 2.2B); Non-G7 (Figure 2.2C); Latin America (Figure 2.2D); Eastern Europe (Figure 2.2E); Sub-Saharan Africa (Figure 2.2F), and North Africa and Middle East (Figure 2.2G). These figures plot the 119 economies based on their income ranks in 1990 (on the horizontal axis) and in 2010 (on the vertical axis). The seven figures are identical except for the labeling of the economies in each of the seven groups, for the sake of clarity. The 119 economies are divided into six categories based on three criteria: the median income rank in 1990, the median income rank in 2010, and the income rank change between 1990 and 2010. The classification of the six categories is described below and summarized in Table 2.4.

Based on the median income rank in 1990, the 119-economy sample can be divided into two groups: Poor1990, which includes the economies with income ranks below the sample's median income rank in 1990, and Rich1990, which includes the rest of the sample. In Figures 2.2A–2.2G, the vertical median line divides the space into two parts: Poor1990 (on the left-hand side) and Rich1990 (on the right-hand side).

Similarly, based on the median income rank in 2010, the 119-economy sample can be divided into two groups: Poor2010, which includes the economies with income ranks below the sample's median income rank in 2010; and Rich2010, which includes the rest of the sample. In Figures 2.2A–2.2G, the horizontal median line divides the space into two parts: Poor2010 (below) and Rich2010 (above).

Based on the income rank change over the period 1990–2010, the 119-economy sample can be divided into two groups: Catching-up, which includes the economies with income rank improvement over 1990–2010; and Falling-behind, which includes the economies with rank deterioration. In Figures 2.2A–2.2G, the 45-degree line divides the space into two parts: catching up (upper part) and falling behind (lower part). The vertical distance of an economy from the 45-degree line indicates how far it caught up or fell behind during 1990–2010.

In addition, Tables 2.5A–2.5G provide details on the catching-up performance of individual economies over 1990–2010 for the seven groups. These tables (2.5A for Developing Asia, 2.5B for G7, 2.5C for Non-G7, 2.5D for Latin America, 2.5E for Eastern Europe, 2.5F for Sub-Saharan Africa and 2.5G for North Africa and Middle East) provide details on the progress of the economies in each of the two sub-periods, 1990–2000 and 2000–2010, with respect to the overall rank change over the 1990–2010 period.

The subsections below examine the performance of individual economies in each of the seven groups in the global dynamics of catching up and

*Table 2.4   The six categories of economies in the 1990–2010 global
              dynamics of catching up and falling behind*

Category	Overlapping Sub-sample	Description of the economies in the category
I	Catching-up Poor 1990 Poor 2010	• These economies improved their income ranks over 1990–2010. • These economies were below the sample's median in income level in both 1990 and 2010.
II	Catching-up Poor 1990 Rich 2010	• These economies improved their income ranks over 1990–2010. • These economies were below the sample's median in income level in 1990 but above it in 2010.
III	Catching-up Rich 1990 Rich 2010	• These economies improved their income ranks over 1990–2010. • These economies were above the sample's median in income level in both 1990 and 2010.
IV	Falling-behind Rich 1990 Rich 2010	• These economies declined in their income ranks over 1990–2010. • These economies were above the sample's median in income level in both 1990 and 2010.
V	Falling-behind Rich 1990 Poor 2010	• These economies declined in their income ranks over 1990–2010. • These economies were above the sample's median in income level in 1990 but fell below it in 2010.
VI	Falling-behind Poor 1990 Poor 2010	• These economies declined in their income ranks over 1990–2010. • These economies were below the sample's median in income level in both 1990 and 2010.

falling behind over the 1990–2010 period. The presentation is based on Figures 2.2A–2.2G and Tables 2.5A–2.5G.

2.4.1   Developing Asia (Figure 2.2A and Table 2.5A)

The performance of the 16 Developing Asia economies is examined in comparative views of their four subgroups: China–India; Tigers-4; ASEAN-6; and SAC-4. Figure 2.2A shows the robust catching-up performance of the group over 1990–2010, with 14 of the 16 economies in the catching-up area (above the 45-degree line). The two economies that did not make progress in catching up were the Philippines and Nepal.

The two economic giants, China and India, both substantially advanced their income rank over 1990–2010. China, the leading performer among the 16 Developing Asia economies, improved its income rank by 31 places (from 101st to 70th), while India moved up by 10 places (from 99th to 89th). Furthermore, the catching-up performance of both China and India was consistent between the two sub-periods, 1990–2000 and 2000–2010. The contribution to the total number of ranks changed over 1990–2010 was 55 per cent in the first sub-period and 45 per cent in the second sub-period for China and 50–50 per cent in both sub-periods for India (Table 2.5A).

It is worth noting, however, that in spite of their impressive catching-up performance over 1990–2010, China and India, especially India, still remained notably below the world's median level of per capita income in 2010 (Figure 2.2A).

The Tigers-4 economies—Hong Kong, Singapore, South Korea, and Taiwan—which have become rich as a result of their outstanding catching-up performance in previous decades, continued to make considerable

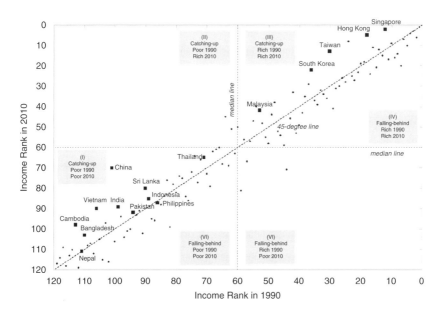

Source: Author's calculations.

Figure 2.2A *The global dynamics of catching up and falling behind, 1990–2010: Developing Asia economies*

Table 2.5A   Change in global income rank, 1990–2010: Developing Asia economies

Economy	Income Rank			Income Rank Change			Share in 1990–2010 Ranks Changed	
	1990	2000	2010	1990–2000	2000–2010	1990–2010	1990–2000	2000–2010
	(1)	(2)	(3)	(4) = (1)−(2)	(5) = (2)−(3)	(6) = (1)−(3)	(7) = (4)/(6)	(8)=(5)/(6)
China–India								
China	101	84	70	17	14	31	55%	45%
India	99	94	89	5	5	10	50%	50%
Tigers-4								
Taiwan	30	23	13	7	10	17	41%	59%
South Korea	36	29	22	7	7	14	50%	50%
Hong Kong	18	14	5	4	9	13	31%	69%
Singapore	12	4	2	8	2	10	80%	20%
ASEAN-6								
Vietnam	106	95	90	11	5	16	69%	31%
Cambodia	113	104	98	9	6	15	60%	40%
Malaysia	53	41	42	12	−1	11	109%	−9%
Thailand	71	65	65	6	0	6	100%	0%
Indonesia	89	85	85	4	0	4	100%	0%
Philippines	86	83	87	3	−4	−1	−300%	400%
SAC-4								
Sri Lanka	90	80	80	10	0	10	100%	0%
Bangladesh	110	105	103	5	2	7	71%	29%
Pakistan	94	92	92	2	0	2	100%	0%
Nepal	111	108	111	3	−3	0	–	–

Note: The economies in each subgroup appear in decreasing order of income rank change over 1990–2010.

Source: Author's calculations.

strides in moving up in the global income ranking over the 1990–2010 period. Taiwan was the leading performer, with its income rank elevated by 17 places (from 30th to 13th), followed by South Korea (14 places, from 36th to 22nd). At the same time, Hong Kong, with its income rank elevated by 13 places (from 18th to 5th), and Singapore, with its income rank elevated by10 places (from 12th to 2nd), have ascended to the league of the world's five highest income economies over the 1990–2010 period. It is also worth noting that the catching-up performance of the four Asian Tiger economies was consistent between the two sub-periods, 1990–2000 and 2000–2010. In fact, the share of the total number of ranks elevated over 1990–2010 by each of the individual economies was distributed fairly equally between the two sub-periods: 41 per cent in 1990–2000 and 59 per cent in 2000–2010 for Taiwan; 50–50 per cent for South Korea; 31–69 per cent for Hong Kong; and 80–20 per cent for Singapore. This implies that the four Asian Tiger economies were successful in overcoming the severe adverse effects of the 1997–1998 Asian financial crisis and sustaining their strong catching-up performance (Table 2.5A).

The ASEAN-6 economies exhibited mixed catching-up performance over 1990–2010. Differences in performance were notable among the economies in the group and between the two sub-periods. The leading performers in the group in income rank change over 1990–2010 were Vietnam, with its rank elevated by 16 places (from 106th to 90th), Cambodia (15 places, from 113th to 98th), and Malaysia (11 places, from 53rd to 42nd). Thailand and Indonesia recorded less robust perform-ance, with an income rank improvement of six places (from 71st to 65th) for Thailand and four places (from 89th to 85th) for Indonesia, while the Philippines was the laggard: its rank deteriorated by one place (from 86th to 87th). At the same time, it is important to note that most of the ASEAN-6 economies achieved their strong catching-up performance in the first sub-period, 1990–2000, and failed to sustain this momentum in the second sub-period, 2000–2010. In fact, Malaysia declined in its rank by one place in 2000–2010, while Thailand and Indonesia made no progress over this sub-period. Similarly, the Philippines moved up by three places in the first sub-period and declined by four places in the second. On the other hand, Vietnam and Cambodia continued to record strong catching-up performance in the second sub-period, although there were some signs of slowdown. In fact, the share of the sub-period in the total number of places elevated over 1990–2010 decreased from 69 per cent in 1990–2000 to 31 per cent in 2000–2010 for Vietnam and from 60 to 40 per cent for Cambodia. The findings for the ASEAN-6 economies tend to suggest that sustaining robust catching-up performance over time is a great chal-lenge that may be too difficult for some countries to overcome. It is worth noting that Malaysia was the only ASEAN-6 economy that had an income above the world's median level in both 1990 and 2010.

No SAC-4 economy fell behind during 1990–2010, but the catching-up performance of the SAC-4 economies was modest compared to the performance of the ASEAN-6 economies. Sri Lanka was the best performer, with its rank elevated by ten places (from 90th in 1990 to 80th in 2010), followed by Bangladesh (seven places, from 110th to 103rd). At the same time, Pakistan improved its rank by only two places (from 94th to 92nd), while Nepal—the poorest economy of Developing Asia—stayed at the same place (111th) over 1990–2010. Again, it is important to note that the catching-up performance of the SAC-4 economies tended to deteriorate from the first sub-period to the second, which was similar to the trend observed for the ASEAN-6 economies. The share of the sub-period in the total places moved up over the 1990–2010 period decreased from 100 per cent in 1990–2000 to 0 per cent in 2000–2010 for Sri Lanka and Pakistan and from 71 to 29 per cent for Bangladesh. Nepal, on the other hand, moved up by three places in 1990–2000, moved down by three places in 2000–2010, and stayed at the same income rank over 1990–2010.

2.4.2   G7 (Figure 2.2B and Table 2.5B)

It is a great challenge for economies with high income levels to maintain their income ranks in the vibrant global dynamics of catching up and falling behind. In fact, five of the seven G7 economies declined in their income ranks over 1990–2010: Japan (by 13 places, from 7th in 1990 to 20th in 2010), Italy (by seven places, from 17th to 24th), Germany (by six places, from 8th to 14th), France (by six places, from 15th to 21st) and Canada (by five places, from 5th to 10th). It is important to note that the recent global financial crisis that erupted in 2008 was not the main reason behind this notable decline in income ranks of the G7 economies over 1990–2010. In fact, the share of the first sub-period, 1990–2000, in the total number of places moved down over the 1990–2010 period was substantial for the declining economies: 85 per cent for Japan, 67 per cent for Germany and France, 43 per cent for Italy, and 40 per cent for Canada. Some salient possible factors may have played a role in the income rank decline of Japan and Germany. For Japan, its aging population may have been a factor, while for Germany, reunification between West Germany and East Germany in 1990, which required substantial restructuring efforts and costs, may have been a factor.

The United Kingdom was the only G7 economy that improved its income rank slightly, moving up by one place (from 19th to 18th). Meanwhile, the United States remained in the 4th place over the period. Again, it is worth

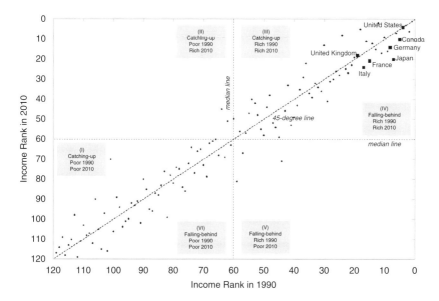

Source: Author's calculations.

Figure 2.2B   *The global dynamics of catching up and falling behind, 1990–2010: G7 economies*

noting that the performance of these two countries deteriorated in the second sub-period relative to the first. The United Kingdom improved its rank by three places in 1990–2000 but declined by two places in 2000–2010, while the United States moved up by one place in the first sub-period and then moved down by one place in the second sub-period.

2.4.3   Non-G7 (Figure 2.2C and Table 2.5C)

All the Non-G7 economies are high-income economies. Of these 17 economies, 10 were falling behind, five were catching up, and two moved neither up nor down in the global income ranking over the 1990–2010 period. The decline of the falling-behind economies, however, was not severe: Iceland moved down by seven places (from 9th in 1990 to 16th in 2010), Denmark by six places (from 11th to 17th), New Zealand by five places (from 22nd to 27th), Switzerland by four places (from 2nd to 6th), Greece by three places (from 25th to 28th), Portugal by three places (from 28th to 31st), Belgium by two places (from 13th to 15th), Israel by two places (from 23th to 25th), Spain by two places (from 21st to 23rd) and the Netherlands by one place (from 6th to 7th). It is worth noting that Portugal and Greece

Table 2.5B   Change in global income rank, 1990–2010: G7 economies

Economy	Income Rank			Income Rank Change			Share in 1990–2010 Ranks Changed	
	1990	2000	2010	1990–2000	2000–2010	1990–2010	1990–2000	2000–2010
	(1)	(2)	(3)	(4) = (1)–(2)	(5) = (2)–(3)	(6) = (1)–(3)	(7) = (4)/(6)	(8) = (5)/(6)
United Kingdom	19	16	18	3	–2	1	300%	–200%
United States	4	3	4	1	–1	0	–	–
Canada	5	7	10	–2	–3	–5	40%	60%
France	15	19	21	–4	–2	–6	67%	33%
Germany	8	12	14	–4	–2	–6	67%	33%
Italy	17	20	24	–3	–4	–7	43%	57%
Japan	7	18	20	–11	–2	–13	85%	15%

Note: The economies appear in the decreasing order of income rank change over 1990–2010.

Source: Author's calculations.

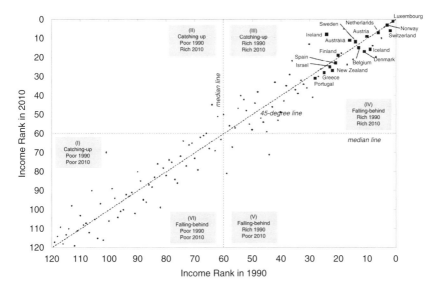

Source: Author's calculations.

Figure 2.2C   *The global dynamics of catching up and falling behind, 1990–2010: Non-G7 economies*

were the lowest-income economies in the group in both 1990 and 2010, and the declines in their ranks were significant.

Ireland was the leading performer among the five catching-up economies of the group (with its rank elevated by 16 places, from 24th in 1990 to 8th in 2010), followed by Australia (five places, from 16th to 11th) and Sweden (two places, from 14th to 12th). At the same time, Austria and Finland improved their ranks by only one place, from 10th to 9th for Austria, and from 20th to 19th for Finland. The catching-up performance of these five Non-G7 economies over 1990–2010 was impressive in different ways. Ireland elevated its income rank by 16 places, which was comparable to improvement of the economies of the four Asian Tigers. Ireland, however, lost its steam in the second sub-period, making no improvement in its income rank over 2000–2010. Australia improved its income rank in both sub-periods, rising by one place in 1990–2000 and four places in 2000–2010.[6] Sweden and Finland, on the other hand, made turnarounds

---

[6]   Some may point out that Australia, with its rich natural resources, has benefited greatly from the rise of China. China has a huge demand for Australia's commodities, such as iron ore and coal.

Table 2.5C   Change in global income rank, 1990–2010: Non-G7 economies

Economy	Income Rank			Income Rank Change			Share in 1990–2010 Ranks Changed	
	1990	2000	2010	1990–2000	2000–2010	1990–2010	1990–2000	2000–2010
	(1)	(2)	(3)	(4) = (1)–(2)	(5) = (2)–(3)	(6) = (1)–(3)	(7) = (4)/(6)	(8) = (5)/(6)
Ireland	24	8	8	16	0	16	100%	0%
Australia	16	15	11	1	4	5	20%	80%
Sweden	14	17	12	-3	5	2	-150%	250%
Austria	10	9	9	1	0	1	100%	0%
Finland	20	21	19	-1	2	1	-100%	200%
Luxembourg	1	1	1	0	0	0	–	–
Norway	3	2	3	1	-1	0	–	–
Netherlands	6	6	7	0	-1	-1	0%	100%
Belgium	13	11	15	2	-4	-2	-100%	200%
Israel	23	24	25	-1	-1	-2	50%	50%
Spain	21	22	23	-1	-1	-2	50%	50%
Greece	25	27	28	-2	-1	-3	67%	33%
Portugal	28	26	31	2	-5	-3	-67%	167%
Switzerland	2	5	6	-3	-1	-4	75%	25%
New Zealand	22	25	27	-3	-2	-5	60%	40%
Denmark	11	10	17	1	-7	-6	-17%	117%
Iceland	9	13	16	-4	-3	-7	57%	43%

Note: The economies appear in the decreasing order of income rank change over 1990–2010.

Source: Author's calculations.

from falling behind in the first sub-period to catching up in the second. In fact, Sweden moved down by three places in 1990–2000 and rose by five places in 2000–2010, while Finland moved down by one place in the first sub-period but rose by two places in the second.

Luxembourg and Norway, which were already the world's richest nations, retained their ranks, 1st for Luxembourg and 3rd for Norway, over the 1990–2010 period. These are the only two economies of the group that remained in leading positions in the global dynamics of catching up.

2.4.4   Latin America (Figure 2.2D and Table 2.5D)

The Latin America economies varied largely in their catching-up performance over the 1990–2010 period. While the best performer (Chile) rose by 14 places, the worst player (Venezuela) moved down by 12 places. Furthermore, all 20 Latin American economies changed their income ranks over 1990–2010; nine economies were catching up and 11 economies were falling behind.

Among the nine catching-up economies, the leading performers that

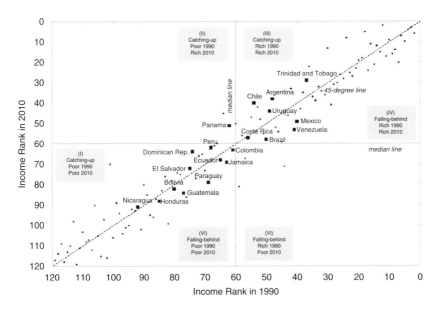

Figure 2.2D   The global dynamics of catching up and falling behind, 1990–
            2010: Latin America economies

Table 2.5D Change in global income rank, 1990–2010: Latin America economies

Economy	Income Rank			Income Rank Change			Share in 1990–2010 Ranks Changed	
	1990	2000	2010	1990–2000	2000–2010	1990–2010	1990–2000	2000–2010
	(1)	(2)	(3)	(4) = (1)−(2)	(5) = (2)−(3)	(6) = (1)−(3)	(7) = (4)/(6)	(8) = (5)/(6)
Chile	54	39	40	15	−1	14	107%	−7%
Panama	62	52	51	10	1	11	91%	9%
Argentina	48	40	38	8	2	10	80%	20%
Dominican Rep.	74	63	64	11	−1	10	110%	−10%
Trinidad and Tobago	37	31	29	6	2	8	75%	25%
Peru	68	64	62	4	2	6	67%	33%
Uruguay	49	43	44	6	−1	5	120%	−20%
El Salvador	75	68	72	7	−4	3	233%	−133%
Nicaragua	92	89	91	3	−2	1	300%	−200%
Costa Rica	56	51	57	5	−6	−1	−500%	600%
Bolivia	80	78	82	2	−4	−2	−100%	200%
Colombia	61	58	63	3	−5	−2	−150%	250%
Ecuador	65	67	68	−2	−1	−3	67%	33%
Honduras	85	82	88	3	−6	−3	−100%	200%
Jamaica	63	59	69	4	−10	−6	−67%	167%
Guatemala	77	73	84	4	−11	−7	−57%	157%
Brazil	50	53	58	−3	−5	−8	38%	63%
Mexico	40	36	49	4	−13	−9	−44%	144%
Paraguay	69	74	79	−5	−5	−10	50%	50%
Venezuela	41	44	53	−3	−9	−12	25%	75%

Note: The economies appear in the decreasing order of income rank change over 1990–2010.

Source: Author's calculations.

moved up by at least five places over 1990–2010 were Chile (14 places, from 54th in 1990 to 40th in 2010); Panama (11 places, from 62nd to 51st), Argentina (10 places, from 48th to 38th), the Dominican Republic (10 places, from 74th to 64th), Trinidad and Tobago (eight places, from 37th to 29th), Peru (six places, from 68th to 62nd) and Uruguay (five places, from 49th to 44th). Of the nine catching-up economies, four economies (Chile, Argentina, Trinidad and Tobago, and Uruguay) met the criteria for being rich economies in both 1990 (Rich 1990) and 2010 (Rich 2010); four economies (Peru, Dominican Republic, El Salvador, and Nicaragua) would be categorized as poor in both 1990 (Poor 1990) and 2010 (Poor 2010), and one economy (Panama) shifted from 'poor' in 1990 to 'rich' in 2010. It is interesting to note that the four Rich 1990 economies (Chile, Argentina, Trinidad and Tobago, and Uruguay) were among the leading catching-up performers of the Latin America group.

Among the 11 falling-behind economies, the countries with the most severe rank deterioration were Venezuela (down by 12 places, from 41st in 1990 to 53rd in 2010), Paraguay (10 places, from 69th to 79th), Mexico (nine places, from 40th to 49th), Brazil (eight places, from 50th to 58th), Guatemala (seven places, from 77th to 84th) and Jamaica (six places, from 63rd to 69th). Of the 11 falling-behind economies, four economies (Venezuela, Mexico, Brazil, and Costa Rica) were 'rich' in both 1990 and 2010, and the remaining seven economies (Paraguay, Guatemala, Jamaica, Honduras, Ecuador, Colombia, and Bolivia) were 'poor' in both 1990 and 2010. It is worth noting that among the falling-behind economies, the declines of the 'rich' economies tended to be more severe than those of the 'poor' economies.

It is also worth noting that most of the income rank improvement attained by the nine catching-up Latin American economies took place in the first sub-period, 1990–2000. On the other hand, most of the deterioration in income rank of the 11 falling-behind Latin American economies occurred in the second sub-period, 2000–2010. This suggests that it has become increasingly challenging for Latin American economies to succeed in catching up and avoid the risk of falling behind.

2.4.5   Eastern Europe (Figure 2.2E and Table 2.5E)

Eastern Europe suffered a severe decline over 1990–2010. One main reason behind the notable decline of many economies in this group was the political and economic turmoil they suffered after the collapse of the communist regime during 1989–1991. Over 1990–2010, only seven of the 21 economies in the group were catching up, while 13 were falling behind and one stayed at the same rank.

Among the seven catching-up economies, five economies rose by more than five places: Poland (up by nine places, from 42nd to 33rd), Belarus (eight places, from 55th to 47th), Armenia (seven places, from 83rd to 76th), Albania (six places, from 72nd to 66th) and Azerbaijan (six places, from 66th to 60th). It is worth noting that among these five leading performers, Poland and Albania exhibited consistent catching-up performance during the two sub-periods. Poland improved its rank by five places in 1990–2000 and four places in 2000–2010, while Albania rose by three places in each of the two sub-periods.

Among the 13 falling-behind economies, eight economies fell by at least five places over 1990–2010: Ukraine (down by 27 places, from 44th to 71st), Georgia (22 places, from 59th to 81st), Tajikistan (17 places, from 82nd to 99th), the Kyrgyz Republic (nine places, from 87th to 96th), Romania (eight places, from 46th to 54th), Russia (five places, from 34th to 39th), Croatia (five places, from 31st to 36th) and Bulgaria (five places, from 47th to 52nd). Two economies, Ukraine and Georgia, fell from 'rich' status in 1990 to 'poor' status in 2010.

It is worth noting that most Eastern Europe economies suffered from a sharp decline in the first sub-period, 1990–2000, but bounced back strongly

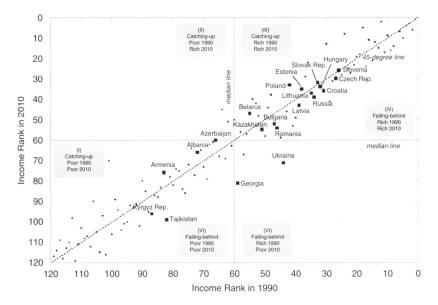

Source: Author's calculations.

Figure 2.2E   The global dynamics of catching up and falling behind, 1990–2010: Eastern Europe economies

Table 2.5E   Change in global income rank, 1990–2010: Eastern Europe economies

Economy	Income Rank			Income Rank Change			Share in 1990–2010 Ranks Changed	
	1990	2000	2010	1990–2000	2000–2010	1990–2010	1990–2000	2000–2010
	(1)	(2)	(3)	(4) = (1)–(2)	(5) = (2)–(3)	(6) = (1)–(3)	(7) = (4)/(6)	(8) = (5)/(6)
Poland	42	37	33	5	4	9	56%	44%
Belarus	55	62	47	–7	15	8	–88%	188%
Armenia	83	88	76	–5	12	7	–71%	171%
Albania	72	69	66	3	3	6	50%	50%
Azerbaijan	66	87	60	–21	27	6	–350%	450%
Estonia	38	38	35	0	3	3	0%	100%
Slovak Rep.	33	34	32	–1	2	1	–100%	200%
Slovenia	26	28	26	–2	2	0		–
Hungary	32	32	34	0	–2	–2	0%	100%
Lithuania	35	46	37	–11	9	–2	550%	–450%
Czech Rep.	27	30	30	–3	0	–3	100%	0%
Kazakhstan	51	66	55	–15	11	–4	375%	–275%
Latvia	39	50	43	–11	7	–4	275%	–175%
Bulgaria	47	56	52	–9	4	–5	180%	–80%
Croatia	31	35	36	–4	–1	–5	80%	20%
Russia	34	49	39	–15	10	–5	300%	–200%
Romania	46	57	54	–11	3	–8	138%	–38%
Kyrgyz Rep.	87	98	96	–11	2	–9	122%	–22%
Tajikistan	82	106	99	–24	7	–17	141%	–41%
Georgia	59	86	81	–27	5	–22	123%	–23%
Ukraine	44	76	71	–32	5	–27	119%	–19%

Note: The economies appear in the decreasing order of income rank change over 1990–2010.

Source: Author's calculations.

in the second sub-period, 2000–2010. There were notable examples of both catching-up and falling-behind economies. Among the catching-up economies, Azerbaijan, Belarus, and Armenia showed remarkable turnarounds. In particular, Azerbaijan fell by 21 places in 1990–2000 but surged up by 27 places in 2000–2010, which enabled it to shift from 'poor' status in 1990 to the border of 'rich' status in 2010. Among the falling-behind economies, Kazakhstan, Russia, and Lithuania rebounded strongly in the second sub-period. In particular, Russia fell by 15 places in 1990–2000 but rose by 10 places in 2000–2010.

Slovenia was the only economy in the Eastern Europe that remained at the same rank, 26th, in the global income ranking over 1990–2010. This economy declined only slightly (down by two places) in the first sub-period and returned to its earlier rank in the second sub-period.

2.4.6   Sub-Saharan Africa (Figure 2.2F and Table 2.5F)

Most economies in this group of 27 economies are clustered at low income levels. In fact, 23 of the 27 economies in this group were 'poor' in both

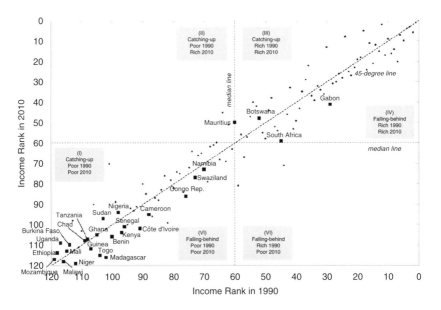

Source: Author's calculations.

*Figure 2.2F   The global dynamics of catching up and falling behind, 1990–
2010: Sub-Saharan Africa economies*

Table 2.5F Change in global income rank, 1990–2010: Sub-Saharan Africa economies

Economy	Income Rank			Income Rank Change			Share in 1990–2010 Ranks Changed	
	1990	2000	2010	1990–2000	2000–2010	1990–2010	1990–2000	2000–2010
	(1)	(2)	(3)	(4) = (1)−(2)	(5) = (2)−(3)	(6) = (1)−(3)	(7) = (4)/(6)	(8) = (5)/(6)
Mauritius	60	47	50	13	−3	10	130%	−30%
Uganda	117	113	109	4	4	8	50%	50%
Sudan	103	100	97	3	3	6	50%	50%
Botswana	52	45	48	7	−3	4	175%	−75%
Burkina Faso	114	111	110	3	1	4	75%	25%
Ethiopia	118	118	114	0	4	4	0%	100%
Nigeria	98	99	94	−1	5	4	−25%	125%
Mali	115	114	113	1	1	2	50%	50%
Mozambique	119	119	117	0	2	2	0%	100%
Chad	109	115	108	−6	7	1	−600%	700%
Tanzania	108	112	107	−4	5	1	−400%	500%
Ghana	105	103	105	2	−2	0	–	–
Malawi	116	116	118	0	−2	−2	0%	100%
Namibia	70	70	73	0	−3	−3	0%	100%
Swaziland	73	71	77	2	−6	−4	−50%	150%
Guinea	107	109	112	−2	−3	−5	40%	60%
Senegal	96	97	101	−1	−4	−5	20%	80%

Table 2.5F (continued)

| Economy | Income Rank | | | Income Rank Change | | | Share in 1990–2010 Ranks Changed | |
| | 1990 | 2000 | 2010 | 1990–2000 | 2000–2010 | 1990–2010 | 1990–2000 | 2000–2010 |
	(1)	(2)	(3)	(4) = (1)−(2)	(5) = (2)−(3)	(6) = (1)−(3)	(7) = (4)/(6)	(8) = (5)/(6)
Benin	100	101	106	−1	−5	−6	17%	83%
Cameroon	88	91	95	−3	−4	−7	43%	57%
Kenya	97	102	104	−5	−2	−7	71%	29%
Niger	112	117	119	−5	−2	−7	71%	29%
Congo Rep.	76	79	86	−3	−7	−10	30%	70%
Côte d'Ivoire	91	93	102	−2	−9	−11	18%	82%
Togo	104	110	115	−6	−5	−11	55%	45%
Gabon	29	33	41	−4	−8	−12	33%	67%
Madagascar	102	107	116	−5	−9	−14	36%	64%
South Africa	45	54	59	−9	−5	−14	64%	36%

Note: The economies appear in the decreasing order of income rank change over 1990–2010.

Source: Author's calculations.

54

1990 and 2010. Among the remaining four economies, three economies were 'rich' in both 1990 and 2010, while one economy (Mauritius) shifted from the median income level in 1990 to 'rich' status in 2010.

Decline was the dominant trend observed for the group. Among its 27 economies, only 11 economies were catching up, while 15 economies were falling behind and only one economy stayed at the same rank over 1990–2010. In addition, the performance of the catching-up economies was not strong relative to those in the other developing groups. In fact, only three catching-up economies moved up by more than five places: Mauritius (up by 10 places, from 60th in 1990 to 50th in 2010), Uganda (eight places, from 117th to 109th) and Sudan (six places, from 103rd to 97th). On the other hand, the decline of the falling-behind economies was severe, with 12 economies moving down by at least five places. Among them were six economies that dropped by 10 or more places: South Africa (down by 14 places, from 45th in 1990 to 59th in 2010), Madagascar (14 places, from 102nd to 116th), Gabon (12 places, from 29th to 41st), Togo (11 places, from 104th to 115th), Côte d'Ivoire (11 places, from 91st to 102nd) and the Congo Republic (10 places, from 76th to 86th).

It is interesting to see the large variation in the performance of the four 'rich' economies of the group. While Mauritius and Botswana moved up by ten and four places, respectively, South Africa and Gabon moved down by 14 and 12 places, respectively. This implies that the global dynamics of catching up and falling behind over 1990–2010 had a more notable impact on the 'rich' economies of the group, which is similar to what was observed for the Latin America group.

One important feature of the performance of the Sub-Saharan Africa group in the global dynamics of catching up and falling behind was the consistency between the two sub-periods. For most economies in the group, the performance in the second sub-period was in the same direction as in the first sub-period. This feature was particularly pronounced for the falling-behind economies. In fact, all the falling-behind economies that moved down by five or more places over 1990–2010 experienced declines in both sub-periods.

2.4.7   North Africa and Middle East (Figure 2.2G and Table 2.5G)

The economies in this group were notably affected by the global dynamics of catching up and falling behind. Lebanon in particular, as the top catching-up performer, with its rank increased by 19 places over 1990–2010, shifted its status from 'poor' in 1990 to 'rich' in 2010. In contrast, Algeria, as the worst performer with a decline of 10 places in its rank, dropped from 'rich' status in 1990 to 'poor' status in 2010.

Overall, with seven of the group's 11 economies moving up in the income ranking over 1990–2010, the group exhibited good performance in the global dynamics of catching up and falling behind during this period. However, there were signs of concern in the sharp worsening of the group's performance from the first sub-period, 1990–2000, to the second sub-period, 2000–2010. In fact, eight of the group's 11 economies fell in the income ranking in the second sub-period. Among them, six economies (Egypt, Syria, Iran, Morocco, Yemen, and Turkey) turned from rank improvement in the first sub-period to rank deterioration in the second sub-period, and the other two economies (Mauritania and Algeria) declined in both sub-periods, although their decline in the second sub-period was far more severe than in the first sub-period. This pattern was also observed for the two leading performers of the group, Lebanon and Tunisia. Lebanon rose by sixteen places in 1990–2000 but only by three places in 2000–2010, while Tunisia improved its rank by six places in the first sub-period but none in the second.

It is worth noting that the sharp worsening in the catching-up

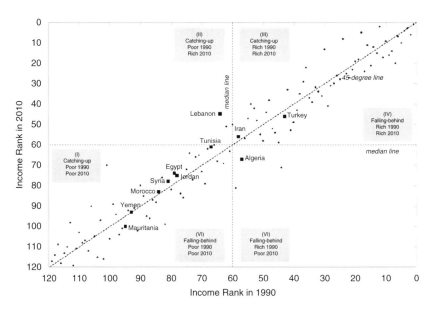

Source: Author's calculations.

Figure 2.2G *The global dynamics of catching up and falling behind, 1990–2010: North Africa & Middle-East economies*

Table 2.5G   Change in global income rank, 1990–2010: North Africa & Middle-East economies

Economy	Income Rank			Income Rank Change			Share in 1990–2010 Ranks Changed	
	1990	2000	2010	1990–2000	2000–2010	1990–2010	1990–2000	2000–2010
	(1)	(2)	(3)	(4) = (1)–(2)	(5) = (2)–(3)	(6) = (1)–(3)	(7) = (4)/(6)	(8) = (5)/(6)
Lebanon	64	48	45	16	3	19	84%	16%
Tunisia	67	61	61	6	0	6	100%	0%
Egypt	79	72	74	7	-2	5	140%	-40%
Jordan	78	77	75	1	2	3	33%	67%
Syria	81	75	78	6	-3	3	200%	-100%
Iran	58	55	56	3	-1	2	150%	-50%
Morocco	84	81	83	3	-2	1	300%	-200%
Yemen	93	90	93	3	-3	0	–	–
Turkey	43	42	46	1	-4	-3	-33%	133%
Mauritania	95	96	100	-1	-4	-5	20%	80%
Algeria	57	60	67	-3	-7	-10	30%	70%

Note: The economies appear in the decreasing order of income rank change over 1990–2010.

Source: Author's calculations.

performance of the North Africa and Middle East group from the first
to the second sub-period may have been a contributing economic factor
in the widespread uprisings in the region in 2011 known as the Arab
Spring. This link, in particular, is strong for Egypt (which rose in rank
by seven places in 1990–2000 but fell by two places in 2000–2010), Syria
(up by six places and then down by three places), Tunisia (up by six
places and then stagnated), and Yemen (up by three places and then
down by three places). These findings suggest an important policy impli-
cation. For a developing country, making catching-up efforts must go
hand in hand with good governance and building a vibrant democratic
society, both of which are important not only to fostering a country's
catching-up performance but also to the country remaining peaceful and
stable during declining periods, which the country will experience sooner
or later.

2.5   THE PERFORMANCE OF DEVELOPING ASIA IN THE GLOBAL DYNAMICS OF CATCHING-UP: A CLOSER LOOK

As described in the previous section, the catching-up performance of
individual economies fluctuated notably during the 1990–2010 period, as
reflected in the changes in their performance between the two sub-periods,
1990–2000 and 2000–2010. This section presents a more detailed picture
of the catching-up performance of the 16 Developing Asia economies
between the two sub-periods, 1990–2000 and 2000–2010, and on an annual
basis during the 1990–2010 period.

Figure 2.3 depicts the global income rank change of the 16 Developing
Asia in 1990–2000 (on the x axis) and 2000–2010 (on the y axis). The
vertical median line divides the 16 Developing Asia economies into two
subgroups by their performance in the first sub-period, 1990–2000 and
the horizontal median line divides the economies by their performance in
the second sub-period, 2000–2010. At the same time, the 45-degree line
divides the space into two parts. The upper part contains the economies
that performed better in the second sub-period than in the first sub-period
in terms of the number of ranks changed, while the lower part contains
the economies whose performance slowed down in the second sub-period
relative to the first.

Figure 2.3 shows that the performance of most economies slowed
down in the second sub-period relative to the first. In fact, only Taiwan
and Hong Kong improved their performance from the first sub-period to
the second, and South Korea and India sustained the same performance

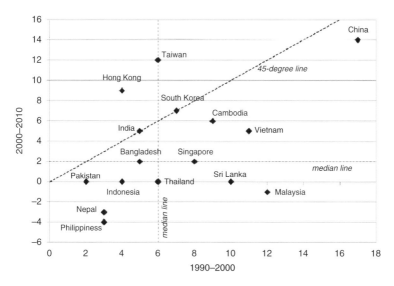

Source: Author's calculations.

Figure 2.3   Change in global income rank – Developing Asia: 2000–2010 versus 1990–2000

in the two sub-periods. The Philippines, Nepal, Pakistan, and Indonesia were among the laggards of the group in both sub-periods: their performance worsened notably from the first sub-period to the second. Malaysia and Sri Lanka performed outstandingly in the first sub-period but poorly in the second. China was the top performer in both sub-periods, although its performance slowed down in the second sub-period relative to the first.

Figures 2.4A–2.4D portray the annual global income rank during the 1990–2010 period for individual economies of Developing Asia, which are split into four subgroups: China–India (Figure 2.4A), Tigers-4 (Figure 2.4B), ASEAN-6 (Figure 2.4C), and SAC-4 (Figure 2.4D).

2.5.1   China–India (Figure 2.4A)

China surpassed India in income rank in 1992 and achieved outstanding improvement in income rank during 1992–1996. After a notable slowdown in 1997–1998, which was most likely caused by the consequences of the Asian financial crisis, China's catching-up performance improved robustly from 2000 to 2009 before flatting out in 2010. India's catching-up progress was strong during 1992–1995 and 2000–2006, but the

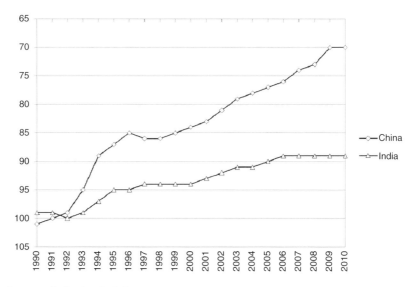

Source: Author's calculations.

Figure 2.4A   Annual income rank, 1990–2010: China–India

country nearly did not achieve significant improvements in other years. In particular, India has stayed at the same rank in recent years, from 2006 to 2010.

2.5.2   Tigers-4 (Figure 2.4B)

Singapore made its major catch-up progress between 1990 and 1995 and its income rank has been among the top five since 1995. The economy stayed at the same rank through 1996–2003, during which the country suffered from the notable effects of the Asian financial crisis and the worldwide economic slowdown in 2000–2001, caused by the consequences of the dotcom bust and the 9/11 terrorist attacks.

Hong Kong achieved outstanding catch-up performance during 1990–1993, but its performance slowed down and then worsened considerably during 1993–1999. The Asian financial crisis appears to have had a severe adverse effect on Hong Kong's income rank during this period. Hong Kong exhibited solid catch-up performance again during 2002–2008, and since 2008, its income rank became stable at 5th place.

Both Taiwan and South Korea made notable catch-up progress during 1990–1996, but the Asian financial crisis appears to have had strong

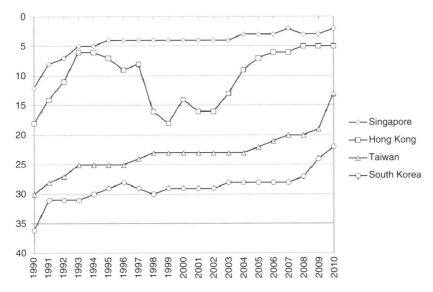

Source: Author's calculations.

Figure 2.4B   Annual income rank, 1990–2010: Tigers-4

adverse effects on their catching-up momentum. Taiwan did not regain its robust catching-up performance until 2005, while South Korea only returned to strong catching-up performance in 2007.

2.5.3   ASEAN-6 (Figure 2.4C)

The catching-up performance of the six ASEAN-6 economies exhibited distinctive trends. On the one hand, Malaysia, Thailand, and Indonesia made notable progress during 1990–1997, but all experienced sharp declines during the Asian financial crisis in 1997–1998, and their perform-ance has flattened out since then. The Philippines, to some extent, also followed the pattern observed for Malaysia, Thailand, and Indonesia, but Vietnam and Cambodia made impressive progress in moving up in the global income ranking throughout 1990–2010. The catching-up perform-ance of these two economies was not significantly affected by the Asian financial crisis. However, their catching-up performance appeared to lose momentum after 2007, and they have been staying at the same income ranks since then.

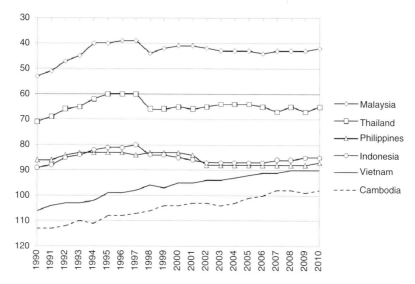

Source: Author's calculations.

Figure 2.4C   Annual income rank, 1990–2010: ASEAN-6

2.5.4   SAC-4 (Figure 2.4D)

Sri Lanka and Bangladesh exhibited rather similar patterns in catching-up performance. These two economies made significant progress in catching up during 1990–2000 but experienced notable declines during 2001–2006, before regaining their catching-up momentum in 2007. This pattern was more pronounced for Sri Lanka, the leading performer of the SAC-4 group.

On the other hand, Pakistan and Nepal exhibited another pattern. These two economies made significant progress during 1990–1994 and then lost their momentum. Pakistan's income rank declined during 1994–1996, and has remained almost unchanged since 1996. Nepal declined in its income rank during 1994–1999 and experienced an improvement in 2000. However, this rank improvement was short-lived. The country's rank declined to the 111th place in 2003 and has mostly stayed at this same rank since then.

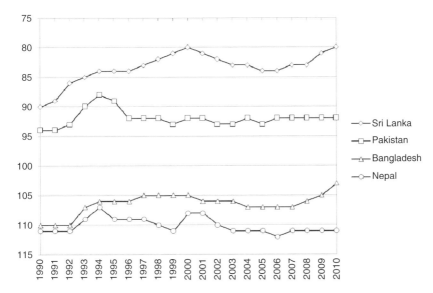

Source: Author's calculations.

Figure 2.4D   *Annual income rank, 1990–2010: SAC-4*

2.6   SUMMARY

This chapter examines the performance of 119 economies in seven groups—Developing Asia, G7, Non-G7, Latin America, Eastern Europe, Sub-Saharan Africa, and North Africa and Middle East—in the global dynamics of catching up during the 1990–2010 period. The global rank based on per capita GDP, measured in PPP$, is used for this purpose. The chapter documents several notable findings.

First, almost all economies were affected by the shake-up of the global dynamics of catching up. Over the 1990–2010 period, 45 per cent of the 119 economies studied moved up and 49 per cent moved down, while the ranks of only 6 per cent of the economies remained unchanged.

Second, the catching-up performance over 1990–2010 varied largely in three respects: among the seven groups, among the economies in each group, and between the two sub-periods, 1990–2000 and 2000–2010, by group as well as by individual economy. In terms of the performance variation by group over the 1990–2010 period, Developing Asia was the best performer, followed by North Africa and Middle East and Latin America. In contrast, G7 was the worst performer, followed by Eastern Europe and

Sub-Saharan Africa. Within each of the seven groups, the variation by economy was striking. The gap in rank change between the best and the worst performer was 32 for Developing Asia (China, the best performer, moved up by 31 places, while the Philippines, the worst performer, moved down by one place), 14 for G7 (United Kingdom, up by one place; Japan, down by 13 places), 23 for Non-G7 (Ireland, up by 16 places; Iceland, down by seven places), 26 for Latin America (Chile, up by 14 places; Venezuela, down by 12 places), 36 for Eastern Europe (Poland, up by nine places; Ukraine, down by 27 places), 24 for Sub-Saharan Africa (Mauritius, up by 10 places; South Africa, down by 14 places) and 29 places for North Africa and Middle East (Lebanon, up by 19 places; Algeria, down by 10 places). The variation between the two sub-periods by group as well as by economy was also notable. In particular, most economies in Eastern Europe suffered sharp declines in the first sub-period but resurged in the second. At the same time, almost all economies in the North Africa and Middle East group performed poorly in the second sub-period, although they did reasonably well in the first.

Third, a closer look at the catching-up performance of the 16 Developing Asia economies reveals that most economies in the group performed very well before the Asian financial crisis erupted in 1997. The adverse impact of this crisis, however, varied significantly among the economies in this group. China, India, Vietnam and Cambodia performed well in both sub-periods. At the same time, Malaysia, Thailand, and Indonesia appeared to lose considerable momentum beginning in 1997. The four Asian Tigers showed robust catching-up performance, although they suffered significantly from the consequence of the crisis. Among the SAC-4 economies, Sri Lanka and Bangladesh have shown encouraging catching-up performance in recent years, while Pakistan and Nepal have apparently stagnated in their catching-up since 1996.

3. The rise of Asia

3.1 INTRODUCTION

Profound transformational changes have been occurring in the Developing Asia countries over the past six decades. The pace of these changes have notably accelerated in the past two decades with the outstanding economic performance of the two giants, China and India, which together account for over one third of the world's population. These changes have ushered in a new era of Asia's ascent, which is expected to have powerful and unprecedented impacts on the world economy and on every nation's economic prospects.

There has been a wealth of studies discussing the rise of Asia in the global economic landscape and projecting its potential impact in the future. Kawai and Petri (2010) observed that the growth of emerging and developing economies tended to be higher than that of advanced economies in the 1970s. However, the gap narrowed over time and essentially disappeared between 1985 and 1995. Since the second half of the 1990s, the growth of emerging and developing economies has been rising, while that of advanced economies has been declining. This phenomenon was termed by Kawai and Petri (2010) as 'trend decoupling.'

In a more recent study, Jorgenson and Vu (2011) predicted that the rise of Asia would be firmly established sometime by the year 2020. Asia's economic performance is thought to have created a new model for economic growth that is built on globalization and the rapid accumulation of human and non-human capital over decades, notwithstanding the skillful roles of public and private authorities. It has been forecasted that with the current levels of productivity and economic performance, by 2020, China will overtake the US in terms of gross domestic product (GDP), measured in terms of purchasing power parity. At the same time, Developing Asia is expected to overtake the group of the seven largest industrialized economies (G7), while India is expected to overtake Japan.

ADB (2011) predicted that the next four decades (2010–2050) would witness the march of Asia to prosperity. In its optimistic scenario, by 2050, the average per capita income of Asia would be $45,800 in purchasing power parity (PPP) terms, compared with $37,300 for the world as a whole. In addition, seven economies, including Japan and six Developing Asia economies—China, India, Indonesia, South Korea, Thailand, and Malaysia—will be the engines of this transformation. Together, they are expected to account for 91 per cent of total GDP growth in Asia and 53 per cent of global GDP growth between 2010 and 2050.

This chapter seeks to provide an in-depth understanding of the rise of Developing Asia over the period 1990–2010. The chapter examines the share of the region in the world economy and its contribution to the world's economic growth over this period. This examination is focused on the key items of the national account, which include GDP, private consumption, government consumption, fixed investment, exports and imports. In addition, the chapter presents a deeper examination of the rise of Developing Asia in the measures shaping the dynamics of the world economy, which include inward foreign direct investment (FDI) and international trade related to manufactures, commercial services, and information and communication technology (ICT) products.

The table for examining the performance of Developing Asia with respect to a given indicator is constructed in a format intended to make it easy for readers to follow. The world is divided into three groups: Developing Asia,[1] Industrialized Economies,[2] and the group of remaining economies, which is referred to as the Rest of the World (ROW).[3] The table covers the 1990–2010 period, which is split into two sub-periods, 1990–2000 and 2000–2010, and includes two panels. The upper panel reports the summary statistics at the group level, while the lower panel presents the statistics for the individual Developing Asia economies. As in the other chapters of this book, to facilitate comparisons, the results for the 16 individual Developing Asia economies are presented in four subgroups: China–India, which includes China and India; Tigers-4, which includes Hong Kong, Singapore, South Korea, and Taiwan; ASEAN-6, which includes Cambodia, Indonesia, Malaysia, the Philippines, Thailand, and Vietnam; and SAC-4, which includes Bangladesh, Nepal, Pakistan, and Sri Lanka.

To make cross-country comparisons meaningful, the values of GDP, private consumption, government consumption, and fixed investment for individual economies are expressed in terms of purchasing power parity (PPP) using their corresponding PPP conversion factors. The main data are from the World Bank's World Development Indicators (WDI) database. The PPP conversion factors for private consumption, govern-

---

[1]   The Developing Asia group consists of the 16 economies introduced in Chapter 1.
[2]   The Industrialized Economies group consists of 24 economies introduced in Section 2.1 (Chapter 2), which include seven G7 economies and 17 non-G7 industrialized economies.
[3]   The number of economies in the ROW group may vary by table depending on their data availability for the measure of interest.

BOX 3.1   A NOTE ON COMPUTATION: THE AGGREGATE GROWTH RATE OF A GROUP AND THE CONTRIBUTION OF INDIVIDUAL ECONOMIES TO THE GROUP'S AGGREGATE GROWTH

1–The growth rate g_{Group} of a group of n economies over period [0, T] on a given variable X is computed as the weighted average growth rates of the n economies:

$$g_{Group} = \sum_{k=1}^{n} \bar{w}_k \, g_k$$

where g_k is growth rate of economy k ($k = 1,2,\ldots n$) over period [0, T], $\bar{w}_k$ is the average share of economy k in the group on variable X over the period, $\bar{w}_k = (w_k^0 + w_k^T) / 2$.

2–The contribution of economy k to the group's aggregate growth over period [0, T] is computed as

$$C_k = \bar{w}_k \, g_k / g_{Group} * 100\%$$

It is worth noting that $\sum_{k=1}^{n} C_k = 100\%$

---

ment consumption, and fixed investment are from the World Bank's International Comparison Program (ICP) 2005 Report. The data for Taiwan, which are not available in the WDI database, are extrapolated from information in the Asian Development Bank database and the ICP 2005 Report.

The role of a group of economies such as Developing Asia in the world economy with respect to a given indicator during a given period can be captured by two measures. One is its share in the world economy and the other is its contribution to the world economy's growth. Similarly, the role of an economy in a group with respect to a given indicator is measured by its share in the group and its contribution to the group's growth. Box 3.1 provides a short technical note on calculation of the contribution of an economy to its group's growth for a given indicator. This method can also be applied to the calculation of the contribution of a group to the world economy's growth.

The remaining sections of this chapter examine the rise of Developing

Asia by investigating the performance of the group and its individual economies in the world economy with respect to key economic indicators, including GDP (Section 3.2), private consumption (Section 3.3), government consumption (Section 3.4), fixed investment (Section 3.5), and exports and imports of goods and services (Section 3.6). To capture a more in-depth picture of the impact of Developing Asia in the globalization trend, Section 3.7 looks at the rise of Asia and its two major economic giants, China and India, with respect to the four indicators that have been the emblems of globalization in the past two decades: exports of ICT hardware, exports of manufactures, exports of commercial services, and FDI stock. Finally, Section 3.8 combines the main results from Sections 3.2 to 3.7 to form a comprehensive picture of the rise of Developing Asia and its two giant economies, China and India, in the world economy during the two-decade period of 1990–2010.

3.2   THE RISE OF DEVELOPING ASIA IN WORLD GDP

This section examines the rise of Asia in the world economy in terms of GDP. The value of GDP is measured in terms of purchasing power parity, using conversion factors obtained from the World Bank Development Indicators database.

The role of a group such as Developing Asia in the world economy can be captured by two GDP-related measures. One is its share in world GDP and the other is its contribution to the world's GDP growth. These statistics for Developing Asia and other parts of the world for the 1990–2010 period and its two sub-periods, 1990–2000 and 2000–2010, are reported in Table 3.1 (Panel A). Panel B of the table presents similar statistics for individual economies of the Developing Asia group.

3.2.1   Performance of Developing Asia as a Group in Terms of GDP

Developing Asia's GDP grew at 6.8 per cent during 1990–2010, well above the world average of 3.1 per cent (Table 3.1, Panel A). In contrast, the Industrialized Economies grew at 2 per cent, and the ROW grew at 2.5 per cent. Furthermore, Developing Asia's growth accelerated between the two sub-periods, from 5.9 per cent in 1990–2000 to 7.9 per cent in 2000–2010. The Industrialized Economies experienced a declining trend, from 2.6 per cent in the first sub-period to 1.4 per cent in the second. However, the ROW also exhibited a solid acceleration in growth, from 1.1 per cent in 1990–2000 to 4 per cent in 2000–2010.

Table 3.1 The rise of Developing Asia in the world economy, 1990–2010: GDP

(A) Groups in the World

Group	Growth and Contribution						Share in World		
	1990–2010		1990–2000		2000–2010		1990	2000	2010
	Growth	Contb.	Growth	Contb.	Growth	Contb.			
World (119 Economies)	**3.1**	**100.0**	**2.8**	**100.0**	**3.5**	**100.0**	**100.0**	**100.0**	**100.0**
Developing Asia	6.8	46.1	5.9	34.7	7.9	53.8	13.3	19.3	28.2
Industrialized Economies	2.0	34.9	2.6	56.7	1.4	21.1	62.6	60.1	48.7
Rest of World (ROW)	2.5	19.0	1.1	8.6	4.0	25.1	24.1	20.6	23.1

(B) Developing Asia

Economy	1990–2010			1990–2000			2000–2010			Share in Group			Share in World		
	Growth Rate	Contb. to Growth		Growth Rate	Contb. to Growth		Growth Rate	Contb. to Growth		1990	2000	2010	1990	2000	2010
		Group	World		Group	World		Group	World						
Developing Asia	**6.8**	**100.0**	**46.1**	**5.9**	**100.0**	**34.7**	**7.9**	**100.0**	**53.8**	**100.0**	**100.0**	**100.0**	**13.3**	**19.3**	**28.2**
China–India															
China	9.0	50.4	25.0	14.0	39.3	14.0	10.9	59.7	32.6	27.6	37.6	48.7	3.7	7.3	13.7
India	6.4	20.6	9.0	6.8	20.0	6.8	7.4	19.0	10.1	23.3	20.1	20.1	3.1	3.9	5.7
Tigers-4															
Hong Kong	3.9	1.3	0.5	3.9	1.7	0.6	4.0	1.0	0.5	3.0	2.2	1.6	0.4	0.4	0.4
Singapore	6.5	1.5	0.7	7.3	2.1	0.7	5.8	1.1	0.6	1.7	1.7	1.4	0.2	0.3	0.4
South Korea	5.2	6.6	2.7	6.3	11.1	3.8	4.1	4.4	2.3	10.4	10.2	6.8	1.4	2.0	1.9
Taiwan	4.9	3.9	1.6	6.0	6.5	2.2	3.8	2.5	1.3	6.5	6.2	4.3	0.9	1.2	1.2

Table 3.1 (continued)

(B) Developing Asia

Economy	1990–2010			1990–2000			2000–2010			Share in Group			Share in World		
	Growth Rate	Contb. to Growth		Growth Rate	Contb. to Growth		Growth Rate	Contb. to Growth		1990	2000	2010	1990	2000	2010
		Group	World		Group	World		Group	World						
ASEAN-6															
Cambodia	7.4	0.2	0.1	7.0	0.2	0.1	7.7	0.1	0.1	0.1	0.1	0.1	0.02	0.03	0.04
Indonesia	4.6	4.5	1.8	4.1	5.1	1.7	5.1	3.6	1.9	8.2	6.3	5.0	1.1	1.2	1.4
Malaysia	5.7	2.0	0.8	6.9	3.1	1.1	4.5	1.3	0.7	2.7	2.7	2.0	0.4	0.5	0.6
Philippines	3.8	1.4	0.6	2.9	1.4	0.5	4.7	1.2	0.6	3.5	2.3	1.8	0.5	0.5	0.5
Thailand	4.3	2.5	1.0	4.4	3.3	1.1	4.2	1.8	0.9	5.0	3.9	2.8	0.7	0.7	0.8
Vietnam	7.2	1.4	0.6	7.3	1.7	0.6	7.0	1.2	0.6	1.3	1.4	1.3	0.2	0.3	0.4
SAC-4															
Bangladesh	5.2	1.1	0.5	4.7	1.2	0.4	5.6	0.9	0.5	1.7	1.4	1.2	0.2	0.3	0.3
Nepal	4.3	0.2	0.1	4.9	0.2	0.1	3.8	0.1	0.1	0.3	0.2	0.2	0.04	0.05	0.05
Pakistan	4.5	2.1	0.8	4.3	2.5	0.9	4.7	1.6	0.8	4.0	3.0	2.2	0.5	0.6	0.6
Sri Lanka	5.1	0.5	0.2	5.1	0.6	0.2	5.1	0.4	0.2	0.8	0.6	0.5	0.1	0.1	0.1

Note: GDP is measured in PPPs for GDP.

Source: Author's calculations; data from WDI, ADB, TED.

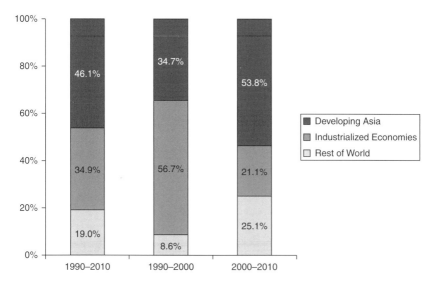

Source: Author's calculations; data from WDI, ADB, TED.

*Figure 3.1   Contribution to the world's GDP growth: Developing Asia
versus other parts of the world*

The role of Developing Asia as the major driver of the world's GDP
growth is apparent. As shown in Figure 3.1, Developing Asia's contribution to the world's GDP growth for 1990–2010 was 46.1 per cent, exceeding that of the Industrialized Economies (34.9 per cent) and that of the
ROW (19.0 per cent). Moreover, the contribution of Developing Asia
exhibited a notable rising trend, from 34.7 per cent in the first sub-period,
1990–2000, to 53.8 per cent in 2000–2010, while this measure sharply
declined from 56.7 to 21.1 per cent for the Industrialized Economies.
These findings indicate the increasingly important role of Developing
Asia as the main driver of world economic growth. It is also worth noting
that the contribution of the ROW increased, growing from 8.6 per cent in
1990–2000 to 25.1 per cent in 2000–2010, which means that other developing economies also enhanced their contribution to the world's GDP
growth.

The share of Developing Asia in world GDP rose rapidly, from 13.3 per
cent in 1990 to 19.3 per cent in 2000 and 28.2 per cent in 2010 (Table 3.1,
Panel A). In contrast, the share of the Industrialized Economies group
declined at an accelerating rate, from 62.6 per cent in 1990 to 60.1 per
cent in 2000 and 48.7 per cent in 2010. However, the share of the ROW
group exhibited a different pattern, falling from 24.1 per cent in 1990

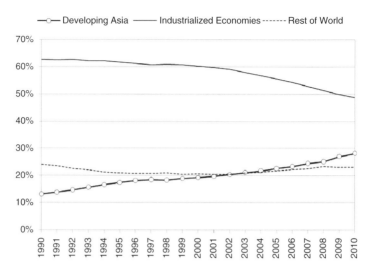

Source: Author's calculations; data from WDI, ADB, TED.

Figure 3.2 Share in world GDP, 1990–2010: Developing Asia versus other parts of the world

to 20.6 per cent in 2000 and then recovering to 23.1 per cent, which was slightly below its 1990 level. This trend in the ROW group was primarily associated with the shrinking of the Eastern European and former Soviet Union economies in the early 1990s and their strong recovery in the 2000s. Figure 3.2 illustrates a clear upward trend in Developing Asia's share of world GDP during 1990–2010. In contrast, the share of the Industrialized Economies declined continuously over this period, particularly after 2000. As a result, the gap between Developing Asia and the Industrialized Economies in terms of their shares of world GDP narrowed significantly over 1990–2010, especially after 2000. On the other hand, the ROW share of world GDP exhibited an increasing trend after 2000, although the pace was much slower than that of Developing Asia. As a result, Developing Asia surpassed the ROW with respect to this indicator in 2002 and has continuously widened this gap since then.

3.2.2 Performance of Individual Developing Asia Economies in Terms of GDP

China–India
China and India—the two economies with giant populations and out-standing performance in 1990–2010—played important roles in driving

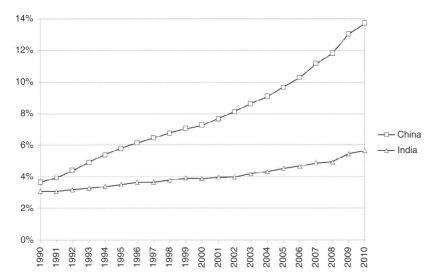

Source: Author's calculations; data from WDI, ADB, TED.

Figure 3.3A   Share in world GDP, 1990–2010: China–India

the world's GDP growth during this period. China's GDP grew at 9 per cent during 1990–2010, contributing 25 per cent to the world's GDP growth over this period; India's GDP growth rate and GDP growth contribution were 6.4 per cent and 9 per cent, respectively (Table 3.1, Panel B). Furthermore, for both countries, GDP growth and GDP growth contribution were notably stronger in the second sub-period than in the first. China's growth accelerated by nearly 4 percentage points, from 7.1 per cent in 1990–2000 to 10.9 per cent in 2000–2010, and its contribution to world GDP growth increased from 14.0 per cent in the first sub-period to 32.6 per cent in the second. India's GDP growth accelerated by 2 percentage points, from 5.4 to 7.4 per cent, enlarging its contribution to the world's GDP growth from 6.8 per cent in the first sub-period to 10.1 per cent in the second.

Together with their outstanding growth, the shares of China and India in world GDP expanded rapidly. This share increased by 10 percentage points, from 3.7 per cent in 1990 to 13.7 per cent in 2010, for China and by close to 3 percentage points, from 3.1 to 5.7 per cent over the same period, for India (Table 3.1, Panel B). As shown in Figure 3.3A, the shares of both China and India in world GDP followed solid upward trends. Moreover, this expanding trend accelerated after 2000 for China and after 2002 for India. China's share in world GDP, however, increased much faster than India's throughout 1990–2010. As a result, the gap between the two countries in terms of this measure widened substantially, from less than 1 percentage point in 1990 to more than 8 percentage points in 2010.

Tigers-4

The four Asian Tiger economies outperformed the world average in terms of GDP growth during 1990–2010. The GDP growth rate over the period was 3.9 per cent for Hong Kong, 6.5 per cent for Singapore, 5.2 per cent for South Korea, and 4.9 per cent for Taiwan, while the world average rate was only 3.1 per cent (Table 3.1, Panel B). However, the degree to which these four economies outperformed the world average was greater in the first sub-period than in the second. The growth rate was nearly unchanged for Hong Kong, at approximately 4 per cent, but decreased notably between the two sub-periods for Singapore (from 7.3 per cent in 1990–2000 to 5.8 per cent in 2000–2010), South Korea (from 6.3 to 4.1 per cent), and Taiwan (from 6 to 3.8 per cent), while the world average rate increased from 2.8 per cent in the first sub-period to 3.5 per cent in the second sub-period. Among the four Asian Tiger economies, South Korea was the largest contributor to the world's GDP growth, followed by Taiwan, while Singapore exceeded Hong Kong with respect to this measure in 1990–2010 as well as in the two sub-periods, 1990–2000 and 2000–2010.

With the exception of Hong Kong, the shares of the Asian Tiger economies in world GDP increased during 1990–2010. This share increased from 1.4 per cent to 1.9 per cent for South Korea, from 0.9 to 1.2 per cent for Taiwan, and from 0.2 per cent to 0.4 per cent for Singapore, while it remained stable at 0.4 per cent for Hong Kong (Table 3.1, Panel B). However, this expansion took place mostly before the eruption of the Asian financial crisis in 1997 (Figure 3.3B). South Korea appeared to be hit hard by the Asian financial crisis but also exhibited a strong recovery after the crisis. South Korea's share in world GDP plunged in 1998, bounced back during 1999–2002, and then declined again during 2002–2010. Taiwan was not directly affected by the Asian financial crisis, but its expansion seemed to lose steam after 2000. Taiwan's share in world GDP increased steadily during 1990–2000 but flattened out during 2000–2010. Hong Kong's share of world GDP decreased during 1997–1998, picked up slightly during 1998–2000, and fluctuated around the same level during 2000–2010. Singapore's share, on the other hand, increased consistently during 1990–2010, although it declined slightly during the Asian financial crisis period of 1997–1998.

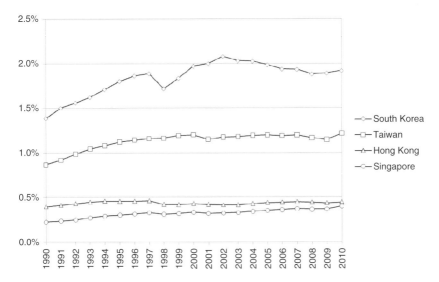

Source: Author's calculations; data from WDI, ADB, TED.

Figure 3.3B   Share in world GDP, 1990–2010: Tigers-4

ASEAN-6

The ASEAN-6 economies all outperformed the world average in terms of GDP growth during 1990–2010, as well as in the two sub-periods, 1990–2000 and 2000–2010. The leading performers of the subgroup in terms of GDP growth over 1990–2010 were Cambodia (7.4 per cent), Vietnam (7.2 per cent), and Malaysia (5.7 per cent); the Philippines was the laggard, growing at 3.8 per cent (Table 3.1, Panel B). These economies, however, followed different trends in GDP growth over the two sub-periods. GDP growth accelerated for Cambodia (from 7 per cent in 1990–2000 to 7.7 per cent in 2000–2010), Indonesia (from 4.1 to 5.1 per cent), and the Philippines (from 2.9 to 4.7 per cent), while it slowed down for Malaysia (from 6.9 to 4.5 per cent), Thailand (from 4.4 to 4.2 per cent), and Vietnam (7.3 to 7 per cent). Indonesia and Thailand were the two ASEAN-6 economies that contributed more than 1 per cent to the world's GDP growth over 1990–2010.

The shares of all the ASEAN-6 economies in world GDP increased over 1990–2010 (Figure 3.3C). However, the patterns and magnitudes of their expansion differed vastly among the six economies. The Asian financial crisis appeared to have notable effects on Indonesia, Thailand, and Malaysia. The shares of these three economies rapidly expanded before the crisis but sharply declined during the crisis (1997–1998 for

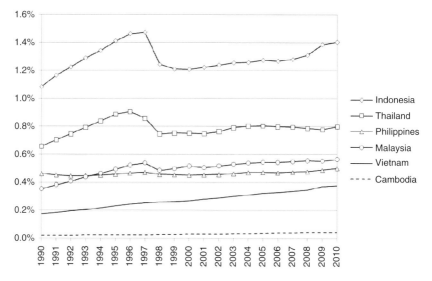

Source: Author's calculations; data from WDI, ADB, TED.

Figure 3.3C   Share in world GDP, 1990–2010: ASEAN-6

Thailand, 1998–1999 for Indonesia, and 1998 for Malaysia). These three high-performing Asian economies[4] then slowly recovered and continued to expand their shares of world GDP during 1999–2010. It is worth noting that although the resurgence of Indonesia during 2000–2010 was sizable, its share of world GDP in 2010 was still significantly lower than in 1997. On the other hand, the Philippines' share of world GDP was rather stable throughout 1990–2010, which indicates that it was less affected by the region's booms and busts during the period. However, its share exhibited some slight increase in the late 2000s. Vietnam and Cambodia were not affected by the Asian financial crisis. Their shares of world GDP rapidly expanded in solid upward trends throughout 1990–2010.

SAC-4

The SAC-4 economies also outperformed the world average in terms of GDP growth over 1990–2010, with Bangladesh and Sri Lanka being the

[4]   The World Bank (1993) identified eight high-performing Asian economies (HPAEs) to draw observations concerning economic development success. The eight HPAEs are Japan, Hong Kong, Singapore, South Korea, Taiwan, Indonesia, Thailand, and Malaysia.

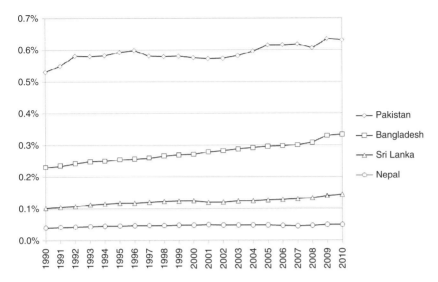

Source: Author's calculations; data from WDI, ADB, TED.

Figure 3.3D   Share in world GDP, 1990–2010: SAC-4

leading performers, growing at 5.2 per cent and 5.1 per cent, respectively (Table 3.1, Panel B). Nepal, which grew at 4.3 per cent over 1990–2010, was the only economy in the subgroup that experienced a slowdown in GDP growth between the two sub-periods, from 4.9 per cent in 1990–2000 to 3.8 per cent in 2000–2010. Pakistan and Bangladesh were the two economies of the subgroup with contributions of more than 0.5 per cent to the world's GDP growth over 1990–2010.

The shares of world GDP of all four SAC-4 economies followed an upward trend during 1990–2010 (Figure 3.3D). This trend was notable for Pakistan during 1990–1996 and 2002–2010, while it was consistent for Bangladesh throughout 1990–2010. Sri Lanka's share of world GDP also followed a consistent slightly expanding trend, except for a small decline in 2001.

3.3   PRIVATE CONSUMPTION

The data on private consumption derive from the 'household final consumption expenditure' indicator data from the World Development Indicators (WDI) database. Household final consumption expenditure, as defined by the World Bank, includes all household current expenditures for purchases of goods and services.[5] The value of the private consumption of individual economies is converted to purchasing power parity (PPP) terms, using the PPP conversion factors for private consumption provided in the 2005 ICP report.

Statistics on the shares and contributions of Developing Asia to world private consumption during 1990–2010 and its two sub-periods, 1990–2000 and 2000–2010, are reported in Table 3.2. Panel A of the table presents statistics at the group level, while Panel B presents statistics for individual Developing Asia economies.

3.3.1 Performance of Developing Asia as a Group In Terms of Private Consumption

Developing Asia's private consumption grew 5.7 per cent per year, on average, during 1990–2010, far above the world average growth rate of 3.0 per cent. In contrast, the private consumption of the Industrialized Economies group grew at 2.2 per cent, well below the world average (Table 3.2, Panel A). Developing Asia maintained its robust growth of 5.7 per cent between the two sub-periods, 1990–2000 and 2000–2010, while the growth of the Industrialized Economies declined from 2.7 per cent in the first sub-period to 1.6 per cent in the second. On the other hand, the ROW group exhibited a solid increase in growth, from 2.3 per cent in 1990–2000 to 4.6 per cent in 2000–2010, averaging 3.4 per cent for the entire period of 1990–2010.

Although Developing Asia contributed only 33.8 per cent to the world's private consumption growth over 1990–2010, notably below the contribution of 46.1 per cent claimed by Industrialized Economies, the contribution of Developing Asia increased by more than 10 percentage points between the two sub-periods, from 27.8 per cent in 1990–2000 to 38.4 per cent in 2000–2010. The contribution of Industrialized Economies declined sharply, from 60.4 per cent in the first sub-period to 34.9 per cent in the second (Figure 3.4). As a result, in the second sub-period, 2000–2010, Developing Asia surpassed Industrialized Economies to become the largest driver of the world's growth in private consumption.

---

[5]   The complete definition is 'Household final consumption expenditure (formerly private consumption) is the market value of all goods and services, including durable products (such as cars, washing machines, and home computers), purchased by households. It excludes purchases of dwellings but includes imputed rent for owner-occupied dwellings. It also includes payments and fees to governments to obtain permits and licenses. Here, household consumption expenditure includes the expenditures of nonprofit institutions serving households, even when reported separately by the country.' Source: WDI (2012).

Table 3.2   The rise of Developing Asia in the world economy, 1990–2010: private consumption

(A) Groups in the World

Group	Growth and Contribution						Share in World		
	1990–2010		1990–2000		2000–2010		1990	2000	2010
	Growth	Contb.	Growth	Contb.	Growth	Contb.			
World (79 Economies)	**3.0**	**100.0**	**3.1**	**100.0**	**3.0**	**100.0**	**100.0**	**100.0**	**100.0**
Developing Asia*	5.7	33.8	5.7	27.8	5.7	38.4	13.2	17.1	22.6
Industrialized Economies**	2.2	46.1	2.7	60.4	1.6	34.9	69.8	67.3	59.0
Rest of World (ROW)	3.4	20.1	2.3	11.8	4.6	26.7	17.0	15.6	18.5

(B) Developing Asia

Economy	1990–2010			1990–2000			2000–2010			Share in Group			Share in World		
	Growth Rate	Contb. to Growth		Growth Rate	Contb. to Growth		Growth Rate	Contb. to Growth		1990	2000	2010	1990	2000	2010
		Group	World		Group	World		Group	World						
Developing Asia*	**5.7**	**100.0**	**33.8**	**5.7**	**100.0**	**27.8**	**5.7**	**100.0**	**38.4**	**100.0**	**100.0**	**100.0**	**13.2**	**17.1**	**22.6**
China–India															
China	7.7	41.1	14.5	7.9	38.5	10.8	7.4	43.8	17.0	24.5	30.7	36.5	3.2	5.3	8.2
India	5.6	27.0	9.0	4.6	21.0	5.8	6.7	30.2	11.6	27.7	24.7	27.2	3.7	4.2	6.1
Tigers-4															
Hong Kong	3.7	1.5	0.5	4.1	1.9	0.5	3.2	1.2	0.5	2.8	2.4	1.9	0.4	0.4	0.4
Singapore	5.2	0.9	0.3	6.2	1.2	0.3	4.3	0.8	0.3	1.0	1.1	0.9	0.1	0.2	0.2
South Korea	4.1	6.9	2.2	5.2	9.7	2.7	3.1	5.0	1.9	10.9	10.4	8.0	1.4	1.8	1.8
Taiwan	4.0	4.4	1.3	6.7	7.1	2.0	2.2	2.1	0.8	5.8	6.4	4.5	0.8	1.1	1.0

Table 3.2   (continued)

(B) Developing Asia

Economy	1990–2010			1990–2000			2000–2010			Share in Group			Share in World		
	Growth Rate	Contb. to Growth		Growth Rate	Contb. to Growth		Growth Rate	Contb. to Growth		1990	2000	2010	1990	2000	2010
		Group	World		Group	World		Group	World						
ASEAN-6															
Indonesia	5.0	6.7	2.2	5.8	8.4	2.3	4.2	5.7	2.2	8.2	8.3	7.1	1.1	1.4	1.6
Malaysia	5.9	2.1	0.7	5.4	1.9	0.5	6.4	2.3	0.9	2.0	1.9	2.1	0.3	0.3	0.5
Philippines	4.0	2.4	0.8	3.8	2.4	0.7	4.2	2.2	0.9	4.0	3.3	2.8	0.5	0.6	0.6
Thailand	3.8	2.8	0.9	3.8	3.1	0.9	3.7	2.5	1.0	5.1	4.2	3.5	0.7	0.7	0.8
SAC-4															
Bangladesh	3.5	1.5	0.5	2.5	1.1	0.3	4.6	1.6	0.6	2.9	2.1	1.9	0.4	0.4	0.4
Pakistan	4.0	3.1	1.0	4.3	3.7	1.0	3.7	2.6	1.0	5.1	4.5	3.7	0.7	0.8	0.8

Notes:
* Developing Asia excludes Cambodia, Nepal, Sri Lanka, and Vietnam;
** Industrialized Economies excludes Israel; private consumption is measured in PPPs for private consumption.

Source: Author's calculations; data from WDI, ADB, ICP.

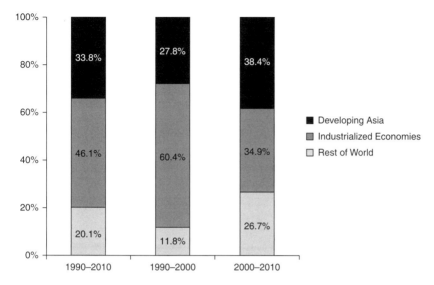

Source: Author's calculations; data from WDI, ADB, ICP.

*Figure 3.4   Contribution to the world's private consumption growth:
Developing Asia versus other parts of the world*

Thanks to its rapid growth, Developing Asia expanded its share of world private consumption by close to 10 percentage points over 1990–2010, from 13.2 per cent in 1990 to 22.6 per cent in 2010. In contrast, the share of Industrialized Economies contracted by more than 10 percentage points, from 69.8 to 59 per cent over the same period (Table 3.2, Panel A). As depicted in Figure 3.5, Developing Asia's share of world private consumption exhibited a consistent expanding trend, while the Industrialized Economies' share decreased steadily. As a result, the gap between Developing Asia and Industrialized Economies with respect to this measure narrowed steadily over 1990–2010. Furthermore, Developing Asia surpassed the ROW in terms of its share of world private consumption in 1995, although the ROW also consistently expanded its share of world private consumption over 1990–2010. However, it is worth noting that in 2010, Industrialized Economies still claimed a dominant share of world private consumption, which was approximately 60 per cent, while this share was still approximately 20 per cent for Developing Asia and for the ROW.

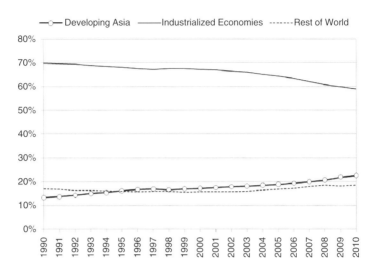

Source: Author's calculations; data from WDI, ADB, ICP.

Figure 3.5   *Share in world private consumption, 1990–2010: Developing Asia versus other parts of the world*

3.3.2   Performance of Individual Developing Asia Economies in Terms of Private Consumption

China–India

Both China and India played important roles in driving the world's private consumption growth. China's private consumption grew at 7.7 per cent during 1990–2010, contributing 14.5 per cent to the world's private consumption growth during this period, while India's private consumption grew at 5.6 per cent and contributed 9 per cent to the world's private consumption growth (Table 3.2, Panel B). Furthermore, both countries increased their contributions to the world's growth between the two sub-periods, from 10.8 per cent in 1990–2000 to 17 per cent in 2000–2010 for China and from 5.8 to 11.6 per cent for India.

Thanks to their rapid growth, China and India's shares of world private consumption expanded notably over 1990–2010. China's share increased by 5 percentage points, from 3.2 per cent in 1990 to 8.2 per cent in 2010, while India's share increased by more than 2 percentage points, from 3.7 to 6.1 per cent, over the same period (Table 3.2, Panel B). In addition, the shares of both China and India increased steadily over 1990–2010 (Figure 3.6A). These upward trends accelerated notably for both China and India beginning in 2004. However, China, with its much faster growth, sur-

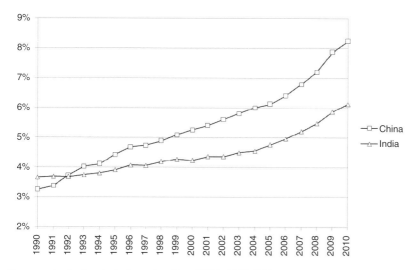

Source: Author's calculations; data from WDI, ADB, ICP.

*Figure 3.6A   Share in world private consumption, 1990–2010:
China–India*

passed India in 1992, and the gap between the two countries with respect
to this measure has widened since then. In 2010, this gap exceeded 2 percentage points.

Tigers-4
The Asian Tiger economies outperformed the world average for private
consumption growth over 1990–2010. Singapore was the leading performer, growing at 5.2 per cent, followed by Taiwan (4.4 per cent), South
Korea (4.1 per cent), and Hong Kong (3.7 per cent), while the world
average grew at 3 per cent over the same period (Table 3.2, Panel B).

The strong performance of the four Asian Tiger economies with respect
to this measure, however, was driven primarily by their performance in
the first sub-period. In fact, the growth rate declined from 4.1 per cent in
1990–2000 to 3.2 per cent in 2000–2010 for Hong Kong, from 6.2 to 4.3
per cent for Singapore, from 5.2 to 3.1 per cent for South Korea, and from
6.7 to 2.2 per cent for Taiwan, while it was stable at approximately 3 per
cent for the world average in the two sub-periods.

The four Asian Tiger economies' shares of world private consumption
expanded robustly during 1990–1997 but started to decline or stagnate
when the Asian financial crisis occurred (Figure 3.6B). As a result, South
Korea, Taiwan, and Hong Kong were in lower positions in 2010 than in

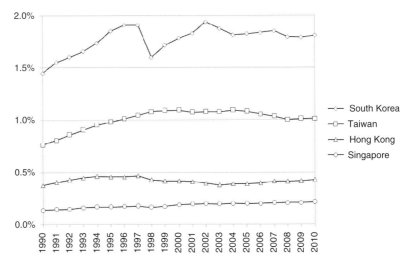

Source: Author's calculations; data from WDI, ADB, ICP.

Figure 3.6B   Share in world private consumption, 1990–2010: Tigers-4

1997 in terms of their shares of world private consumption. Singapore was the only economy of the Tigers-4 group that maintained a consistent expansion of its share of world private consumption during 1990–2000, although this expansion was insignificant during the second sub-period, 2000–2010.

ASEAN-6

Data on private consumption are available for only four ASEAN-6 economies: Indonesia, Malaysia, the Philippines, and Thailand. All four economies outperformed the world average in private consumption growth during 1990–2010, as well as in the two sub-periods, 1990–2000 and 2000–2010. Malaysia was the leading performer, growing at 5.9 per cent, followed by Indonesia (5 per cent), the Philippines (4 per cent), and Thailand (3.8 per cent). Among these four economies, private consumption growth accelerated between the two sub-periods for Malaysia (from 5.4 per cent in 1990–2000 to 6.4 per cent in 2000–2010) and the Philippines (from 3.8 to 4.2 per cent). In contrast, the growth decelerated for Indonesia (from 5.8 to 4.2 per cent) and Thailand (from 3.8 to 3.7 per cent). Among the four economies, only Indonesia contributed more than 1 per cent to the world's private consumption growth over 1990–2010.

The shares of these economies in world private consumption expanded rapidly before the Asian financial crisis but plunged during the crisis fallout (Figure 3.6C). This implies that these economies, with the exception of the

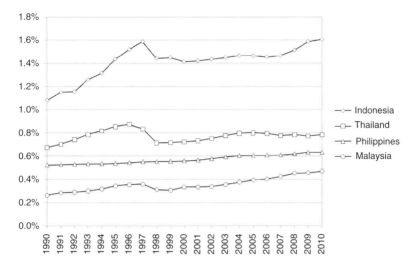

Source: Author's calculations, data from WDI, ADB, ICP.

Figure 3.6C   Share in world private consumption, 1990–2010: ASEAN-6

Philippines, were hit hard by the Asian financial crisis. However, the economies of Indonesia, Thailand, and Malaysia exhibited clear recoveries after the crisis, with their shares of world private consumption back in expansion modes. In particular, the expansion trend was strong and consistent during 2000–2010 for Indonesia and Malaysia, while it was weaker and less consistent for Thailand. It is worth noting that relative to their peaks during 1990–2010 (1996 for Thailand and 1997 for Indonesia), Indonesia and Thailand were not in stronger positions in 2010 in terms of their shares of world private consumption. On the other hand, the Philippines' share of world private consumption exhibited a consistent but modest upward trend during 1990–2010. Although the expansion of the Philippines with respect to this measure was unimpressive, it tended to accelerate after 2000.

SAC-4
Data on private consumption is available for only two SAC-4 economies: Pakistan and Bangladesh. These two economies both grew faster in terms of private consumption than the world average during 1990–2010, but with different trends. Bangladesh accelerated its growth from 2.5 per cent in the first sub-period, which was below the world average growth rate of 3.1 per cent for this sub-period, to 4.6 per cent in the second sub-period, while the growth of Pakistan's private consumption slowed from 4.3 to 3.7 per cent from the first to the second sub-period (Table 3.2, Panel B).

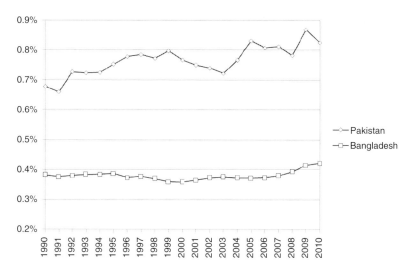

Source: Author's calculations; data from WDI, ADB, ICP.

Figure 3.6D   Share in world private consumption, 1990–2010: SAC-4

Pakistan, however, contributed 1 per cent to the world's private consumption growth over 1990–2010.

Pakistan's share of world private consumption fluctuated but followed a clear upward trend during 1990–2010 (Figure 3.6D). At the same time, Bangladesh's share shifted from a decreasing trend during 1990–2000 to an increasing trend during 2000–2010, more notably so from 2006 onward.

3.4   GOVERNMENT CONSUMPTION

The data on government consumption derive from the 'general government final expenditure' indicator data in the World Development Indicators (WDI) database. General government final expenditure, as defined by the World Bank, includes all government current expenditures for purchases of goods and services.[6] Government consumption is converted to purchasing power parity (PPP) terms using the PPP conversion factors for government consumption provided in the 2005 ICP report.

---

[6]   The complete definition is 'General government final consumption expenditure (formerly general government consumption) includes all government current expenditures for purchases of goods and services (including compensation of employees). It also includes most expenditures on national defense and security, but excludes government military expenditures that are part of government capital formation.' Source: WDI (2012).

Statistics on the shares and contributions of Developing Asia to world government consumption during 1990–2010 and its two sub-periods, 1990–2000 and 2000–2010, are presented in Table 3.3. Panel A of the table is for the group level, while Panel B is for individual Developing Asia economies.

3.4.1   Performance of Developing Asia as a Group in Terms of Government Consumption

Developing Asia's government consumption grew, on average, at a rate of 7 per cent during 1990–2010, more than double the world's growth rate of 3.2 per cent. In contrast, Industrialized Economies grew at only 1.8 per cent, far below the world average, while the ROW grew at only 2 per cent (Table 3.3, Panel A). It is worth noting that the world average growth of government consumption increased significantly between the two sub-periods, from 2.4 per cent in 1990–2000 to 3.8 per cent in 2000–2010. This acceleration was driven not only by Developing Asia but also by other groups. This growth accelerated from 6.9 to 7.1 per cent for Developing Asia, from 1.5 to 2.1 per cent for Industrialized Economies, and from 0.8 to 3.2 per cent for the ROW over the two sub-periods.

Developing Asia played a major role in driving growth in world government consumption over 1990–2010. The contribution of the group to the world's growth with respect to this measure was 55.8 per cent during 1990–2010 and the contribution of the group was rather stable between the two sub-periods, at 56.8 per cent for 1990–2000 and 54.4 per cent for 2000–2010 (Figure 3.7). On the other hand, the contribution of Industrialized Economies was 30.7 per cent for 1990–2010, declining from 36.3 per cent for the first sub-period to 28.2 per cent for the second, while the contribution of the ROW was 13.5 per cent for 1990–2010, increasing from 6.9 to 17.4 per cent between the two sub-periods (Figure 3.7).

The share of Developing Asia in world government consumption rapidly expanded, increasing almost 20 percentage points, from 15.3 per cent in 1990 to 33.7 per cent in 2010 (Table 3.3, Panel A). In contrast, this share fell sharply from 59.7 per cent to 46.4 per cent for the Industrialized Economies and from 25 per cent to nearly 20 per cent for the ROW over the same period. As depicted in Figure 3.8, the share of Developing Asia in world government consumption followed a solid increasing trend, while the Industrialized Economies' share steadily contracted over 1990–2010. As a result, the gap between Developing Asia and the Industrialized Economies with respect to this measure narrowed rapidly during this period. On the other hand, Developing Asia surpassed the ROW with respect to this measure in 1998, and its gap with the ROW has widened markedly since then.

Table 3.3 *The rise of Developing Asia in the world economy, 1990–2010: government consumption*

(A) Groups in the World

Group	Growth and Contribution						Share in World		
	1990–2010		1990–2000		2000–2010		1990	2000	2010
	Growth	Contb.	Growth	Contb.	Growth	Contb.			
World (83 Economies)	**3.2**	**100.0**	**2.4**	**100.0**	**3.8**	**100.0**	**100.0**	**100.0**	**100.0**
Developing Asia*	7.0	55.8	6.9	56.8	7.1	54.4	15.3	24.0	33.7
Industrialized Economies**	1.8	30.7	1.5	36.3	2.1	28.2	59.7	54.8	46.4
Rest of World (ROW)	2.0	13.5	0.8	6.9	3.2	17.4	25.0	21.2	19.9

(B) Developing Asia

Economy	1990–2010			1990–2000			2000–2010			Share in Group			Share in World		
	Growth Rate	Contb. to Growth		Growth Rate	Contb. to Growth		Growth Rate	Contb. to Growth		1990	2000	2010	1990	2000	2010
		Group	World		Group	World		Group	World						
Developing Asia*	**7.0**	**100.0**	**55.8**	**7.1**	**100.0**	**56.8**	**7.1**	**100.0**	**54.4**	**100**	**100**	**100**	**15.3**	**24.0**	**33.7**
China–India															
China	9.2	67.5	39.4	9.9	67.9	39.2	8.5	69.6	38.1	40.4	54.4	62.4	6.2	13.1	21.0
India	5.9	14.1	7.3	5.7	14.5	8.0	6.1	13.4	7.2	18.7	16.5	14.9	2.9	4.0	5.0

Tigers-4															
Hong Kong	3.3	0.7	0.3	4.4	1.1	0.6	2.2	0.4	0.2	2.0	1.6	1.0	0.3	0.4	0.3
Singapore	6.8	1.1	0.6	9.0	1.7	1.0	4.6	0.8	0.4	1.2	1.4	1.1	0.2	0.3	0.4
South Korea	4.6	4.3	2.1	4.5	4.8	2.6	4.6	3.7	2.0	8.4	6.5	5.1	1.3	1.6	1.7
Taiwan	1.9	1.8	0.8	2.9	3.3	1.8	1.0	0.7	0.3	9.7	6.5	3.5	1.5	1.6	1.2
ASEAN-6															
Indonesia	4.2	2.4	1.2	0.8	0.4	0.2	7.7	3.1	1.7	5.1	2.8	2.9	0.8	0.7	1.0
Malaysia	6.3	2.3	1.2	5.2	1.9	1.1	7.4	2.5	1.3	2.8	2.4	2.4	0.4	0.6	0.8
Philippines	2.5	0.8	0.3	1.6	0.6	0.3	3.3	0.7	0.4	3.0	1.8	1.2	0.5	0.4	0.4
Thailand	4.9	2.1	1.0	4.8	2.2	1.2	5.0	1.8	1.0	3.6	2.9	2.3	0.6	0.7	0.8
SAC-4															
Bangladesh	6.4	0.4	0.2	4.5	0.3	0.2	8.2	0.5	0.3	0.5	0.4	0.4	0.1	0.1	0.1
Pakistan	4.3	1.7	0.8	0.7	0.3	0.1	8.0	2.2	1.2	3.6	1.9	2.1	0.5	0.5	0.7
Sri Lanka	6.2	0.7	0.4	7.3	0.9	0.5	5.1	0.6	0.3	0.9	0.9	0.7	0.1	0.2	0.2

Notes:
*   Developing Asia excludes Cambodia, Nepal, and Vietnam;
** Industrialized Economies excludes Israel; government consumption is measured in PPPs for government consumption.

Source: Author's calculations; data from WDI, ADB, ICP.

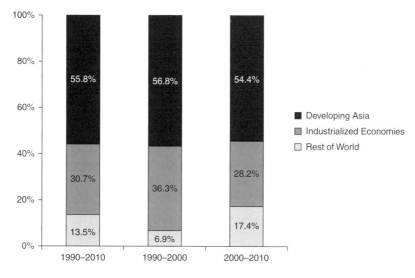

Source: Author's calculations; data from WDI, ADB, ICP.

Figure 3.7   Contribution to the world's government consumption growth: Developing Asia versus other parts of the world

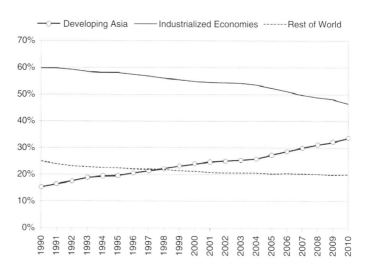

Source: Author's calculations; data from WDI, ADB, ICP.

Figure 3.8   Share in world government consumption, 1990–2010: Developing Asia versus other parts of the world

3.4.2 Performance of Individual Developing Asia Economies in Terms of Government Consumption

China–India

China's government consumption grew at an outstanding rate of 9.2 per cent during 1990–2010, contributing 39.4 per cent to the world's government consumption growth over this period, while India's government consumption grew at a rate of 5.9 per cent and contributed 7.3 per cent to the world's growth over the same period (Table 3.3, Panel B). The contribution to the world's growth was nearly the same between the two sub-periods for China, at approximately 38–39 per cent, as well as for India, at approximately 7–8 per cent.

China's share in world government consumption soared by almost 15 percentage points, from 6.2 per cent in 1990 to 21 per cent in 2010, while India's share increased by 2 percentage points, from 2.9 to 5 per cent (Table 3.3, Panel B). Figure 3.9A indicates that this share followed a solid increasing trend throughout 1990–2010 for both China and India. However, the pace of expansion was much higher and more solid for China than for India. As a result, the gap between China and India on this measure widened rapidly during 1990–2010, with notable acceleration

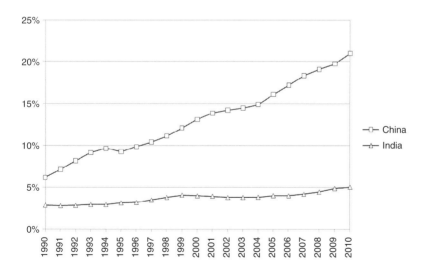

Source: Author's calculations; data from WDI, ADB, ICP.

Figure 3.9A   Share in world government consumption, 1990–2010: China–India

since 2000. In 2010, China's share in world government consumption exceeded that of India by more than 15 percentage points.

Tigers-4
The four Asian Tiger economies sharply differed in government consumption growth rates over 1990–2010 (Table 3.3, Panel B). Singapore and South Korea, which grew at 6.8 per cent and 4.6 per cent, respectively, over the period, far outperformed the world average at 3.2 per cent. In contrast, Taiwan, with its growth rate of merely 1.9 per cent, was notably below the world average, while Hong Kong was on par with the world average, growing at 3.3 per cent. On the other hand, the growth of the four Asian Tiger economies, with the exception of South Korea, slowed down between the two sub-periods, from 4.4 per cent in 1990–2000 to 2.2 per cent in 2000–2010 for Hong Kong, from 9 to 4.6 per cent for Singapore, and from 2.9 to 1 per cent for Taiwan. South Korea, on the other hand, grew at nearly the same rate of 4.5–4.6 per cent in both sub-periods. In addition, South Korea was the only economy of this subgroup that contributed more than 1 per cent to the world's government consumption growth over 1990–2010.

The four Asian Tiger economies' shares of world government consumption expanded robustly during 1990–1997 but changed in different ways after the fallout of the Asian financial crisis (Figure 3.9B). South Korea's

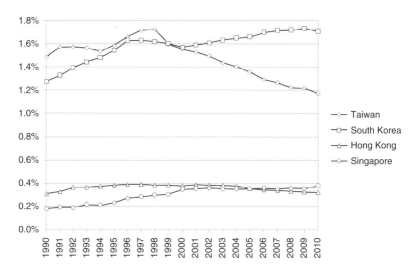

Source: Author's calculations; data from WDI, ADB, ICP.

Figure 3.9B   Share in world government consumption, 1990–2010: Tigers-4

share of world government consumption plunged during 1998–2000 but returned to a strong increasing trend during 2000–2010. In contrast, Taiwan's share fell into a steep declining trend beginning in 1998. Hong Kong's share also followed a decreasing trend, which started in 1997 but was more gradual than that of Taiwan. On the other hand, Singapore's share followed a consistent upward trend throughout 1990–2010, but its expansion slowed during the second sub-period, 2000–2010. South Korea and Taiwan were the two economies in the group that contributed more than 1 per cent to world government consumption.

ASEAN-6

Data on government consumption are available only for Indonesia, Malaysia, the Philippines, and Thailand. These economies, with the exception of the Philippines, grew faster than the world average in government consumption over 1990–2010 (Table 3.3, Panel B). This growth rate was 4.2 per cent for Indonesia, 6.3 per cent for Malaysia, and 4.9 per cent for Thailand, while it was only 2.5 per cent for the Philippines. On the other hand, all four economies accelerated their growth with respect to this measure between the two sub-periods: from 0.8 per cent in 1990–2000 to 7.7 per cent in 2000–2010 for Indonesia, from 5.2 to 7.4 per cent for Malaysia, from 1.6 to 3.3 per cent for the Philippines, and from 4.8 to 5

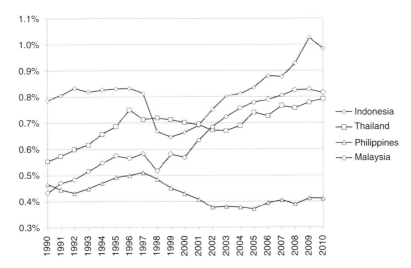

Source: Author's calculations; data from WDI, ADB, ICP.

Figure 3.9C   *Share in world government consumption, 1990–2010: ASEAN-6*

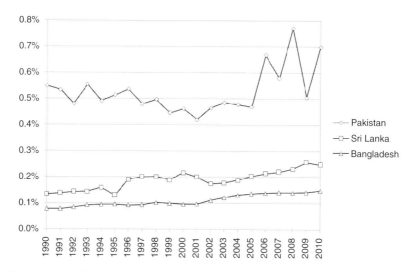

Source: Author's calculations; data from WDI, ADB, ICP.

Figure 3.9D   Share in world government consumption, 1990–2010: SAC-4

per cent for Thailand. It is worth noting that Indonesia, Malaysia, and Thailand contributed more than 1 per cent to the world's government consumption growth over 1990–2010.

These four economies' shares of world government consumption followed rather similar patterns: expansion during 1990–1997, contraction during the Asian financial crisis, and recovery in the 2000s (Figure 3.9C). Among these four economies, Malaysia was the economy that experienced the largest share expansion during 1990–2010, with a strong increasing trend during 1990–1997 and 1999–2010. Indonesia's share of world government consumption has also followed a robust expanding trend since 1999. Thailand's share did not recover until 2004, with a more gradual expansion during 2004–2010. The Philippines' share declined during 1997–2002 and improved slightly during 2002–2010. It is worth noting that the Philippines' share of world government consumption contracted over 1990–2010.

SAC-4

Data on government consumption were available only for Bangladesh, Pakistan, and Sri Lanka. These three economies grew faster in terms of government consumption than the world average over 1990–2010. This growth rate was highest for Bangladesh (6.4 per cent), followed by Sri Lanka (6.2 per cent) and Pakistan (4.3 per cent) (Table 3.3, Panel B). The growth notably accelerated between the two sub-periods for Bangladesh (from 4.5 per cent in 1990–2000 to 8.2 per cent in 2000–2010) and Pakistan (from 0.7 to 8 per cent), while it slowed down for Sri Lanka (from 7.3 to 5.1 per cent).

These three economies' shares of world government consumption expanded significantly over 1990–2010 (Figure 3.9D). Pakistan's share, however, fluctuated sharply, with a declining trend during 1990–2001 and an upward trend during 2001–2010, while the shares of Bangladesh and Sri Lanka followed rather consistent increasing trends during 1990–2010 that were more pronounced in the 2000s.

3.5   FIXED INVESTMENT

The data on fixed investment are derived from the 'gross fixed capital formation (GFCF)' indicator data in the World Development Indicators (WDI) database. GFCF, as defined by the World Bank, includes land improvements; plant, machinery, and equipment purchases; and the construction of roads, railways, and the like, including schools, offices, hospitals, private residential dwellings, and commercial and industrial buildings.[7] The GFCF of individual economies is measured in terms of purchasing power parity (PPP), using the PPP conversion factors for GFCF provided in the 2005 ICP report.

Statistics on the shares and contributions of Developing Asia to the world fixed investment during 1990–2010 and its two sub-periods, 1990–2000 and 2000–2010, are reported in Table 3.4. Panel A of the table is for the group level, while Panel B is for individual Developing Asia economies.

3.5.1   Performance of Developing Asia as a Group in Terms of Fixed Investment

Developing Asia's fixed investment grew, on average, at a rapid rate of 8.6 per cent per year during 1990–2010, far exceeding the world average growth rate of 3.8 per cent. In contrast, Industrialized Economies grew at a notably low rate of 1.4 per cent during the same period (Table 3.4, Panel A). Moreover, this growth notably accelerated for Developing Asia

---

[7]   The complete definition is 'Gross fixed capital formation (formerly gross domestic fixed investment) includes land improvements (fences, ditches, drains, and so on); plant, machinery, and equipment purchases; and the construction of roads, railways, and the like, including schools, offices, hospitals, private residential dwellings, and commercial and industrial buildings. According to the 1993 SNA, net acquisitions of valuables are also considered capital formation.' Source: WDI (2012).

Table 3.4   The rise of Developing Asia in the world economy, 1990–2010: fixed investment

(A) Groups in the World

Group	Growth and Contribution						Share in World		
	1990–2010		1990–2000		2000–2010				
	Growth	Contb.	Growth	Contb.	Growth	Contb.	1990	2000	2010
World (82 Economies)	**3.8**	**100.0**	**3.0**	**100.0**	**4.0**	**100.0**	**100.0**	**100.0**	**100.0**
Developing Asia*	8.6	76.8	7.7	56.6	9.5	86.6	16.6	26.1	45.7
Industrialized Economies**	1.4	18.3	3.2	65.1	-0.3	-4.3	62.2	61.8	40.3
Rest of World (ROW)	1.4	4.9	-2.8	-21.7	5.5	17.7	21.2	12.1	14.0

(B) Developing Asia

Economy	1990–2010			1990–2000			2000–2010			Share in Group			Share in World		
	Growth Rate	Contb. to Growth		Growth Rate	Contb. to Growth		Growth Rate	Contb. to Growth							
		Group	World		Group	World		Group	World	1990	2000	2010	1990	2000	2010
Developing Asia*	**8.6**	**100.0**	**76.8**	**7.7**	**100.0**	**56.6**	**9.5**	**100.0**	**86.6**	**100.0**	**100.0**	**100.0**	**16.6**	**26.1**	**45.7**
China–India															
China	13.1	68.3	57.1	13.7	65.6	38.2	12.5	72.8	63.9	26.2	47.6	63.5	4.3	12.4	29.0
India	7.9	16.2	11.0	5.3	11.6	6.2	10.6	17.3	14.8	18.8	14.8	16.3	3.1	3.9	7.5

Tigers-4

Hong Kong	3.4	0.9	0.5	4.7	1.7	0.9	2.2	0.4	0.3	3.2	2.4	1.1	0.5	0.6	0.5
Singapore	6.0	1.1	0.7	8.4	2.3	1.3	3.6	0.6	0.5	2.0	2.2	1.2	0.3	0.6	0.5
South Korea	3.5	4.6	2.5	4.5	8.2	4.3	2.6	2.4	1.8	16.5	11.9	5.9	2.7	3.1	2.7
Taiwan	3.3	1.6	0.9	7.2	5.6	3.0	-0.6	-0.3	-0.2	6.2	5.8	2.1	1.0	1.5	1.0
ASEAN-6															
Indonesia	4.7	2.8	1.6	2.5	1.8	0.9	7.0	2.7	2.2	6.9	4.1	3.2	1.2	1.1	1.4
Malaysia	4.7	1.3	0.8	6.0	2.4	1.3	3.5	0.8	0.6	3.3	2.8	1.5	0.6	0.7	0.7
Philippines	3.3	0.8	0.4	2.6	0.8	0.4	4.0	0.6	0.5	3.0	1.8	1.0	0.5	0.5	0.5
Thailand	1.1	0.8	0.4	-2.4	-2.0	-1.0	4.7	1.4	1.1	9.5	3.4	2.1	1.6	0.9	1.0
SAC-4															
Bangladesh	7.7	0.8	0.5	8.1	1.1	0.6	7.2	0.7	0.6	1.0	1.0	0.8	0.2	0.3	0.4
Pakistan	2.4	0.5	0.3	1.8	0.5	0.3	2.9	0.4	0.3	2.9	1.6	0.8	0.5	0.4	0.4
Sri Lanka	6.6	0.3	0.2	7.2	0.4	0.2	6.0	0.2	0.2	0.5	0.4	0.3	0.1	0.1	0.1

Notes:
* Developing Asia excludes Cambodia, Nepal, and Vietnam;
** Industrialized Economies excludes Israel; fixed investment is measured in PPPs for fixed investment.

Source: Author's calculations; data from WDI, ADB, ICP.

between the two sub-periods, increasing from 7.7 per cent in 1990–2000 to 9.5 per cent in 2000–2010, while it changed from a positive 3.2 per cent rate in the first sub-period to a negative rate in the second sub-period for the Industrialized Economies. On the other hand, the growth rate experienced by the ROW was also low, at 1.4 per cent for 1990–2010, but it exhibited a solid turnaround between the two sub-periods, from −2.8 per cent in 1990–2000 to 5.5 per cent in 2000–2010. The contraction of the ROW in terms of fixed investment in the first sub-period was associated with the turmoil that occurred in the Eastern Europe and the former Soviet Union economies in the early 1990s after the collapse of their communist regimes.

Developing Asia played a dominant role in the growth of the world fixed investment over 1990–2010, contributing more than three quarters of the world's growth during this period. Moreover, this contribution of the group substantially increased between the two sub-periods, from 56.6 per cent in 1990–2000 to 86.6 per cent in the second (Figure 3.10). In contrast, the contribution of the Industrialized Economies to the world's growth with respect to this measure was only 18.3 per cent for 1990–2010, with a dramatic decline from 65.1 per cent in 1990–2000 to −4.3 per cent in 2000–2010. The negative growth in fixed investment experienced by

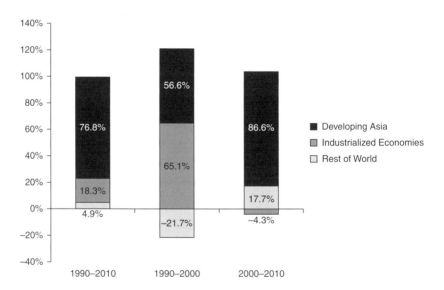

Source: Author's calculations; data from WDI, ADB, ICP.

Figure 3.10   Contribution to the world's fixed investment growth:
Developing Asia versus other parts of the world

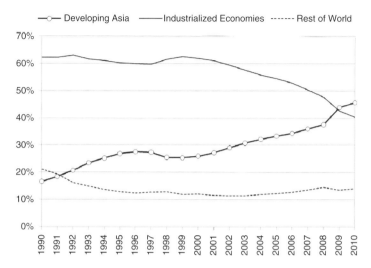

Source: Author's calculations; data from WDI, ADB, ICP.

Figure 3.11   Share in world fixed investment, 1990–2010: Developing Asia versus other parts of the world

the industrialized group during 2000–2010 was due to the global financial crisis that erupted in 2008.

The rise of Developing Asia and the contraction of the Industrialized Economies in terms of their shares of world fixed investment were clear and solid throughout 1990–2010, especially from 2000 on (Figure 3.11). In particular, Developing Asia surpassed the ROW in 1991 and Industrialized Economies in 2009 to become the group with the largest share of world fixed investment in 2010. Developing Asia's share in world fixed investment expanded by nearly 30 percentage points, from 16.6 per cent in 1990 to 45.7 per cent in 2010, while the Industrialized Economies' share contracted by over 20 percentage points, from 62.2 to 40.3 per cent (Table 3.4, Panel A).

3.5.2   Performance of Individual Developing Asia Economies in Terms of Fixed Investment

China–India

China's fixed investment grew at a striking rate of 13.1 per cent during 1990–2010, contributing 57.1 per cent to the world's growth over this period; the growth rate for India was also impressively high, at 7.9 per cent, with a contribution of 11 per cent (Table 3.4, Panel B). China

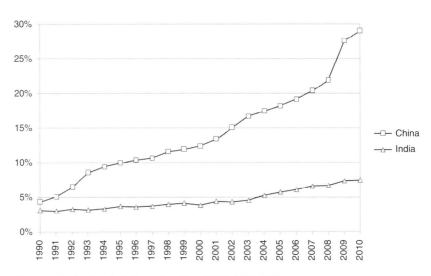

Source: Author's calculations; data from WDI, ADB, ICP.

Figure 3.12A   Share in world fixed investment, 1990–2010: China–India

maintained its two-digit growth rate with respect to this measure in both
sub-periods (13.7 per cent in 1990–2000 and 12.5 per cent in 2000–2010),
while India accelerated its growth from 5.3 per cent in the first sub-period
to 10.6 per cent in the second. As a result, both China and India substantially increased their contributions to the world's growth in fixed investment between the two sub-periods, from 38.2 per cent in 1990–2000 to 63.9
per cent in 2000–2010 for China and from 6.2 to 14.8 per cent for India.

China's share in world fixed investment increased by almost 25 percentage points over 1990–2010, from 4.3 per cent in 1990 to 29 per cent
in 2010, while India's share increased by more than 4 percentage points,
from 3.1 to 7.5 per cent (Figure 3.12A). It is worth noting that although
both countries recorded rapid growth in fixed investment, China far outperformed India in this regard. Consequently, the gap between China and
India in terms of their shares of world fixed investment, which was small
in 1990, widened considerably during 1990–2010. The acceleration of
China's share of world fixed investment during 2008–2010 tends to suggest
a special push by the Chinese government in fixed investment to stimulate
economic growth during this period of the world's recession.

Tigers-4

The four Asian Tiger economies, with the exception of Singapore, under-
performed the world average for fixed investment growth over 1990–2010

(Table 3.4, Panel B). The growth rate over the period was 6 per cent for Singapore, well above the world average rate of 3.8 per cent, but it was only 3.4 per cent for Hong Kong, 3.5 per cent for South Korea, and 3.3 per cent for Taiwan. The Asian financial crisis appears to have had a significant impact on the growth patterns of the four Asian Tiger economies. Their growth with respect to this measure slowed down markedly between the two sub-periods, from 4.7 per cent in 1990–2000 to 2.2 per cent in 2000–2010 for Hong Kong, from 8.4 to 3.6 per cent for Singapore, from 4.5 to 2.6 per cent for South Korea, and from 7.2 to −0.6 per cent for Taiwan. In contrast, the growth rate of the world average accelerated from 3 per cent in the first sub-period to 4 per cent in the second. That is, while the four Asian Tiger economies far outperformed the world average on fixed investment in the first sub-period, they all fell behind the world average by this measure in the second sub-period. South Korea was the only economy in this group that contributed more than 1 per cent to the world's fixed investment growth over 1990–2010.

The four Asian Tiger economies' shares of world fixed investment expanded rapidly during 1990–1997 but appeared to be hit hard by the fallout of the Asian financial crisis (Figure 3.12B). South Korea's share fell sharply in 1997–1998 and recovered during 1999–2002 before it fell into a consistent declining trend from 2002 on. Taiwan's share followed an expanding trend during 1990–2000 but declined from 2000 on. Hong

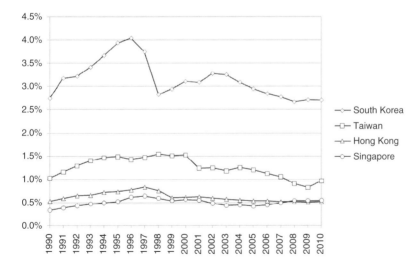

Source: Author's calculations; data from WDI, ADB, ICP.

Figure 3.12B   Share in world fixed investment, 1990–2010: Tigers-4

Kong's share decreased significantly in 1998–1999 and then fell into a gradual declining trend during 2000–2010. Singapore was the only Asian Tiger economy that expanded its share of world fixed investment over 1990–2010. This share, however, declined during 1997–2005 before increasing again during 2005–2010.

ASEAN-6
For the ASEAN-6 subgroup, data on fixed investment are available only for Indonesia, Malaysia, the Philippines, and Thailand. Among these four economies, Indonesia and Malaysia outperformed the world average for fixed investment growth over 1990–2010, while Thailand and the Philippines were below the world average in this regard (Table 3.4, Panel B). Indonesia was the only economy in this subgroup that contributed more than 1 per cent to the world's fixed investment growth over 1990–2010.

These four economies, particularly, Indonesia, Malaysia, and Thailand, were hit hard by the Asian financial crisis. Their shares of world fixed investment expanded before the eruption of the crisis but plummeted in 1997–1999 for Thailand and in 1998–1999 for the other three economies (Figure 3.12C). Indonesia was the only economy in this subgroup that bounced back solidly, with a notable expansion of its share during the second sub-period, 2000–2010. It is worth noting, however, that the shares

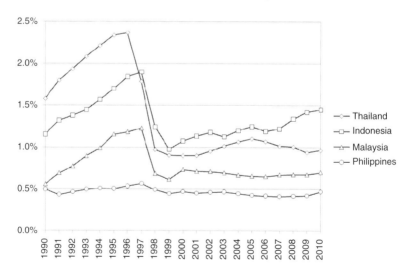

Source: Author's calculations; data from WDI, ADB, ICP.

Figure 3.12C   Share in world fixed investment, 1990–2010: ASEAN-6

of world fixed investment of all four of these economies were noticeably lower in 2010 than at their peaks before the eruption of the Asian financial crisis. In 2010, Indonesia was the only economy in this subgroup that accounted for more than 1 per cent of world fixed investment.

SAC-4

For the SAC-4 subgroup, data on fixed investment are available only for Bangladesh, Pakistan, and Sri Lanka. Bangladesh and Sri Lanka, which grew in fixed investment at 7.7 per cent and 6.6 per cent, respectively, during 1990–2010, far outperformed the world average growth over the period. In addition, the outperformance over the world average by these two economies was notable in both sub-periods. In contrast, Pakistan grew at 2.4 per cent over 1990–2010, which was well below the world average. Furthermore, the underperformance of Pakistan relative to the world average was consistent in both sub-periods (1.8 versus 3 per cent in the first sub-period and 2.9 versus 4 per cent in the second sub-period). The shares of Bangladesh and Sri Lanka followed clear upward trends during 1990–2010, while that of Pakistan followed a strong declining trend (Figure 3.12D). The upward trend for Bangladesh was particularly steep and consistent throughout 1990–2010.

As an additional note, one may find it surprising that Bangladesh and Sri Lanka outperformed most East Asian economies in fixed investment

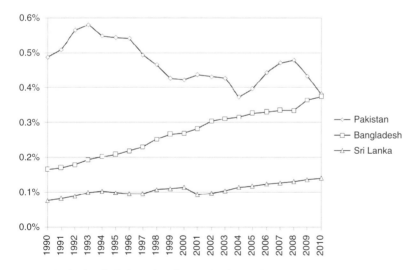

Source: Author's calculations; data from WDI, ADB, ICP.

Figure 3.12D   Share in world fixed investment, 1990–2010: SAC-4

growth over 1990–2010. In fact, while this growth rate over 1990–2010 was 7.7 per cent for Bangladesh and 6.6 per cent for Sri Lanka, it was below 5 per cent for most East Asian economies for which data are available.

3.6   EXPORTS AND IMPORTS OF GOODS AND SERVICES

The data on exports and imports of goods and services are from the World Development Indicators (WDI) database. Exports and imports are measured in current US dollars, and the growth rates presented in this section represent nominal growth. The international trade in goods and services of a given economy consists of two components: trade in merchandise and trade in commercial services. The trade in merchandise includes trade on agricultural products, fuel and mining products, and manufactures, while trade in commercial services is associated with transportation, travelling, telecommunication, information processing, ICT services, finance, royalties and license fees, and construction.

This section describes the rise of Developing Asia and its individual economies in world exports and imports of goods and services. In addition, the section highlights the performance of the region's three important items of international trade: manufactures, commercial services, and ICT hardware.

3.6.1   Exports of Goods and Services

Statistics on the performance of Developing Asia and its individual economies in world exports of goods and services during 1990–2010 and two sub-periods, 1990–2000 and 2000–2010, are reported in Table 3.5. Panel A of the table is for the group level and Panel B for individual Developing Asia economies.

a.   Performance of Developing Asia as a Group in Terms of Exports of Goods and Services

The exports of goods and services of Developing Asia grew, on average, at 11.4 per cent over 1990–2010, well above the world average of 7.5 per cent. This growth rate was much lower for the Industrialized Economies, at 5.8 per cent, and for the ROW, at 8.7 per cent (Table 3.5, Panel A).

Developing Asia contributed 31.8 per cent to the world's growth in exports of goods and services during 1990–2010, experiencing a notable increase between the two sub-periods, from 28 per cent in 1990–2000

Table 3.5   The rise of Developing Asia in the world economy, 1990–2010: exports of goods and services

(A) Groups in the World

Group	Growth and Contribution						Share in World		
	1990–2010		1990–2000		2000–2010		1990	2000	2010
	Growth	Contb.	Growth	Contb.	Growth	Contb.			
World (111 Economies)	**7.5**	**100.0**	**6.2**	**100.0**	**8.5**	**100.0**	**100.0**	**100.0**	**100.0**
Developing Asia	11.4	31.8	10.8	28.0	11.8	33.4	12.5	19.7	27.5
Industrialized Economies	5.8	51.1	5.2	59.1	6.5	47.4	75.0	67.7	56.0
Rest of World (ROW)	8.7	17.1	6.3	12.8	11.1	19.2	12.5	12.7	16.6

(B) Developing Asia

Economy	1990–2010			1990–2000			2000–2010			Share in Group			Share in World		
	Growth Rate	Contb. to Growth		Growth Rate	Contb. to Growth		Growth Rate	Contb. to Growth		1990	2000	2010	1990	2000	2010
		Group	World		Group	World		Group	World						
Developing Asia	**11.4**	**100.0**	**31.8**	**10.8**	**100.0**	**28.0**	**11.8**	**100.0**	**33.4**	**100.0**	**100.0**	**100.0**	**12.5**	**19.7**	**27.5**
China–India															
China	17.3	37.1	13.6	15.8	22.0	6.5	18.7	44.6	15.4	11.2	18.7	37.6	1.4	3.7	10.3
India	14.1	7.7	2.6	9.9	3.9	1.1	18.4	9.4	3.2	4.4	4.1	7.9	0.6	0.8	2.2
Tigers-4															
Hong Kong	8.0	10.6	2.9	8.8	14.8	4.0	7.2	8.2	2.6	19.7	16.3	10.4	2.5	3.2	2.8
Singapore	9.7	9.2	2.6	10.6	12.2	3.4	8.7	7.9	2.5	12.6	12.4	9.1	1.6	2.4	2.5
South Korea	9.9	11.0	3.2	10.3	13.5	3.7	9.5	9.9	3.2	14.5	13.8	11.0	1.8	2.7	3.0
Taiwan	7.2	6.7	1.7	8.3	10.1	2.7	6.1	4.6	1.5	14.8	11.6	6.5	1.8	2.3	1.8

Table 3.5 (continued)

(B) Developing Asia

Economy	1990–2010			1990–2000			2000–2010			Share in Group			Share in World		
	Growth Rate	Contb. to Growth		Growth Rate	Contb. to Growth		Growth Rate	Contb. to Growth		1990	2000	2010	1990	2000	2010
		Group	World		Group	World		Group	World						
ASEAN-6															
Cambodia	22.4	0.1	0.1	32.8	0.2	0.1	12.1	0.1	0.04	0.01	0.1	0.1	0.00	0.02	0.03
Indonesia	9.0	3.7	1.0	8.5	4.0	1.1	9.5	3.3	1.1	5.7	4.5	3.6	0.7	0.9	1.0
Malaysia	9.8	4.8	1.4	12.3	8.0	2.3	7.2	3.8	1.2	6.4	7.5	4.8	0.8	1.5	1.3
Philippines	8.7	1.5	0.4	12.3	3.0	0.8	5.1	0.9	0.3	2.4	2.8	1.4	0.3	0.5	0.4
Thailand	10.3	4.7	1.4	10.3	5.4	1.5	10.2	4.4	1.4	5.7	5.5	4.7	0.7	1.1	1.3
Vietnam	17.8	1.7	0.6	20.0	1.5	0.5	15.7	1.9	0.6	0.5	1.1	1.7	0.1	0.2	0.5
SAC-4															
Bangladesh	11.5	0.4	0.1	12.7	0.5	0.1	10.3	0.4	0.1	0.4	0.4	0.4	0.05	0.1	0.1
Nepal	7.0	0.03	0.01	12.1	0.1	0.03	1.8	0.01	0.00	0.1	0.1	0.03	0.01	0.02	0.01
Pakistan	6.7	0.5	0.1	4.7	0.4	0.1	8.8	0.4	0.1	1.2	0.7	0.5	0.2	0.1	0.1
Sri Lanka	7.6	0.2	0.1	9.7	0.4	0.1	5.5	0.2	0.05	0.5	0.4	0.2	0.1	0.1	0.1

Note: Exports of goods and services is measured in current US$.

Source: Author's calculations; data from WDI, ADB.

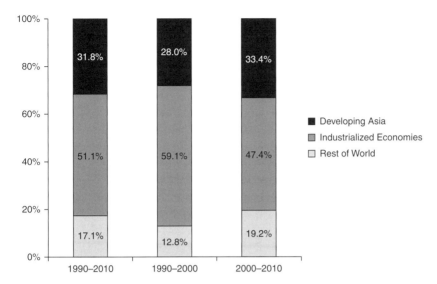

Source: Author's calculations; data from WDI, ADB.

Figure 3.13   *Contribution to the world's exports of goods and services growth: Developing Asia versus other parts of the world*

to 33.4 per cent in 2000–2010 (Figure 3.13). Industrialized Economies remained the main driver of the world's growth in export, contributing 51.1 per cent to the world's exports growth during 1990–2010. However, the contribution of the group declined by more than 10 percentage points between the two sub-periods, from 59.1 per cent in the first sub-period to 47.4 per cent in the second (Figure 3.13).

Developing Asia's share in world exports of goods and services soared by 15 percentage points, from 12.5 per cent in 1990 to 27.5 per cent in 2010. In contrast, the Industrialized Economies' share contracted by 19 percentage points, from 75 per cent in 1990 to 56 per cent in 2010 (Table 3.5, Panel A). In addition, the upward trend for Developing Asia and the downward trend for the Industrialized Economies in their shares of world exports of goods and services were consistent and more notable in the 2000s (Figure 3.14). The gap between the two groups with respect to this measure narrowed rapidly during 1990–2010. However, the Industrialized Economies still commanded a lead of approximately 12 percentage points over all developing economies and a lead of nearly 30 percentage points over Developing Asia in terms of its share of world exports of goods and services in 2010.

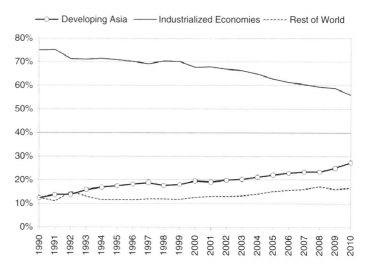

Source: Author's calculations; data from WDI, ADB.

*Figure 3.14   Share in world exports of goods and services, 1990–2010:
            Developing Asia versus other parts of the world*

b.   Performance of Individual Developing Asia Economies in Terms of Exports of Goods and Services

China–India

Both China and India played important roles in world exports of goods
and services. China grew at 17.3 per cent during 1990–2010, contributing
13.6 per cent to the world's growth in this period, while India grew at 14.1
per cent, contributing 2.6 per cent to the world's growth.[8] Furthermore,
the growth of China and India accelerated between the two sub-periods,
from 15.8 per cent in 1990–2000 to 18.7 per cent in 2000–2010 for China
and from 9.9 to 18.4 per cent for India. As a result, the two countries
increased their contributions to the world's growth in exports of goods and
services notably between the two sub-periods, from 6.5 per cent in the first
sub-period to 15.4 per cent in the second for China and from 1.1 to 3.2 per
cent for India.

China's share of world exports of goods and services soared almost
9 percentage points, from 1.4 per cent in 1990 to 10.3 per cent in 2010,

[8]   The contribution of India to the world's growth in exports of goods and services was
modest, despite its outstanding growth rate, because of its small share of world exports of
goods and services.

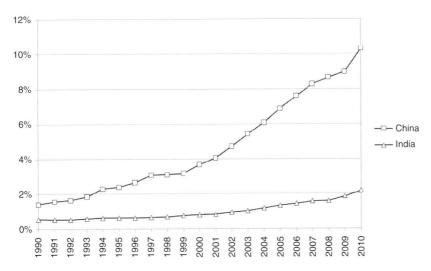

Source: Author's calculations; data from WDI, ADB.

Figure 3.15A   *Share in world exports of goods and services, 1990–2010: China–India*

while India's share increased from 0.6 to 2.2 per cent over the same period (Table 3.5, Panel B). In addition, the upward trend of China's share accelerated during 1999–2010, while India's share followed a stronger increasing trend in the 2000s (Figure 3.15A). The gap between China and India widened noticeably during 1999–2010, and China exceeded India in this respect by more than 8 percentage points in 2010.

Tigers-4

The four Asian Tiger economies did not far outperform the world average for exports of goods and services over 1990–2010. The leading performer was South Korea, which grew at 9.9 per cent over the period, followed by Singapore (9.7 per cent) and Hong Kong (8 per cent), while Taiwan grew at 7.2 per cent, slightly below the world's average growth rate (7.5 per cent). The four Asian Tiger economies, however, with their significant shares of world exports of goods and services, made notable contributions to the world's growth in exports of goods and services over 1990–2010: 2.9 per cent for Hong Kong, 2.6 per cent for Singapore, 3.2 per cent for South Korea, and 1.7 per cent for Taiwan.

The share of world exports of goods and services expanded significantly over 1990–2010 for South Korea (from 1.8 per cent in 1990 to 3 per cent in 2010), Singapore (from 1.6 to 2.5 per cent), and Hong Kong (from 2.5

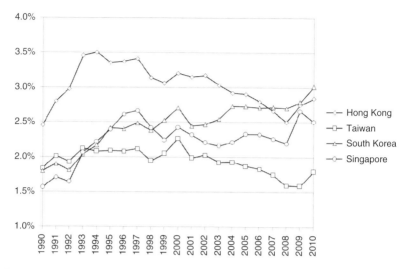

Source: Author's calculations; data from WDI, ADB.

*Figure 3.15B   Share in world exports of goods and services, 1990–2010:
Tigers-4*

to 2.8 per cent), while it stayed nearly unchanged for Taiwan at approximately 1.8 per cent (Table 3.5, Panel B). The shares of the four Asian Tiger economies followed rather similar trends in the 1990s but different trends in the 2000s. In the 1990s, the shares of the four economies rapidly expanded before the eruption of the Asian financial crisis in 1997, plummeted during the crisis and recovered in 2000 (Figure 3.15B). During the 2000s, the share of world exports of goods and services followed a clear upward trend for South Korea but fell into consistent declining trends for Taiwan and Hong Kong and fluctuated for Singapore. It is important to note that the shares of world exports of goods and services of the four economies, with the exception of South Korea, were smaller in 2010 than at their peaks before the eruption of the Asian financial crisis. This pattern tends to suggest that the Asian financial crisis, the rise of China, and globalization with vibrant foreign direct investment flows between Asian economies were important factors that reduced the relative importance of the four Asian Tiger economies in world exports in recent decades.

ASEAN-6
The ASEAN-6 economies all outperformed the world average in the growth of exports of goods and services over 1990–2010. Cambodia and Vietnam were the leading performers, growing over the period at

22.4 per cent and 17.8 per cent, respectively. The growth rate was more
modest at 10.3 per cent for Thailand, 9.8 per cent for Malaysia, 9 per
cent for Indonesia, and 8.7 per cent for the Philippines, all of which were
still higher than the world average rate of 7.5 per cent (Table 3.5, Panel
B). However, the growth rates of these economies, with the exception of
Indonesia, slowed down between the two sub-periods, from 32.8 per cent
in 1990–2000 to 12.1 per cent in 2000–2010 for Cambodia, from 12.3 to
7.2 per cent for Malaysia, from 12.3 to 5.1 per cent for the Philippines,
from 10.3 to 10.2 per cent for Thailand, and from 20 to 15.7 per cent for
Vietnam. The acceleration of Indonesia's growth from 8.5 per cent in the
first sub-period to 9.5 per cent in the second tends to indicate a resurgence
of this economy in the late 2000s. Indonesia, Thailand, and Malaysia
were the three economies of this subgroup that contributed more than
1 per cent to the world's growth in exports of goods and services over
1990–2010.

The shares of the ASEAN-6 economies of world exports of goods and
services expanded significantly over 1990–2010 (Table 3.5, Panel B).
However, their expansion trends followed different patterns, as shown in
Figure 3.15C. While Vietnam and Cambodia followed consistently strong
expansion trends throughout 1990–2010, Indonesia, Malaysia, Thailand,
and the Philippines appeared to be severely affected by the Asian financial

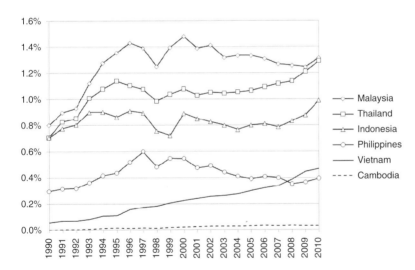

Source: Author's calculations; data from WDI, ADB.

*Figure 3.15C   Share in world exports of goods and services, 1990–2010:
ASEAN-6*

crisis. The rapid expansion of the economies' shares of world exports of goods and services in the early 1990s was interrupted during the crisis, especially in 1998. Indonesia and Thailand, however, exhibited a notable expansion trend in the late 2000s, while Malaysia and the Philippines followed a declining trend in the 2000s, after a short recovery in 1998–2000. It is worth noting that Thailand and Malaysia were the only two economies of this subgroup that contributed more than 1 per cent to world exports of goods and services in 2010.

SAC-4
Among the four SAC-4 economies, only Bangladesh outperformed the world average in exports of goods and services, growing at 11.5 per cent over 1990–2010, 12.7 per cent in 1990–2000, and 10.3 per cent in 2000–2010; the world averages for these three periods were 7.5 per cent, 6.2 per cent, and 8.5 per cent, respectively (Table 3.5, Panel B). Sri Lanka, which grew at 7.6 per cent over 1990–2010, was on par with the world average, while Nepal and Pakistan were below the world average by this measure. Because the shares of the SAC-4 economies in world exports of goods and services were small, their contributions to the world's growth over 1990–2010 by this measure were marginal and comparable to that of Cambodia in the ASEAN-6.

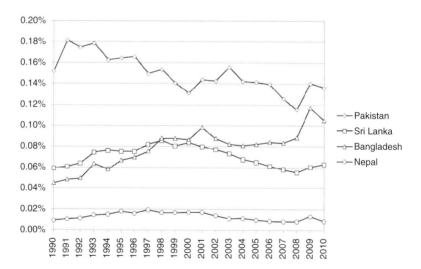

Source: Author's calculations; data from WDI, ADB.

Figure 3.15D   *Share in world exports of goods and services, 1990–2010:*
                  SAC-4

The share of world exports of goods and services followed a consistent increasing trend over 1990–2010 only for Bangladesh; it followed a consistent declining trend over 1990–2010 for Pakistan and shifted from an increasing trend in the 1990s to a decreasing trend in the 2000s for Nepal and Sri Lanka (Figure 3.15D). Notably, Bangladesh surpassed Sri Lanka in terms of its share of world exports of goods and services in 2000.

3.6.2 Imports of Goods and Services

Statistics on the performance of Developing Asia and its individual economies in world imports of goods and services during 1990–2010 and two sub-periods, 1990–2000 and 2000–2010, are reported in Table 3.6. Panel A of the table is for the group level and Panel B for individual Developing Asia economies.

a. Performance of Developing Asia as a Group in Terms of Imports of Goods and Services

The imports of goods and services of Developing Asia grew, on average, at 11.1 per cent over 1990–2010, well above the world average of 7.3 per cent. The growth rate was 5.8 per cent for the Industrialized Economies, lower than the world average, and it was 8.7 per cent for the ROW (Table 3.6, Panel A).

Developing Asia contributed 30.2 per cent to the world's growth in imports of goods and services during 1990–2010, experiencing a notable increase between the two sub-periods, from 25.3 per cent in 1990–2000 to 32.1 per cent in 2000–2010 (Figure 3.16). The Industrialized Economies were the main driver of the world's growth in imports, with a contribution of 52.7 per cent for 1990–2010. However, the contribution of the group declined markedly between the two sub-periods, from 62.1 per cent in 1990–2000 to 48.7 per cent in 2000–2010.

Developing Asia's share of world imports of goods and services expanded by almost 14 percentage points, from 12.1 per cent in 1990 to 25.9 per cent in 2010. In contrast, the Industrialized Economies' share shrank by 18 percentage points, from 75.9 per cent in 1990 to 57.7 per cent in 2010 (Table 3.6, Panel A). In addition, the expansion trend for Developing Asia and the contraction trend for the Industrialized Economies in terms of their shares of world imports of goods and services were consistent throughout 1990–2010 (Figure 3.17). Furthermore, these trends were more pronounced in the 2000s than in the 1990s, which implies that the performance of Developing Asia by this measure accelerated in

Table 3.6   The rise of Developing Asia in the world economy, 1990–2010: imports of goods and services

(A) Groups in the World

Group	Growth and Contribution						Share in World		
	1990–2010		1990–2000		2000–2010				
	Growth	Contb.	Growth	Contb.	Growth	Contb.	1990	2000	2010
World (110 Economies)	**7.3**	**100.0**	**6.1**	**100.0**	**8.3**	**100.0**	**100.0**	**100.0**	**100.0**
Developing Asia	11.1	30.2	10.2	25.3	11.8	32.1	12.1	18.1	25.9
Industrialized Economies	5.8	52.7	5.2	62.1	6.3	48.7	75.9	69.5	57.7
Rest of World (ROW)	8.7	17.1	6.3	12.6	11.0	19.3	12.0	12.4	16.4

(B) Developing Asia

Economy	1990–2010			1990–2000			2000–2010			Share in Group			Share in World		
	Growth Rate	Contb. to Growth		Growth Rate	Contb. to Growth		Growth Rate	Contb. to Growth							
		Group	World		Group	World		Group	World	1990	2000	2010	1990	2000	2010
Developing Asia	**11.1**	**100.0**	**30.2**	**10.2**	**100.0**	**25.3**	**11.8**	**100.0**	**32.1**	**100.0**	**100.0**	**100.0**	**12.1**	**18.1**	**25.9**
China–India															
China	17.6	35.2	12.3	16.8	22.5	6.0	18.4	41.5	13.8	9.3	18.0	35.1	1.1	3.3	9.1
India	14.1	9.8	3.1	8.8	4.3	1.1	19.4	12.1	4.1	5.4	4.7	10.1	0.7	0.8	2.6

Tigers-4															
Hong Kong	8.2	10.9	2.8	9.2	16.1	4.0	7.3	8.6	2.6	18.7	17.0	10.8	2.3	3.1	2.8
Singapore	9.2	8.5	2.3	10.5	12.5	3.2	7.9	7.0	2.1	12.0	12.4	8.5	1.5	2.2	2.2
South Korea	9.4	11.2	3.0	9.1	12.9	3.2	9.7	10.3	3.2	15.2	13.7	11.2	1.8	2.5	2.9
Taiwan	7.2	6.4	1.6	8.9	11.1	2.7	5.5	4.2	1.3	13.6	11.9	6.3	1.6	2.2	1.6
ASEAN-6															
Cambodia	19.2	0.2	0.1	27.6	0.3	0.1	10.9	0.1	0.04	0.03	0.2	0.1	0.00	0.03	0.04
Indonesia	8.9	3.6	1.0	6.2	2.7	0.7	11.7	3.6	1.1	5.4	3.6	3.6	0.7	0.7	0.9
Malaysia	8.9	4.2	1.1	10.8	7.0	1.8	6.9	3.2	1.0	6.3	6.8	4.2	0.8	1.2	1.1
Philippines	8.0	1.6	0.4	10.8	3.2	0.8	5.2	1.1	0.3	2.9	3.1	1.6	0.4	0.6	0.4
Thailand	8.7	4.5	1.2	7.0	4.2	1.0	10.5	4.3	1.3	7.1	5.1	4.5	0.9	0.9	1.2
Vietnam	17.3	2.1	0.7	18.1	1.7	0.4	16.5	2.4	0.8	0.6	1.3	2.1	0.1	0.2	0.5
SAC-4															
Bangladesh	9.1	0.6	0.2	8.0	0.6	0.1	10.2	0.5	0.2	0.8	0.7	0.6	0.1	0.1	0.1
Nepal	10.0	0.1	0.04	8.2	0.1	0.03	11.8	0.1	0.04	0.2	0.1	0.1	0.02	0.02	0.03
Pakistan	6.5	0.8	0.2	1.5	0.2	0.04	11.5	0.8	0.2	1.9	0.8	0.8	0.2	0.1	0.2
Sri Lanka	8.0	0.3	0.1	9.7	0.6	0.1	6.3	0.2	0.1	0.6	0.6	0.3	0.1	0.1	0.1

Note: Imports of goods and services is measured in current US$.

Source: Author's calculations; data from WDI, ADB.

The dynamics of economic growth

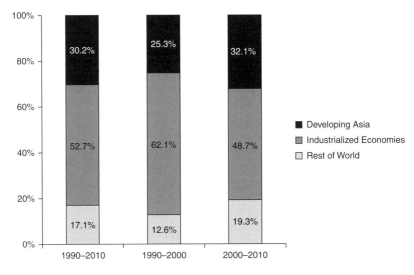

Source: Author's calculations; data from WDI, ADB.

*Figure 3.16   Contribution to the world's imports of goods and services
growth: Developing Asia versus other parts of the world*

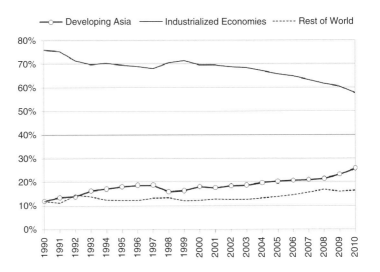

Source: Author's calculations; data from WDI, ADB.

*Figure 3.17   Share in world imports of goods and services, 1990–2010:
Developing Asia versus other parts of the world*

the first decade of the twenty-first century. It is worth noting, however, that the Industrialized Economies still commanded a lead of more than 30 percentage points over Developing Asia in terms of their share of world imports of goods and services in 2010.

b. Performance of Individual Developing Asia Economies in Terms of Imports of Goods and Services

China–India
Both China and India played important roles in the growth of the world's imports of goods and services. China grew at 17.6 per cent during 1990–2010, contributing 12.3 per cent to the world's growth in imports of goods and services during this period, while India grew at 14.1 per cent, contributing 3.1 per cent to the world's growth. In addition, the growth of both China and India accelerated between the two sub-periods, from 16.8 per cent in 1990–2000 to 18.4 per cent in 2000–2010 for China and from 8.8 to 19.4 per cent for India. As a result, the two countries expanded their contributions to the world's growth in imports of goods and services sizably between the two sub-periods, from 6 per cent in the first sub-period to 13.8 per cent in the second for China and from 1.1 to 4.1 per cent for India.

Both China and India notably expanded their shares of world imports of goods and services over 1990–2010. This share expanded by 8 percentage points, from 1.1 per cent in 1990 to 9.1 per cent in 2010, for China, and by 1.9 percentage points, from 0.7 to 2.6 per cent, for India (Table 3.6, Panel B). In addition, the expansion trends of the two countries exhibited significant acceleration during 1998–2004 and 2008–2010 for China, and 2003–2007 and 2008–2010 for India (Figure 3.18A). China appeared to expand much faster than India in terms of its share of world imports of goods and services. China's lead over India widened from less than 1 percentage point in 1990 to more than 6 percentage points in 2010.

Tigers-4
The four Asian Tiger economies, with the exception of Taiwan, grew faster than the world average in imports of goods and services over 1990–2010, but not to an impressive degree. South Korea was the leading performer, growing at 9.4 per cent, followed by Singapore (9.2 per cent) and Hong Kong (8.2 per cent), while Taiwan grew at 7.2 per cent, slightly below the 7.3 per cent world average. However, due to their significant shares of world imports of goods and services, all four Asian Tiger economies made notable contributions to the world's growth in imports

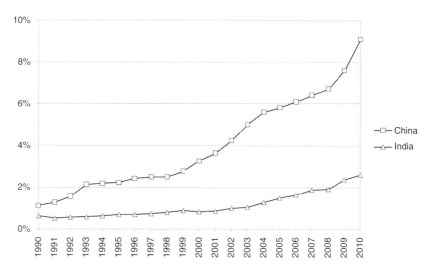

Source: Author's calculations; data from WDI, ADB.

*Figure 3.18A   Share in world imports of goods and services, 1990–2010:
China–India*

of goods and services over 1990–2010: 2.8 per cent for Hong Kong, 2.3 per cent for Singapore, 3 per cent for South Korea, and 1.6 per cent for Taiwan.

The four economies' shares of world imports of goods and services exceeded 1 per cent throughout 1990–2010. This share expanded significantly over 1990–2010 for Hong Kong (from 2.3 per cent in 1990 to 2.8 per cent in 2010), Singapore (from 1.5 to 2.2 per cent), and South Korea (from 1.8 to 2.9 per cent) but was nearly unchanged for Taiwan, at approximately 1.6 per cent (Table 3.6, Panel B). The shares of the four Asian Tiger economies followed rather similar trends during the 1990s but different trends in the 2000s. In the 1990s, the shares of the four economies rapidly expanded before the eruption of the Asian financial crisis in 1997, then plunged during the crisis and recovered in 2000 (Figure 3.18B). During 2000–2010, however, the shares of South Korea and Singapore exhibited upward trends, more solidly and consistently so for South Korea, while the shares of Hong Kong and Taiwan followed declining trends during this sub-period. It is important to note that the four Asian Tiger economies, with the exception of South Korea, had smaller shares of world imports of goods and services in 2010 than at their peaks before the eruption of the Asian financial crisis.

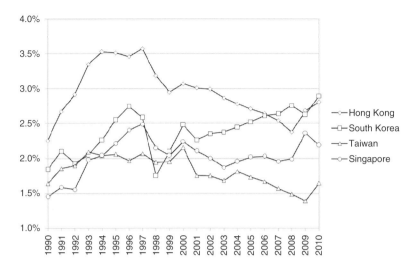

Source: Author's calculations; data from WDI, ADB.

Figure 3.18B   Share in world imports of goods and services, 1990–2010:
Tigers-4

ASEAN-6

Among the ASEAN-6 economies, Cambodia and Vietnam far outperformed the world average in growth in imports of goods and services over 1990–2010, growing at 19.2 per cent and 17.3 per cent, respectively, compared to 7.3 per cent for the world average (Table 3.6, Panel B). Other ASEAN-6 economies grew at approximately 8–9 per cent over the same period, only slightly above the world average. The growth, however, slowed down between the two sub-periods for most economies, from 27.6 per cent in 1990–2000 to 10.9 per cent in 2000–2010 for Cambodia, from 10.8 to 6.9 per cent for Malaysia, from 10.8 to 5.2 per cent for the Philippines, and from 18.1 to 16.5 per cent for Vietnam; while it picked up only for Indonesia (from 6.2 to 11.7 per cent) and Thailand (from 7 to 10.5 per cent). Indonesia, Thailand, and Malaysia were the three economies of this subgroup that contributed 1 per cent or more to the world's growth in imports of goods and services over 1990–2010.

The shares of the ASEAN-6 economies in world imports of goods and services expanded significantly over 1990–2010 but followed notably different patterns (Figure 3.18C). The shares of Vietnam and Cambodia followed solid expansion trends throughout 1990–2010. In contrast, the shares of Indonesia, Malaysia, Thailand, and the Philippines suffered sharp contractions during the Asian financial crisis of 1997–1998, after a

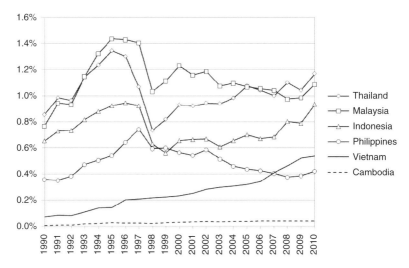

Source: Author's calculations; data from WDI, ADB.

Figure 3.18C   Share in world imports of goods and services, 1990–2010: ASEAN-6

rapid expansion in the early 1990s. In the 2000s, the shares of Indonesia and Thailand exhibited strong expanding trends after recovery from the Asian financial crisis, while the shares of Malaysia and the Philippines exhibited a clear declining trend. It is worth noting that the shares of Thailand, Malaysia, and the Philippines were lower in 2010 than at their peaks before the eruption of the Asian financial crisis. Furthermore, Vietnam's share of world imports of goods and services has exceeded that of the Philippines since 2007 and Thailand's share has exceeded that of Malaysia since 2008. Thailand and Malaysia were the only two ASEAN-6 economies that contributed more than 1 per cent to the world's growth in imports of goods and services over 1990–2010.

SAC-4
The SAC-4 economies, with the exception of Pakistan, grew faster than the world average in imports of goods and services over 1990–2010: 9.1 per cent for Bangladesh, 10 per cent for Nepal, and 8 per cent for Sri Lanka, compared to 7.3 per cent for the world average; while this rate was 6.5 per cent for Pakistan (Table 3.6, Panel B). In addition, the SAC-4 economies, with the exception of Sri Lanka, accelerated their growth between the two sub-periods, from 8 per cent in 1990–2000 to 10.2 per cent in 2000–2010 for Bangladesh, from 8.2 to 11.8 per cent for Nepal,

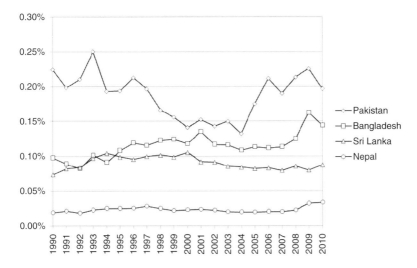

Source: Author's calculations; data from WDI, ADB.

Figure 3.18D   *Share in world imports of goods and services, 1990–2010: SAC-4*

and from 1.5 to 11.5 per cent for Pakistan. This rate, however, declined from 9.7 to 6.3 per cent between the two sub-periods for Sri Lanka.

The shares of world imports of goods and services followed different patterns for the SAC-4 economies over 1990–2010. The trend for Bangladesh was rather consistently upward, while the trend for Pakistan exhibited a sharp decline during 1990–2004 and turned upward during 2004–2010 (Figure 3.18D). The trend for Sri Lanka shifted from expansion during 1990–2000 to contraction during 2000–2010, while the trend for Nepal changed little during 1990–2010, with a small increase in 2008–2010.

3.7 THE RISE OF DEVELOPING ASIA AND GLOBALIZATION: SELECTED INDICATORS

This section describes the rise of Developing Asia in association with globalization by examining its performance with respect to selected indicators of global integration. Due to limited space, this section focuses on exports of ICT hardware, manufactures and commercial services, and foreign direct investment (FDI) stock, which have been among the key drivers of globalization.

The data is from the World Trade Organization (WTO) database for international trade, and from the United Nations Conference on Trade and Development (UNCTAD) database for FDI stock.[9]

3.7.1   Exports of ICT Hardware[10]

ICT hardware is one of the major product categories driving the rapid acceleration of globalization. The ICT hardware includes the manufacture products in three categories of the Standard International Trade Classification (SITC) classified by the United Nations:

● Electronic data processing and office equipment (SITC division 75),
● Telecommunications and sound recording and reproducing apparatus and equipment (SITC division 76), and
● Integrated circuits and electronic components (SITC group 776).

Performance of Developing Asia on exports of ICT hardware
Developing Asia's share of world ICT hardware exports soared by 34 percentage points, from 22.1 per cent in 1990 to 56.2 per cent in 2010 (Figure 3.19). In contrast, the Industrialized Economies' share contracted by almost 40 percentage points, from 75.6 per cent in 1990 to 36.3 per cent in 2010. It should be noted that the increasing trend for Developing Asia and the decreasing trend for the Industrialized Economies with respect to this measure became steeper beginning in 2001 when the progress of the ICT revolution and the penetration of ICT across countries began to accelerate notably. At the same time, the share of the ROW in world ICT hardware exports expanded significantly, from 2.3 per cent in 1990 to 7.5 per cent in 2010.

Performance of China and India in terms of exports of ICT hardware
China recorded a remarkable expansion in its share of world ICT hardware exports, which increased by almost 30 percentage points over 1990–2010, from 1.1 per cent in 1990 to 30.2 per cent in 2010 (Figure 3.20). India, on the other hand, performed unimpressively with respect to this indicator. India's share of world ICT hardware exports was notably below 1 per cent throughout 1990–2010, with some insignificant periods of pickup.

---

[9]   The WTO database can be retrieved from the WTO website (http://www.wto.org/). The UNCTAD database is available at the UNCTAD statistics website (http://unctad.org/en/Pages/Statistics.aspx). The data on trade and FDI stock are measured in current US dollars.
[10]   Table A3.1 (Appendix 3.1) provides the key performance statistics of Developing Asia and its individual economies on exports of ICT hardware during 1990–2010.

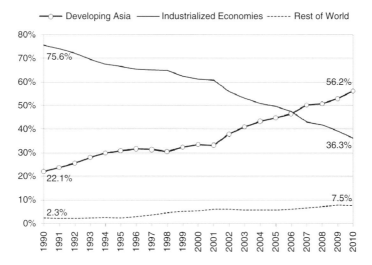

Source: Author's calculations; data from WTO.

*Figure 3.19   Share in world exports of ICT hardware, 1990–2010:
Developing Asia versus other parts of the world*

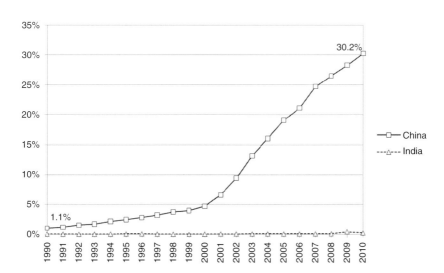

Source: Author's calculations; data from WTO.

*Figure 3.20   Share in world exports of ICT hardware, 1990–2010:
China–India*

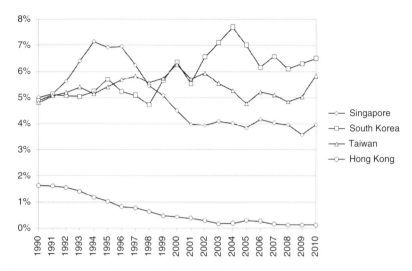

Source: Author's calculations; data from WTO.

Figure 3.21   Share in world exports of ICT hardware, 1990–2010: Tigers-4

It should be noted that while China surged dramatically in terms of its share of world ICT hardware exports, the other key Asian players in this industry, with the exception of South Korea, experienced notable decreasing trends with respect to this measure, especially from 2000 on (Figure 3.21). This means that the performance of Developing Asia in exports of ICT hardware was mostly driven by China.

3.7.2   Exports of Manufactures[11]

Performance of Developing Asia in terms of exports of manufactures
Developing Asia's share of world exports of manufactures soared by almost 20 percentage points, from 12.2 per cent in 1990 to 30.6 per cent in 2010 (Figure 3.22). In contrast, the Industrialized Economies' share contracted by almost 23 percentage points, from 83.5 per cent in 1990 to 60.5 per cent in 2010. It is worth noting that the upward trend for Developing Asia and the downward trend for the Industrialized Economies with respect to this measure both became steeper after 2001.

---

[11]   Table A3.2 (Appendix 3.1) provides the key performance statistics for Developing Asia and its individual economies in exports of manufactures during 1990–2010.

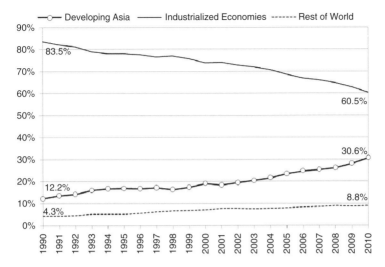

Source: Author's calculations; data from WTO.

Figure 3.22   *Share in world exports of manufactures, 1990–2010:*
Developing Asia versus other parts of the world

Performance of China and India in terms of exports of manufactures

China's share of world manufacture exports followed a steep upward
trend, increasing from 1.9 per cent in 1990 to 16.1 per cent in 2010,
while India's share increased modestly, from 0.5 in 1990 to 1.5 per cent
in 2010 (Figure 3.23). The acceleration of the growth of China's share of
world manufacture exports was prominent during 1999–2010. The faster
pace of expansion of China than of India with respect to this measure
widened the gap between the two countries substantially over 1990–2010,
from 1.4 percentage points in 1990 to more than 14 percentage points
in 2010.

3.7.3   Exports of Commercial Services[12]

Performance of Developing Asia in terms of exports of commercial services

Developing Asia's share of world commercial services expanded by
more than 11 percentage points, from 10.1 per cent in 1990 to 21.6 per
cent in 2010 (Figure 3.24). In contrast, the Industrialized Economies'
share contracted by more than 12 percentage points, from 81.9 per cent

[12]   Table A3.3 (Appendix 3.1) provides the key performance statistics for Developing
Asia and its individual economies in exports of commercial services during 1990–2010.

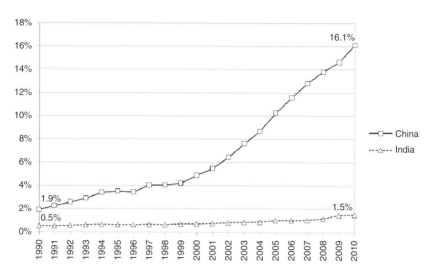

Source: Author's calculations; data from WTO.

*Figure 3.23   Share in world exports of manufactures, 1990–2010:
China–India*

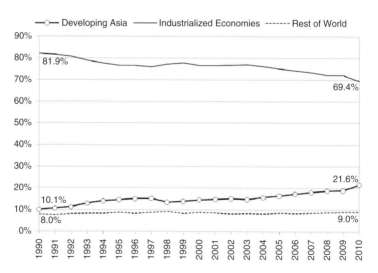

Source: Author's calculations; data from WTO.

*Figure 3.24   Share in world exports of commercial services, 1990–2010:
Developing Asia versus other parts of the world*

in 1990 to 69.4 per cent in 2010. At the same time, the ROW increased its share by 1 percentage point, from 8 per cent to 9 per cent over the same period.

Performance of China and India in terms of exports of commercial services
Both China and India rapidly increased their shares of world exports of commercial services over 1990–2010. China's share rose by approximately 4 percentage points, from 0.8 per cent in 1990 to 4.9 per cent in 2010, while India's share rose by almost 3 percentage points, from 0.6 to 3.5 per cent over the same period (Figure 3.25). It is worth noting that India performed comparably to China with respect to this measure. The strong performance of India in exports of commercial services during 1990–2010 was associated with the country's outstanding growth in exports of computer software and computer services over the period.[13]

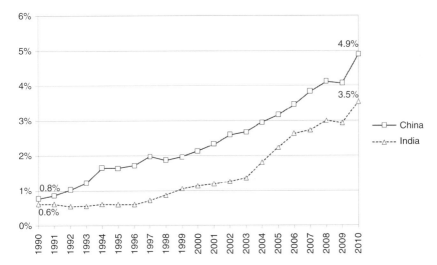

Source: Author's calculations; data from WTO.

Figure 3.25 Share in world exports of commercial services, 1990–2010: China–India

---

[13] India's software and computer services have recorded phenomenal growth, at a rate exceeding 30 per cent per year, since the late 1980s, with a strong focus on exports. The industry's export revenues rose from about US$50 million in 1988 to a projected figure of US$60 billion in 2008, or more than a quarter of India's total exports (Madhani, 2008).

3.7.4   FDI Stock[14]

Performance of Developing Asia in terms of accumulation of FDI stock
Developing Asia did not exhibit outstanding expansion in its share of
world FDI stock. The region's share increased by only 1.6 percentage
points over 1990–2010, from 15.0 per cent in 1990 to 16.6 per cent in 2010
(Figure 3.26), while the ROW's share increased by 10 percentage points,
from 8.6 to 18.5 per cent, over the same period. In fact, the ROW has
surpassed Developing Asia in terms of its world share of FDI stock since
2003. On the other hand, the share of the Industrialized Economies contracted by more than 11 percentage points, from 76.4 per cent in 1990 to
65 per cent in 2010 (Figure 3.26).

The modest expansion of Developing Asia in its share of world FDI
stock was due not to its slow growth but rather to the rapid growth of
other parts of the world with respect to this indicator. In fact, Developing
Asia grew at 12.1 per cent over 1990–2010 in terms of its share of world
FDI stock, while this growth rate was 10.7 per cent for the Industrialized
Economies and 15.9 per cent for the ROW (Table A3.4, Appendix 3.1).

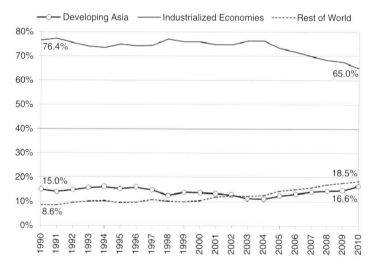

Source: Author's calculations; data from UNCTAD.

Figure 3.26   Share in world FDI stock, 1990–2010: Developing Asia
versus other parts of the world

---

[14]   Table A3.4 (Appendix 3.1) provides key performance statistics for Developing Asia
and its individual economies in terms of FDI stock during 1990–2010.

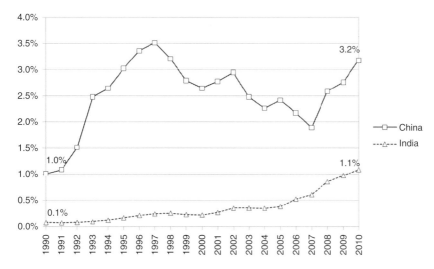

Source: Author's calculations; data from UNCTAD.

Figure 3.27   Share in world FDI stock, 1990–2010: China–India

Performance of China and India in terms of accumulation of FDI stock
Both China and India expanded their shares of world FDI stock over 1990–2010. For China, however, this expansion did not follow a solid trend. It surged during 1990–1997 but then declined during 1997–2007 before rebounding during 2008–2010. As a result, China's share of world FDI stock expanded by just a little more than 2 percentage points over 1990–2010, which was very modest compared to its world share expansions by other measures (Figure 3.27). On the other hand, India experienced a solid upward trend in its share of world FDI stock over 1990–2010, increasing by 1 percentage point from 0.1 per cent in 1990 to 1.1 per cent in 2010.

3.8   INSIGHTS FROM THE COMBINED RESULTS

This chapter examines the rise of Developing Asia during the 1990–2010 period. This examination focuses on key national account items, including GDP, private consumption, government consumption, fixed investment, and exports and imports of goods and services. In addition, this exercise also examines the performance of Developing Asia in terms of indicators of globalization over the past two decades. These indicators include exports of manufactures, ICT hardware, and commercial services and accumulation of FDI capital stock.

Combining the results presented in the previous sections reveals important insights. First, Developing Asia substantially expanded its share of the world economy with respect to GDP and its related indicators (Figure 3.28). In 1990, the shares of Developing Asia with respect to these indicators were modest, with a narrow variation between 12.1 per cent for imports and 16.6 per cent for fixed investment. In 2010, these shares increased and varied more widely, from 22.6 per cent for private consumption to 45.7 per cent for fixed investment.

Second, among the key national accounts, Developing Asia's world share expanded fastest in fixed investment (29.1 percentage points) and slowest in private consumption (9.3 percentage points), as shown in Figure 3.29. Over the same period, the region's share of world exports expanded on a par with its GDP (15 versus 14.9 percentage points) but faster than its share of world imports (13.8 percentage points). This expansion of Developing Asia in the world economy was outstanding, but does suggest that the region needs to make some adjustments to sustain its high growth in the decade to come. One such adjustment is to reduce the large disparity in the pace of growth between fixed investment and private consumption. Another adjustment is to facilitate the growth of imports to narrow the trade imbalance between the region and other parts of the world.

Figure 3.29 also indicates that the decline of the industrialized group during 1990–2010 was most severe for fixed investments. The group's share of world fixed investments decreased by 21.9 percentage points, which was much larger than the decrease in its share of world GDP (13.9 percentage points).

Third, China and India far outperformed the world average with respect to all the national account items examined (Figure 3.30, upper panel). This outperformance was most pronounced in fixed investment and international trade (Figure 3.30, lower panel), which means capital accumulation and openness played important roles in driving outstanding growth in the two countries.

Fourth, embracing the globalization trend, Developing Asia rapidly expanded its world share in international trade in key product categories, especially in ICT hardware exports, increasing from 22.1 per cent in 1990 to 56.2 per cent in 2010, followed by exports of manufactures, from 12.2 to 30.6 per cent, and exports of commercial services, from 10.1 to 21.6 per cent (Figure 3.31). However, the expansion of the region in world FDI stock was unimpressive, from 15 per cent in 1990 to 16.6 per cent in 2010 (Figure 3.31). The reason for this modest expansion in Developing Asia was the rapid growth in other parts of the world with respect to this indicator, fuelled by the acceleration of globalization during the past two

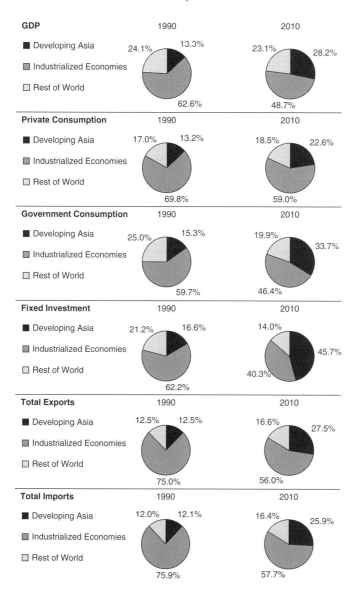

Source: Author's calculations.

Figure 3.28 Developing Asia's shares in world on key national account items: 1990 versus 2010

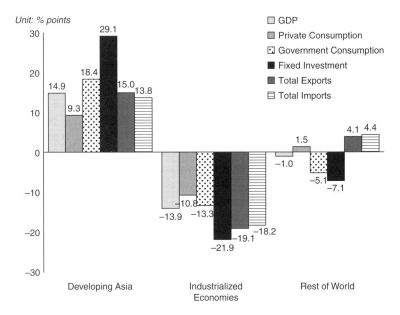

Source: Author's calculations.

Figure 3.29   Change in world share by group, 1990–2010

decades. As Figure 3.32 shows, FDI stock growth in 1990–2010 was rather comparable between Developing Asia (12.1 per cent) and the world aggregate (11.6 per cent).

Fifth, China and India, the two leading performers in Developing Asia in growth during 1990–2010, outperformed the region average in growth with respect to all four of the globalization indicators examined: exports of ICT hardware, exports of manufactures, exports of commercial services, and FDI stock. This superior growth is particularly pronounced for exports of ICT hardware for China and FDI stock for India (Figure 3.32).

However, the change in India's world share for each of the four indicators examined was modest because each started from a low base in 1990 (Figure 3.33). This insight suggests that India still has ample room to promote growth by embracing globalization in the decades to come. The same is true of China with respect to exports of commercial services and FDI stock.

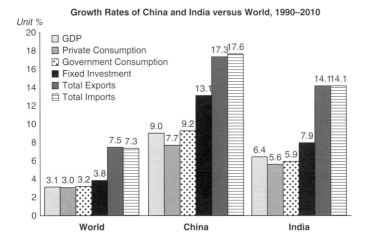

Source: Author's calculations.

*Figure 3.30   Performance of China and India versus the world average,
1990–2010*

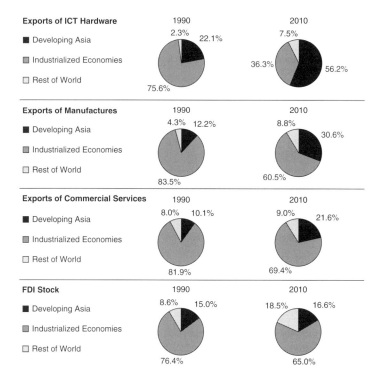

Source: Author's calculations.

*Figure 3.31   Developing Asia's shares in world on selected globalization
indicators: 1990 versus 2010*

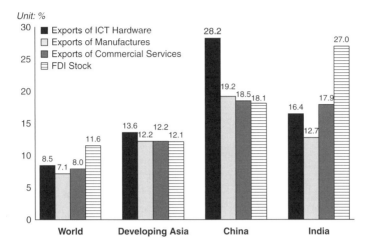

Source: Author's calculations.

Figure 3.32 Growth rates of the world, Developing Asia, China, and India on selected globalization indicators, 1990–2010

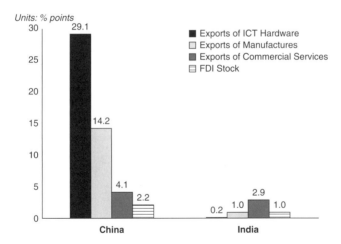

Source: Author's calculations.

Figure 3.33 Changes in the world shares of China and India on selected globalization indicators, 1990–2010

APPENDIX 3.1: DEVELOPING ASIA AS A DRIVER OF GLOBALIZATION: SELECTED INDICATORS

Table A3.1   The rise of Developing Asia, 1990–2010: exports of ICT hardware

(A) Groups in the World

Group	Growth and Contribution						Share in World		
	1990–2010		1990–2000		2000–2010		1990	2000	2010
	Growth	Contb.	Growth	Contb.	Growth	Contb.			
World (67 Economies)	**8.5**	**100.0**	**12.2**	**100.0**	**4.9**	**100.0**	**100.0**	**100.0**	**100.0**
Developing Asia*	13.6	64.5	16.9	38.9	10.5	93.1	22.1	33.5	56.2
Industrialized Economies	4.6	26.7	9.8	54.5	-0.4	-4.2	75.6	61.2	36.3
Rest of World (ROW)	15.1	8.8	22.0	6.7	8.7	11.2	2.3	5.3	7.5

(B) Developing Asia

Economy	Period 1990–2010			Period 1990–2000			Period 2000–2010			Share in Group*			Share in World		
	Growth (CAGR)	Contb. to Growth		Growth (CAGR)	Contb. to Growth		Growth (CAGR)	Contb. to Growth		1990	2000	2010	1990	2000	2010
		Group*	World		Group*	World		Group*	World						
Developing Asia*	**13.6**	**100.0**	**64.5**	**16.9**	**100.0**	**38.9**	**10.5**	**100.0**	**93.1**	**100.0**	**100.0**	**100.0**	**22.1**	**33.5**	**56.2**
China–India															
China	28.2	57.8	37.3		16.5	6.4	26.3	77.0	71.7	4.8	14.1	53.7	1.1	4.7	30.2
India	16.4	0.5	0.3		0.1	0.03	25.6	0.6	0.6	0.3	0.1	0.5	0.1	0.04	0.3

Tigers-4															
Hong Kong	-4.7	-0.4	-0.2	-1.8	-0.3	-0.1	-7.5	-0.4	-0.4	7.4	1.3	0.2	1.6	0.4	0.1
Singapore	7.2	5.7	3.7	11.0	11.0	4.3	3.6	3.3	3.1	22.6	13.4	7.0	5.0	4.5	4.0
South Korea	10.0	10.7	6.9	15.1	18.1	7.0	5.1	7.2	6.7	22.1	19.0	11.5	4.9	6.4	6.5
Taiwan	9.5	9.4	6.1	15.2	17.9	6.9	4.2	5.5	5.1	21.7	18.7	10.4	4.8	6.3	5.8
ASEAN-6															
Indonesia	23.1	1.0	0.7	50.2	2.9	1.1	0.9	0.1	0.1	0.2	2.4	1.0	0.04	0.8	0.5
Malaysia	11.1	7.7	4.9	20.4	18.1	7.0	2.5	2.8	2.6	12.6	16.9	8.0	2.8	5.7	4.5
Philippines	14.6	3.4	2.2	29.9	9.5	3.7	1.1	0.5	0.5	2.8	8.1	3.3	0.6	2.7	1.9
Thailand	12.3	4.2	2.7	18.1	6.2	2.4	6.8	3.3	3.1	5.4	6.0	4.3	1.2	2.0	2.4
SAC-4															
Bangladesh	34.8	0.00	0.00	53.5	0.00	0.00	18.3	0.00	0.00	0.00	0.00	0.00	0.00	0.00	0.00
Pakistan	13.1	0.01	0.00	5.2	0.00	0.00	21.5	0.01	0.01	0.01	0.00	0.01	0.00	0.00	0.00
Sri Lanka	6.1	0.00	0.00	34.4	0.04	0.01	-16.2	-0.01	-0.01	0.01	0.03	0.00	0.00	0.01	0.00

Note: * Developing Asia excludes Cambodia, Nepal and Vietnam.

Source: Author's calculations; data from WTO's Statistics database.

Table A3.2   The rise of Developing Asia, 1990–2010: exports of manufactures

(A) Groups in the World

Group	Growth and Contribution						Share in World		
	1990–2010		1990–2000		2000–2010		1990	2000	2010
	Growth	Contb.	Growth	Contb.	Growth	Contb.			
World (74 Economies)	**7.1**	**100.0**	**6.8**	**100.0**	**7.4**	**100.0**	**100.0**	**100.0**	**100.0**
Developing Asia*	12.2	36.9	11.7	26.4	12.6	41.7	12.2	19.1	30.6
Industrialized Economies	5.4	52.8	5.5	63.5	5.3	47.8	83.5	73.8	60.5
Rest of World (ROW)	11.1	10.4	12.4	10.1	9.8	10.5	4.3	7.1	8.8

(B) Developing Asia

Economy	Period 1990–2010			Period 1990–2000			Period 2000–2010			Share in Group*			Share in World		
	Growth (CAGR)	Contb. to Growth		Growth (CAGR)	Contb. to Growth		Growth (CAGR)	Contb. to Growth		1990	2000	2010	1990	2000	2010
		Group*	World		Group*	World		Group*	World						
Developing Asia*	**12.2**	**100.0**	**36.9**	**11.7**	**100.0**	**26.4**	**12.6**	**100.0**	**41.7**	**100.0**	**100.0**	**100.0**	**12.2**	**19.1**	**30.6**
China–India															
China	19.2	56.6	20.9	17.4	30.7	8.1	21.0	64.3	26.8	15.7	25.7	52.5	1.9	4.9	16.1
India	12.7	5.0	1.8	10.1	3.6	0.9	15.4	5.4	2.2	4.4	3.9	4.9	0.5	0.7	1.5

Tigers-4															
Hong Kong	−6.7	−0.8	−0.3	−2.1	−0.9	−0.2	−11.0	−0.8	−0.3	9.7	2.6	0.2	1.2	0.5	0.1
Singapore	8.4	3.7	1.3	10.6	7.0	1.8	6.2	2.7	1.1	8.2	7.4	4.1	1.0	1.4	1.3
South Korea	10.1	13.9	5.1	9.8	16.5	4.3	10.3	13.1	5.5	21.5	18.1	14.6	2.6	3.5	4.5
Taiwan	7.1	7.2	2.7	8.6	13.8	3.6	5.7	5.3	2.2	22.0	16.5	8.7	2.7	3.1	2.7
ASEAN-6															
Indonesia	9.8	2.0	0.7	15.1	4.9	1.3	4.7	1.1	0.5	3.2	4.3	2.1	0.4	0.8	0.6
Malaysia	11.2	4.6	1.7	17.4	11.0	2.9	5.4	2.8	1.2	5.6	9.2	4.7	0.7	1.8	1.5
Philippines	10.8	1.5	0.6	20.1	5.1	1.3	2.3	0.5	0.2	2.0	4.1	1.6	0.2	0.8	0.5
Thailand	12.0	5.0	1.9	13.5	6.5	1.7	10.6	4.6	1.9	5.2	6.0	5.0	0.6	1.2	1.5
SAC-4															
Bangladesh	14.4	0.7	0.2	17.2	0.8	0.2	11.8	0.6	0.3	0.4	0.7	0.6	0.1	0.1	0.2
Nepal	7.2	0.02	0.01	12.2	0.1	0.01	2.4	0.01	0.00	0.1	0.1	0.02	0.01	0.01	0.01
Pakistan	6.7	0.5	0.2	5.7	0.6	0.1	7.6	0.4	0.2	1.6	0.9	0.6	0.2	0.2	0.2
Sri Lanka	8.8	0.2	0.1	15.1	0.5	0.1	2.9	0.1	0.03	0.4	0.5	0.2	0.04	0.1	0.1

Note: * Developing Asia excludes Cambodia and Vietnam.

Source: Author's calculations; data from WTO's Statistics database.

Table A3.3   *The rise of Developing Asia, 1990–2010: exports of commercial services*

(A) Groups in the World

Group	Growth and Contribution						Share in World		
	1990–2010		1990–2000		2000–2010		1990	2000	2010
	Growth	Contb.	Growth	Contb.	Growth	Contb.			
World (102 Economies)	**8.0**	**100.0**	**6.6**	**100.0**	**9.4**	**100.0**	**100.0**	**100.0**	**100.0**
Developing Asia	12.2	24.7	10.6	19.8	13.7	26.3	10.1	14.7	21.6
Industrialized Economies	7.1	65.9	5.8	70.6	8.3	64.5	81.9	76.6	69.4
Rest of World (ROW)	8.7	9.3	7.6	9.7	9.8	9.2	8.0	8.8	9.0

(B) Developing Asia

Economy	Period 1990–2010			Period 1990–2000			Period 2000–2010			Share in Group			Share in World		
	Growth (CAGR)	Contb. to Growth		Growth (CAGR)	Contb. to Growth		Growth (CAGR)	Contb. to Growth							
		Group	World		Group	World		Group	World	1990	2000	2010	1990	2000	2010
Developing Asia	**12.2**	**100.0**	**24.7**	**10.6**	**100.0**	**19.8**	**13.7**	**100.0**	**26.3**	**100.0**	**100.0**	**100.0**	**10.1**	**14.7**	**21.6**
China–India															
China	18.5	24.4	6.0	18.0	18.5	3.7	18.9	25.8	6.8	7.6	14.5	22.7	0.8	2.1	4.9
India	17.9	17.6	4.3	13.3	8.7	1.7	22.6	19.7	5.2	6.1	7.7	16.4	0.6	1.1	3.5

Tigers-4															
Hong Kong	9.2	13.0	3.2	8.2	16.7	3.3	10.1	12.1	3.2	24.1	19.4	14.1	2.4	2.8	3.0
Singapore	11.5	14.7	3.6	8.4	11.9	2.4	14.7	15.4	4.0	16.8	13.7	14.9	1.7	2.0	3.2
South Korea	11.5	11.3	2.8	12.2	15.9	3.1	10.9	10.2	2.7	12.9	14.8	11.5	1.3	2.2	2.5
Taiwan	9.2	4.9	1.2	11.1	9.8	1.9	7.3	3.7	1.0	9.1	9.6	5.3	0.9	1.4	1.2
ASEAN-6															
Cambodia	22.4	0.2	0.1	30.7	0.3	0.1	14.7	0.2	0.1	0.04	0.2	0.2	0.00	0.03	0.05
Indonesia	9.8	2.0	0.5	7.4	2.0	0.4	12.3	2.1	0.5	3.3	2.4	2.2	0.3	0.4	0.5
Malaysia	11.4	4.3	1.1	13.9	7.6	1.5	9.0	3.5	0.9	5.0	6.7	4.3	0.5	1.0	0.9
Philippines	8.2	1.7	0.4	1.5	0.4	0.1	15.4	2.0	0.5	3.8	1.6	1.9	0.4	0.2	0.4
Thailand	8.8	4.1	1.0	8.2	5.7	1.1	9.5	3.7	1.0	8.3	6.6	4.5	0.8	1.0	1.0
Vietnam	20.3	1.1	0.3	31.0	1.9	0.4	10.5	0.9	0.2	0.2	1.3	1.0	0.02	0.2	0.2
SAC-4															
Bangladesh	7.3	0.1	0.03	-0.4	-0.01	0.00	15.6	0.2	0.04	0.4	0.1	0.2	0.04	0.02	0.03
Nepal	6.5	0.1	0.02	9.4	0.2	0.04	3.6	0.03	0.01	0.2	0.2	0.1	0.02	0.03	0.02
Pakistan	4.5	0.3	0.1	0.5	0.05	0.01	8.7	0.3	0.1	1.6	0.6	0.4	0.2	0.1	0.1
Sri Lanka	9.2	0.3	0.1	8.0	0.4	0.1	10.4	0.3	0.07	0.6	0.4	0.3	0.1	0.1	0.1

Source: Author's calculations; data from WTO's Statistics database.

Table A3.4 The rise of Developing Asia, 1990–2010: FDI capital stock

(A) Groups in the World

Group	Growth and Contribution						Share in World		
	1990–2010		1990–2000		2000–2010		1990	2000	2010
	Growth	Contb.	Growth	Contb.	Growth	Contb.			
World (116 Economies)	**11.6**	**100.0**	**13.6**	**100.0**	**9.6**	**100.0**	**100.0**	**100.0**	**100.0**
Developing Asia	12.1	16.8	12.5	13.2	11.7	18.5	15.0	13.7	16.6
Industrialized Economies	10.7	63.5	13.5	75.8	7.9	57.6	76.4	75.9	65.0
Rest of World	15.9	19.7	15.7	11.1	16.0	23.9	8.6	10.4	18.5

(B) Developing Asia

Economy	Period 1990–2010			Period 1990–2000			Period 2000–2010			Share in Group			Share in World		
	Growth (CAGR)	Contb. to Growth		Growth (CAGR)	Contb. to Growth		Growth (CAGR)	Contb. to Growth		1990	2000	2010	1990	2000	2010
		Group	World		Group	World		Group	World						
Developing Asia	**12.1**	**100.0**	**16.8**	**12.5**	**100.0**	**13.2**	**11.7**	**100.0**	**18.5**	**100.0**	**100.0**	**100.0**	**15.0**	**13.7**	**16.6**
China–India															
China	18.1	20.6	3.5	25.0	25.0	3.3	11.6	19.1	3.5	6.8	19.4	19.2	1.0	2.6	3.2
India	27.0	7.2	1.2	25.7	2.1	0.3	28.3	9.0	1.7	0.5	1.6	6.6	0.1	0.2	1.1

Tigers-4															
Hong Kong	8.8	33.1	5.5	8.5	36.7	4.8	9.2	31.8	5.9	65.9	45.6	36.4	9.9	6.2	6.0
Singapore	14.7	16.2	2.7	13.8	11.6	1.5	15.6	17.8	3.3	10.0	11.1	15.6	1.5	1.5	2.6
South Korea	17.3	4.5	0.8	23.8	5.6	0.7	11.3	4.1	0.8	1.7	4.4	4.2	0.3	0.6	0.7
Taiwan	9.9	2.0	0.3	7.2	1.4	0.2	12.7	2.2	0.4	3.2	2.0	2.1	0.5	0.3	0.4
ASEAN-6															
Cambodia	28.8	0.2	0.04	45.3	0.2	0.03	14.2	0.2	0.04	0.01	0.2	0.2	0.00	0.02	0.03
Indonesia	14.1	4.2	0.7	11.1	2.4	0.3	17.1	4.8	0.9	2.9	2.5	4.0	0.4	0.3	0.7
Malaysia	12.1	3.4	0.6	17.7	6.1	0.8	6.7	2.4	0.4	3.4	5.3	3.4	0.5	0.7	0.6
Philippines	8.9	0.8	0.1	14.9	2.0	0.3	3.2	0.3	0.1	1.5	1.8	0.8	0.2	0.2	0.1
Thailand	14.7	4.4	0.7	13.8	3.1	0.4	15.6	4.8	0.9	2.7	3.0	4.2	0.4	0.4	0.7
Vietnam	20.2	2.4	0.4	28.7	2.7	0.4	12.3	2.2	0.4	0.5	2.1	2.2	0.1	0.3	0.4
SAC-4															
Bangladesh	13.6	0.2	0.03	16.3	0.2	0.03	10.9	0.2	0.04	0.2	0.2	0.2	0.02	0.03	0.03
Nepal	15.5	0.01	0.00	20.0	0.01	0.00	11.0	0.01	0.00	0.00	0.01	0.01	0.00	0.00	0.00
Pakistan	12.9	0.7	0.1	13.8	0.7	0.1	12.0	0.7	0.1	0.6	0.7	0.7	0.1	0.1	0.1
Sri Lanka	10.5	0.2	0.03	8.9	0.1	0.02	12.1	0.2	0.03	0.2	0.2	0.2	0.03	0.02	0.03

Source: Author's calculations; data from UNCTAD's Statistical database.

4. Sources of Developing Asia's economic growth: insights from the standard growth accounting approach

4.1 INTRODUCTION

The previous three chapters depict the catching-up performance of Developing Asia and its rise in the global landscape during the past two decades. This chapter examines the sources of economic growth in the individual economies of the region to identify the key drivers of their economic performance. The chapter then analyses the growth gap between Developing Asia and the rest of the world to understand the sources of the region's high economic performance in comparison to the non-Asian developing economies and the economies of developed countries.

The chapter uses the neo-classical growth accounting framework to decompose the aggregate growth of an individual economy into the contribution of various inputs and the total factor productivity (TFP). This growth accounting methodology was pioneered by Solow (1957) and considerably developed by Jorgenson and associates (Jorgenson and Griliches, 1967; Christensen and Jorgenson, 1969, 1970; Christensen et al., 1975; Diewert, 1976; and Jorgenson et al., 1987).[1] The growth accounting framework has been widely accepted as the most accurate way of measuring the contribution of different economic inputs and is therefore the gold standard for the analysis of productivity and sources of growth.

Using the accounting framework for growth in the information age, this chapter decomposes the aggregate gross domestic product (GDP) growth at the economy level into the contribution of three main sources: capital input, labor input, and total factor productivity (TFP). The capital input consists of the information and communication technology (ICT) capital[2]

---

[1] See OECD (2001) and Caselli (2008) for a comprehensive review.
[2] ICT capital is associated with investment in computer hardware, computer software, and telecommunication equipment.

and non-ICT capital, which includes all of the other types of capital. The contribution of ICT capital captures the impact of the ICT revolution across sectors in the economy. Labor input includes hours worked and labor quality. Hours worked reflects the mobilization of labor through increased labor force participation and longer hours worked per average worker. Labor quality captures the contribution of human capital accumulation, which is proxied by education and experience. TFP growth is considered the contribution of technical progress, efficiency improvement, and other unobservable factors. Comprehensive presentations of the decomposition framework for growth in the information age, in which the split between ICT and non-ICT capital is emphasized, were published by Jorgenson et al. (2005) and Barro and Lee (2010).

Average labor productivity (ALP) of an economy is calculated by dividing its GDP by the total hours worked. ALP is an important indicator of economic performance. Jones (1997) noted that labor productivity is a more reliable measure than per capita income for capturing the wealth level of a nation. Fogel (2011) asserted that 'much of the success of developing countries was due to changes in labor productivity.' The growth accounting framework allows one to decompose ALP growth into the contribution of capital deepening, labor quality, and TFP growth. Capital deepening is a measure of the capital quantity per average worker, which is a major driver of ALP growth in most countries, as will be shown in this chapter.

The decomposition of GDP and ALP growth described in this chapter is based on the growth accounting framework presented by Jorgenson et al. (2003, 2005), which is elaborated in Appendix 4.1. In this exercise, GDP growth is decomposed into the contributions of capital input, which consists of ICT and non-ICT capital, labor input, which includes hours worked and labor quality, and TFP growth. At the same time, ALP growth is decomposed into the contribution of capital deepening, labor quality, and TFP growth.

The decomposition exercise uses the dataset used by Jorgenson and Vu (2011), which is constructed based on the Conference Board's Total Economy Dataset (TED) and the World Bank's World Development Indicators database. The Jorgenson and Vu dataset covers 119 economies that are divided into the seven groups introduced in Chapter 2. Detail of this dataset is provided in Appendix 4.2. Recall that these seven groups are Developing Asia, G7, Non-G7, Latin America, Eastern Europe and former Soviet Union (or Eastern Europe), Sub-Saharan Africa, and Northern Africa and Middle East. The growth decomposition exercise was conducted for the 1990–2010 period, which in turn was divided into two sub-periods: 1990–2000 and 2000–2010.

As in the other chapters of this book, to facilitate comparative analyses, the empirical results obtained for the group composed of 16 Developing Asia economies are arranged into four subgroups. They are: China–India, which includes two giant economies (China and India); Tigers-4, which includes four Asian Tiger economies (Hong Kong, Singapore, South Korea, and Taiwan); ASEAN-6, which includes six ASEAN economies (Cambodia, Indonesia, Malaysia, the Philippines, Thailand, and Vietnam); and SAC-4, which includes four South Asian economies (Bangladesh, Nepal, Pakistan, and Sri Lanka).

The remainder of the chapter proceeds as follows. Section 4.2 examines the sources of GDP growth of the 16 Developing Asia economies at the individual economy level and depicts their performance in a regional picture. Section 4.3 analyses the sources of ALP growth of the 16 Developing Asia economies, and Section 4.4 examines the role of ALP in the driving of GDP growth in these economies. Section 4.5 analyses the factors responsible for the leading economic performance of Developing Asia relative to the group of developed nations and the group of other developing economies. Section 4.6 examines the sources of GDP and ALP growth in a global picture to assess whether the insights gained from the study of Developing Asia can be generalized worldwide. Section 4.7 summarizes the main findings of the chapter.

4.2   SOURCES OF GDP GROWTH IN DEVELOPING ASIA

4.2.1   Empirical Results

The empirical results for the sources of GDP growth for the 16 Developing Asia economies are reported in Table 4.1. Panel A of the table is for the period of 1990–2010, whereas panels B and C are for the two sub-periods 1990–2000 and 2000–2010, respectively.

China–India

China attained an outstanding GDP growth rate of 9 per cent during the period of 1990–2010, of which 5.8 percentage points were due to capital input, 0.5 percentage points were due to labor input, and 2.7 percentage points were due to TFP. Thus, China's GDP growth was largely driven by capital accumulation, which accounted for 64.2 per cent of its growth; TFP growth was also an important source of growth with a share of approximately 30 per cent. In contrast, the labor input accounted for a small share of 6.1 per cent of China's GDP growth, which implies that

Table 4.1 Sources of GDP growth: 1990–2010, 1990–2000, and 2000–2010

(A) Period 1990–2010

Economy	GDP Growth (%)	Contribution to Growth (% ppa)							GDP Growth	Share in Growth (%)						
		Capital Input			Labor Input			TFP		Capital Input			Labor Input			TFP
		All	ICT	Non-ICT	All	Quality	Hours			All	ICT	Non-ICT	All	Quality	Hours	
China–India																
China	9.0	5.8	1.0	4.8	0.5	0.2	0.4	2.7	100.0	64.2	11.0	53.2	6.1	1.7	4.4	29.7
India	6.4	3.4	0.5	2.9	1.2	0.2	1.0	1.9	100.0	52.7	8.1	44.5	18.3	2.4	15.9	29.0
Tigers-4																
Hong Kong	3.9	1.5	0.3	1.2	1.1	0.1	1.0	1.3	100.0	39.4	7.9	31.5	27.6	3.3	24.4	32.9
Singapore	6.5	3.8	0.8	3.0	2.2	0.5	1.7	0.5	100.0	58.7	12.1	46.6	33.7	8.0	25.7	7.7
South Korea	5.2	1.6	0.5	1.1	1.0	0.7	0.3	2.6	100.0	31.0	9.5	21.5	19.8	13.7	6.1	49.2
Taiwan	4.9	2.0	0.5	1.5	0.8	0.3	0.5	2.1	100.0	40.2	10.0	30.1	16.9	6.0	10.9	42.9
ASEAN-6																
Cambodia	7.4	4.9	0.4	4.6	1.8	0.1	1.7	0.6	100.0	66.9	4.8	62.2	24.4	1.3	23.1	8.6
Indonesia	4.6	3.2	0.4	2.8	1.1	0.2	0.9	0.4	100.0	69.3	8.8	60.5	22.9	3.6	19.3	7.8
Malaysia	5.7	2.9	0.6	2.3	1.5	0.2	1.3	1.3	100.0	51.1	11.1	40.0	26.4	4.0	22.4	22.4
Philippines	3.8	1.7	0.3	1.3	1.4	0.2	1.2	0.6	100.0	44.6	8.7	35.9	38.5	6.3	32.2	16.8
Thailand	4.3	2.7	0.3	2.4	0.9	0.3	0.6	0.7	100.0	62.1	6.6	55.5	21.3	7.4	13.9	16.6
Vietnam	7.2	4.5	0.7	3.8	1.4	0.1	1.3	1.3	100.0	62.5	9.2	53.3	19.2	1.3	17.9	8.3
SAC-4																
Bangladesh	5.2	3.7	0.2	3.6	1.1	0.1	1.0	0.3	100.0	72.5	3.6	68.9	21.6	1.4	20.2	5.9
Nepal	4.3	2.4	0.3	2.1	1.6	0.1	1.5	0.3	100.0	55.5	6.1	49.4	36.4	2.1	34.3	8.1
Pakistan	4.5	2.6	0.5	2.1	1.5	0.1	1.4	0.4	100.0	57.9	10.3	47.6	32.4	1.2	31.2	9.7
Sri Lanka	5.1	1.8	0.4	1.4	1.0	0.1	0.9	2.3	100.0	35.6	7.7	27.9	19.9	2.2	17.7	44.5

Table 4.1 (continued)

(B) Period 1990–2000

Economy	GDP Growth (%)	Contribution to Growth (% ppa)							GDP Growth	Share in Growth (%)						
		Capital Input			Labor Input			TFP		Capital Input			Labor Input			TFP
		All	ICT	Non-ICT	All	Quality	Hours			All	ICT	Non-ICT	All	Quality	Hours	
China–India																
China	7.1	5.2	0.8	4.4	0.7	0.2	0.5	1.2	100.0	73.6	11.5	62.1	9.8	2.2	7.6	16.6
India	5.4	2.8	0.3	2.6	1.1	0.2	0.9	1.5	100.0	52.4	5.0	47.4	19.8	3.0	16.8	27.8
Tigers-4																
Hong Kong	3.9	2.1	0.4	1.7	1.5	0.1	1.4	0.3	100.0	54.4	9.6	44.8	38.5	2.2	36.4	7.0
Singapore	7.3	5.0	0.8	4.2	2.2	0.6	1.6	0.1	100.0	68.2	10.8	57.4	30.1	8.6	21.5	1.7
South Korea	6.3	1.8	0.6	1.2	1.6	0.9	0.7	2.9	100.0	28.6	9.7	19.0	25.3	13.6	11.6	46.1
Taiwan	6.0	2.7	0.6	2.1	1.0	0.3	0.7	2.3	100.0	45.3	10.7	34.6	16.3	4.7	11.6	38.4
ASEAN-6																
Cambodia	7.0	4.0	0.4	3.6	2.0	0.1	1.9	1.0	100.0	57.1	5.8	51.3	28.3	0.9	27.5	14.6
Indonesia	4.1	3.5	0.2	3.3	1.0	0.2	0.8	-0.4	100.0	85.2	5.1	80.1	24.5	4.0	20.5	-9.7
Malaysia	6.9	4.0	0.7	3.4	1.9	0.3	1.6	0.9	100.0	58.8	9.6	49.3	28.0	4.2	23.8	13.1
Philippines	2.9	1.7	0.2	1.5	1.2	0.2	1.1	-0.1	100.0	60.6	6.5	54.1	42.4	5.3	37.1	-3.0
Thailand	4.4	3.8	0.2	3.6	0.4	0.2	0.2	0.1	100.0	87.0	4.4	82.7	9.9	4.9	5.0	3.0
Vietnam	7.3	3.5	0.4	3.2	1.3	0.1	1.2	2.5	100.0	48.4	5.1	43.3	17.9	1.0	16.8	33.7
SAC-4																
Bangladesh	4.7	3.7	0.2	3.5	0.7	0.1	0.7	0.3	100.0	78.3	3.3	75.0	15.9	1.7	14.3	5.8
Nepal	4.9	2.7	0.3	2.4	1.5	0.1	1.5	0.6	100.0	55.9	6.1	49.8	31.7	1.2	30.5	12.3
Pakistan	4.3	2.5	0.4	2.1	0.9	-0.1	1.0	0.9	100.0	57.1	8.2	48.8	21.5	-1.3	22.8	21.5
Sri Lanka	5.1	1.5	0.3	1.2	1.2	0.1	1.1	2.5	100.0	28.5	5.0	23.4	23.5	1.7	21.8	48.0

(C) Period 2000–2010

Economy	GDP Growth (%)	Contribution to Growth (% ppa)							GDP Growth	Share in Growth (%)						
		Capital Input			Labor Input			TFP		Capital Input			Labor Input			TFP
		All	ICT	Non-ICT	All	Quality	Hours			All	ICT	Non-ICT	All	Quality	Hours	
China–India																
China	10.9	6.3	1.2	5.1	0.4	0.1	0.3	4.2	100.0	58.0	10.7	47.3	3.7	1.3	2.3	38.3
India	7.4	3.9	0.8	3.2	1.3	0.1	1.1	2.2	100.0	52.9	10.5	42.4	17.2	2.0	15.2	30.0
Tigers-4																
Hong Kong	4.0	1.0	0.2	0.7	0.7	0.2	0.5	2.3	100.0	24.8	6.3	18.5	17.0	4.4	12.6	58.2
Singapore	5.8	2.7	0.8	1.9	2.2	0.4	1.8	0.9	100.0	46.5	13.6	32.9	38.3	7.3	31.0	15.2
South Korea	4.1	1.4	0.4	1.0	0.5	0.6	-0.1	2.2	100.0	34.7	9.3	25.4	11.3	13.8	-2.4	54.0
Taiwan	3.8	1.2	0.3	0.9	0.7	0.3	0.4	1.9	100.0	32.0	9.0	23.0	17.8	8.1	9.7	50.2
ASEAN-6																
Cambodia	7.7	5.8	0.3	5.5	1.6	0.1	1.5	0.2	100.0	75.9	3.8	72.1	20.9	1.7	19.2	3.2
Indonesia	5.1	2.9	0.6	2.3	1.1	0.2	0.9	1.1	100.0	56.4	11.9	44.5	21.6	3.3	18.3	22.0
Malaysia	4.5	1.8	0.6	1.2	1.1	0.2	0.9	1.7	100.0	39.4	13.4	26.0	24.0	3.7	20.3	36.6
Philippines	4.7	1.6	0.5	1.2	1.7	0.3	1.4	1.3	100.0	34.8	10.1	24.8	36.2	6.9	29.2	29.0
Thailand	4.2	1.5	0.4	1.2	1.4	0.4	1.0	1.3	100.0	36.5	8.9	27.6	32.9	9.9	23.0	30.6
Vietnam	7.0	5.4	0.9	4.5	1.4	0.1	1.3	0.2	100.0	77.1	13.4	63.7	20.5	1.6	19.0	2.3
SAC-4																
Bangladesh	5.6	3.8	0.2	3.6	1.5	0.1	1.4	0.3	100.0	67.8	4.0	63.8	26.3	1.2	25.1	5.9
Nepal	3.8	2.1	0.2	1.9	1.6	0.1	1.5	0.1	100.0	55.0	6.0	48.9	42.4	3.2	39.3	2.6
Pakistan	4.7	2.7	0.6	2.2	2.0	0.2	1.8	-0.1	100.0	58.7	12.3	46.4	42.4	3.5	38.9	-1.1
Sri Lanka	5.1	2.2	0.5	1.6	0.8	0.1	0.7	2.1	100.0	42.9	10.4	32.5	16.2	2.6	13.5	41.0

Source: Author's calculations.

149

employment played a minor role in the country's GDP growth during 1990–2010 (Table 4.1, Panel A).

India was also a leading performer in terms of GDP growth over the period of 1990–2010. Its GDP growth of 6.4 per cent during this period was the result of 3.4 percentage points from capital input (accounting for a share of 52.7 per cent), 1.2 percentage points from labor input (18.3 per cent), and 1.9 percentage points from TFP (29.0 per cent; Table 4.1, Panel A).

The sources of GDP growth of China and India exhibited rather similar structures, which demonstrate that the robust growth of these two countries was largely driven by capital accumulation and TFP growth. These two sources together accounted for a lion's share of the two countries' growth over 1990–2010: 93.9 per cent for China and 81.7 per cent for India[3] (Table 4.1, Panel A).

It should be noted, however, that India was well below China in both the contributions of capital input (by 2.4 percentage points) and TFP growth (by 0.8 percentage points). In addition, China also outperformed India in the contribution of ICT capital. In fact, the contribution of ICT capital to China's growth during the period of 1990–2010 was 1 percentage point, which was well above the 0.5 percentage points observed for India (Table 4.1, Panel A).

GDP growth notably accelerated for both China and India from the first sub-period, 1990–2000, to the second sub-period, 2000–2010. In general, the patterns of the source of growth in the two sub-periods were consistent with the results observed for the entire period of 1990–2010. Furthermore, the acceleration of the two countries' growth was also driven by their two major growth engines: capital accumulation and TFP growth. China's GDP growth rate increased from 7.1 per cent in 1990–2000 to 10.9 per cent in 2000–2010; the contribution of capital increased from 5.2 to 6.3 percentage points, and the contribution of TFP growth increased from 1.2 to 4.2 percentage points over the two sub-periods. Similarly, India's GDP growth rate accelerated by 2 percentage points from 5.4 per cent in 1990–2000 to 7.4 per cent in 2000–2010; the contribution of capital increased from 2.8 to 3.9 percentage points, and the contribution of TFP growth improved from 1.5 to 2.2 percentage points over the two sub-periods (Table 4.1, Panels B and C). Thus, for both China and India, the growth acceleration between the two sub-periods was driven not only by the increased contribution of capital input but also by the larger contribution of TFP. This finding demonstrates that,

---

[3] Srinivasan (2011) provided insights that explain why India's reforms since 1990 still had limited effects on employment.

for both countries, the growth of capital accumulation was mainly driven by the economy's strengthened absorptive capability and efficiency improvements.

The decrease in the contribution of hours worked to China's GDP growth from a rather low level of 0.5 percentage points in 1990–2000 to a very low level of 0.25 percentage points in 2000–2010 (Table 4.1, Panels B and C) suggests that the country was facing increasing constraints in its labor supply. Thus, China may face significant wage increases, which would place pressure on labor-intensive industries to move up the value chain or reallocate to other countries. It should be noted that the contribution of hours worked to India's GDP growth increased between the two sub-periods from 0.9 percentage points in 1990–2000 to 1.1 percentage points in 2000–2010. This result demonstrates that the mobilization of labor input is still an important way through which India can promote economic growth.

Tigers-4

Among the four Asian Tiger economies, Singapore was the leading performer in GDP growth during the period of 1990–2010 with a rate of 6.5 per cent, whereas Hong Kong's growth was lowest at 3.9 per cent. Both South Korea and Taiwan's growth rates were approximately 5 per cent. The strong GDP growth rate of Singapore was largely driven by capital and labor inputs with contributions of 3.8 and 2.2 percentage points, respectively. In contrast, the contribution to Hong Kong's GDP growth in this period was only 1.5 percentage points from capital input and 1.1 percentage points from labor input (Table 4.1, Panel A).

The largest sources of GDP growth in South Korea and Taiwan, during the period of 1990–2010, were TFP growth and capital accumulation. The contribution to growth from TFP was 2.6 percentage points (accounting for a share of 49.2 per cent) for South Korea and 2.1 percentage points (42.9 per cent) for Taiwan; the contribution from capital accumulation was 1.6 percentage points (31 per cent) for South Korea and 2.0 percentage points (40.2 per cent) for Taiwan (Table 4.1, Panel A).

There were some salient differences in the sources of GDP growth during the period of 1990–2010 between the four Asian Tiger economies. First, although the hours worked was an important source for both Singapore and Hong Kong's growth, this factor played a minor role in driving the growth of South Korea and Taiwan. The share of hours worked in GDP growth during 1990–2010 was 25.7 per cent for Singapore, 24.4 per cent for Hong Kong, 10.9 per cent for Taiwan, and 6.1 per cent for South Korea. Second, ICT played a more important role in Singapore compared with the other Tigers-4 economies. The share of the contribution of ICT capital to GDP growth during 1990–2010 was 12.1 per cent for Singapore, 10 per cent for Taiwan, 9.5 per cent for South Korea, and 7.9 per cent for Taiwan. Third, improvements in the labor quality were more important in South Korea and Singapore compared with Taiwan and Hong Kong. The share of the contribution of the labor quality to GDP growth during 1990–2010 was 13.7 per cent for South Korea and 8 per cent for Singapore, while it was only 6 per cent for Taiwan and 3.3 per cent for Hong Kong (Table 4.1, Panel A).

As shown in Panels B and C of Table 4.1, there were some notable changes in the growth patterns of the Tigers-4 economies over the two sub-periods. With the exception of Hong Kong, the Tigers-4 economies experienced a notable slowdown in GDP growth over the two sub-periods: from 7.3 per cent in 1990–2000 to 5.8 per cent in 2000–2010 for Singapore, from 6.3 to 4.1 per cent for South Korea, and from 6.0 to 3.8 per cent for Taiwan. In contrast, Hong Kong sustained its GDP growth at a rate of approximately 3.9–4.0 per cent over the two sub-periods.

A common feature observed for all Asian Tiger economies was the notable reduction in the contribution of capital input to the growth over the two sub-periods, which declined from 2.1 percentage points in 1990–2000 to 1 percentage point in 2000–2010 for Hong Kong, from 5.0 to 2.7 percentage points for Singapore, from 1.8 to 1.4 percentage points for South Korea, and from 2.7 to 1.2 percentage points for Taiwan. In contrast, TFP growth significantly increased in Hong Kong (from 0.3 percentage points in 1990–2000 to 2.3 percentage points in 2000–2010) and Singapore (from 0.1 to 0.9 percentage points). TFP growth remained robust at approximately 2 percentage points or higher for South Korea and Taiwan in both sub-periods.

ASEAN-6
Cambodia and Vietnam outperformed the other ASEAN economies in GDP growth over 1990–2010 with growth rates of 7.4 per cent and 7.2 per cent, respectively. During the same period, this growth rate was lowest for the Philippines at 3.8 per cent, whereas it was 4.3 per cent for Thailand, 4.6 per cent for Indonesia, and 5.7 per cent for Malaysia. Capital input was the leading driver of GDP growth during the period of 1990–2010 for all of the economies in this group. The share of capital input in GDP growth was highest for Indonesia (69.3 per cent), followed by Cambodia (66.9 per cent), Vietnam (62.5 per cent), Thailand (62.1 per cent), Malaysia (51.1 per cent), and the Philippines (44.6 per cent) (Table 4.1, Panel A).

Based on their shares in GDP growth during 1990–2010, the contribution of labor input was larger than that of TFP for all of the ASEAN-6 economies: was 24.4 versus 8.6 per cent for Cambodia, 22.9 versus 7.8 per cent for Indonesia, 26.4 versus 22.4 per cent for Malaysia, 38.5 versus 16.8 per cent for the Philippines, 21.3 versus 16.6 per cent for Thailand, and 19.2 versus 18.3 per cent for Vietnam. In particular, the hours worked accounted for a significant share in the growth of the Philippines (32.2 per cent), Cambodia (23.1 per cent), and Malaysia (22.4 per cent; Table 4.1, Panel A).

The dynamic changes in the sources of GDP growth of the ASEAN-6 economies from the first sub-period, 1990–2000, to the second sub-period, 2000–2010, show some striking features. First, Vietnam and Cambodia, which recorded strong GDP growth exceeding 7 per cent in both sub-periods, experienced a sharp drop in TFP growth: from 1 percentage point in 1990–2000 to 0.2 percentage points in 2000–2010 for Cambodia and from 2.5 to 0.2 percentage points for Vietnam. In contrast, the remaining four ASEAN-6 economies exhibited a solid improvement in their TFP growth over the two sub-periods: from −0.4 to 1.1 percentage points for Indonesia, from 0.9 to 1.7 percentage points for Malaysia, from −0.1 to 1.3 percentage points for the Philippines and from 0.1 to 1.3 percentage points for Thailand. Second, the contribution of capital accumulation increased sharply over the two sub-periods for Cambodia (from 57.1 to 75.9 per cent) and Vietnam (from 48.4 to 77.1 per cent). It was notably reduced for Indonesia (from 85.2 to 56.4 per cent), Malaysia (from 58.8 to 39.4 per cent), the Philippines (from 60.6 to 34.8 per cent), and Thailand (from 87 to 36.5 per cent) (Table 4.1, Panels B and C). These findings suggest that the economies that suffered most from the Asian financial crisis of 1997–1998 exhibited a robust improvement in their growth efficiency in the second sub-period of 2000–2010.[4]

SAC-4

The growth rates during the period of 1990–2010 exhibited by the SAC-4 economies were rather strong and similar: the rate was highest for Bangladesh (5.2 per cent), followed by Sri Lanka (5.1 per cent), Pakistan (4.5 per cent), and Nepal (4.3 per cent). With the exception of Sri Lanka,

---

[4]   The improvements in growth efficiency of these economies after the crisis were likely associated with investors' more cautious approach in making capital investment. The fixed investment as a share of GDP declined notably in the 2000s compared to that in the 1990s. In fact, this average rate fell from 35.5 per cent in 1990–2000 to 22.3 per cent in 2000–2010 for Malaysia, from 34.2 to 25.5 per cent for Thailand, from 22.5 to 20.2 per cent for the Philippines, and from 25.8 to 24.5 per cent for Indonesia. In addition, decisive regulatory and structural reforms have also played an important role in enhancing the efficiency of these economies. Haraguchi (2009) illustrated these effects through the case of the Thai Automotive Industry.

capital accumulation was the major source of growth of the economies in this group, with a contribution of 72.5 per cent for Bangladesh, 57.9 per cent for Pakistan, and 55.5 per cent for Nepal. In these three countries, the labor hours worked was the second most important source of growth, whereas these countries' TFP growth only played a minor role with a share of less than 10 per cent. Sri Lanka's growth pattern was rather distinct from the other SAC-4 economies; its growth over 1990–2010 was driven more by TFP than by capital accumulation. TFP accounted for 44.5 per cent of Sri Lanka's GDP growth during this period, whereas the contribution of capital input was 35.6 per cent (Table 4.1, Panel A).

Regarding the growth dynamics over the two sub-periods, GDP growth accelerated from 4.7 per cent in 1990–2000 to 5.6 per cent in 2000–2010 for Bangladesh and from 4.3 to 4.7 per cent for Pakistan, whereas the growth remained unchanged at 5.1 per cent for Sri Lanka. Nepal was the only economy in this group that experienced a decline in GDP growth: from 4.9 per cent in the first sub-period to 3.8 per cent in the second. With the exception of Sri Lanka, capital accumulation played the leading role in GDP growth of the SAC-4 economies, with a contribution share that exceeded 50 per cent during both sub-periods. At the same time, capital accumulation also became notably more important for Sri Lanka: the share of capital input in the growth increased from 28.5 per cent in 1990–2000 to 42.9 per cent in 2000–2010. In contrast, the contribution of its TFP growth remained robust with a share that exceeded 40 per cent in both sub-periods. Note that TFP growth deteriorated over the two sub-periods for the two weaker performers, Nepal and Pakistan: the contribution of TFP growth decreased from 0.6 percentage points in 1990–2000 to 0.1 percentage points in 2000–2010 for Nepal and from 0.9 to −0.1 percentage points for Pakistan (Table 4.1, Panels B and C).

4.2.2 Sources of GDP Growth in Developing Asia: A Regional Picture

This subsection provides a regional picture of the relationship between each of the sources of GDP growth and GDP growth during the period of 1990–2010 for the 16 Developing Asia economies. Figures 4.1, 4.2, and 4.3 depict the correlations between the sources of GDP growth and GDP growth in the 16 Developing Asia economies. Figures 4.1A, 4.1B, and 4.1C represent the total capital input, non-ICT capital, and ICT capital, respectively, whereas Figures 4.2A, 4.2B, 4.2C indicate the total labor input, hours worked, and labor quality, respectively, and Figure 4.3 analyses TFP growth. In the chart for a given source of growth, the x-axis shows the contribution of the source of growth of interest, whereas the y-axis indicates GDP growth.

The fitted line of the sample depicts the relationship between the source of growth and GDP growth within this group. The R^2 value, which ranges from 0 to 1, indicates the robustness of this relationship: a higher R^2 value indicates a stronger relationship. An upward fitted line implies a positive relationship between the growth source of interest and GDP growth, i.e., an economy with a larger contribution from the growth source of interest tends to achieve faster GDP growth. A strong positive relationship between a given source of growth and GDP growth can be established through the following two ways. First, the contribution of the source of growth is a significant part of GDP growth. For example, because capital input is a major source of GDP growth, its positive relationship with GDP growth is expected. Second, the source of growth has a positive causal effect on other sources of growth. For example, investment in ICT capital is believed to produce a positive effect on labor quality growth by fostering learning and on TFP growth by stimulating innovation and improving efficiency. As a result, ICT capital is expected to exhibit a positive relationship with GDP growth.

Capital input

Figure 4.1A shows a strong positive relationship between the contribution of the total capital input and GDP growth in the Developing Asia group. China, Cambodia, and Vietnam were the economies with highest GDP growth during 1990–2010, and these were the economies with largest capital input contribution to GDP growth. In contrast, Hong Kong, South Korea, and the Philippines exhibited the lowest GDP growth, and the low capital input contribution was a key factor underlying their low performance. However, it is worth noting that South Korea's GDP growth in 1990–2010, which was higher than 5 per cent, was less dependent on capital accumulation, whereas its total capital input contributed less than 2 percentage points.

For a more in-depth examination of the correlation between the contribution of capital input to GDP growth and GDP growth in Developing Asia, Figures 4.1B and 4.1C depict this analysis for non-ICT capital and ICT capital, respectively. The correlation between the contribution of non-ICT capital and GDP growth, as shown in Figure 4.1B, exhibits patterns that were similar to those found in the correlation between the contribution of total capital input and GDP growth: this correlation is positive and strong. China, Cambodia, and Vietnam were the three economies with the largest non-ICT capital contribution, whereas Hong Kong, South Korea, and the Philippines exhibited the lowest non-ICT capital contribution.

The correlation between the ICT capital input and GDP growth, however, shows a somewhat different pattern (Figure 4.1C). Whereas the

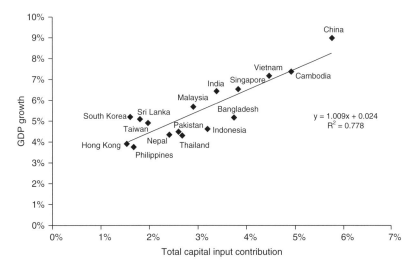

Source: Author's calculations.

Figure 4.1A   Correlation between total capital input and GDP growth in Developing Asia, 1990–2010

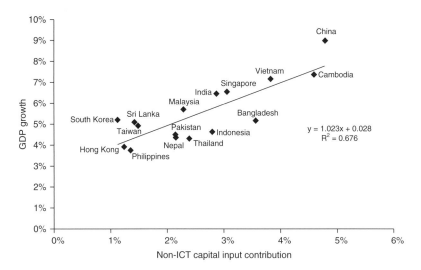

Source: Author's calculations.

Figure 4.1B   Correlation between non-ICT capital and GDP growth in Developing Asia, 1990–2010

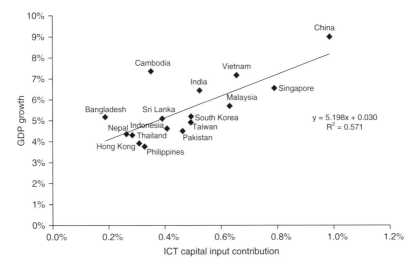

Source: Author's calculations.

Figure 4.1C *Correlation between ICT capital and GDP growth in Developing Asia, 1990–2010*

two variables still show a strong positive relationship, the distribution of the economies on the graph is notably changed. The economies with largest ICT capital contribution were China, Singapore, and Vietnam, whereas Cambodia has a rather low ICT capital contribution. Moreover, Bangladesh, Nepal, and Thailand also had low ICT capital contributions, whereas South Korea was among the economies with higher ICT capital contribution.

Labor input

There was no significant correlation between the contribution of total labor input and GDP growth: the fitted line is horizontal, and its R^2 is approximately equal to zero (Figure 4.2A). Similar patterns were obtained for the number of hours worked (Figure 4.2B) and the labor quality (Figure 4.2C). These findings indicate that, within the Developing Asia group, the labor inputs are not a good predictor of GDP growth. For example, as shown in Figure 4.2A, both high-growing economies (such as Singapore and Cambodia) and low-growing economies (such as Nepal and the Philippines) can have a strong contribution of the total labor input. At the same time, a low contribution of the total labor input was observed for China, which is the economy with strongest

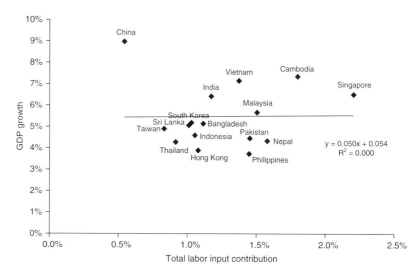

Source: Author's calculations.

Figure 4.2A   *Correlation between total labor input and GDP growth in Developing Asia, 1990–2010*

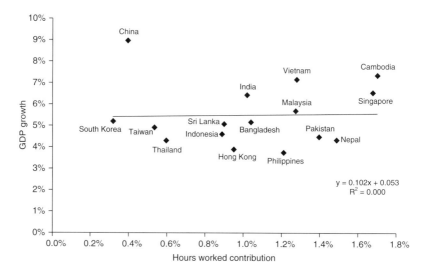

Source: Author's calculations.

Figure 4.2B   *Correlation between hours worked and GDP growth in Developing Asia, 1990–2010*

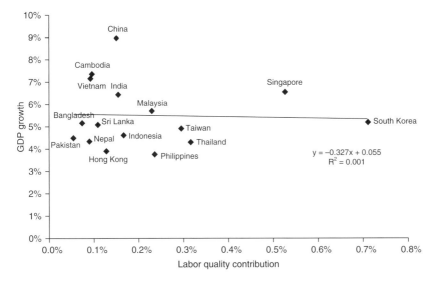

Source: Author's calculations.

Figure 4.2C   Correlation between labor quality and GDP growth in Developing Asia, 1990–2010

growth, and for the economies with weaker growth, such as Taiwan and Thailand.

TFP growth

Figure 4.3 shows a significant positive correlation between TFP growth and GDP growth in the Developing Asia group. However, this relationship ($R^2 = 0.148$) is weaker compared with that between the capital input and GDP growth ($R^2 = 0.778$ for total capital input, $R^2 = 0.676$ for non-ICT capital, and $R^2 = 0.571$ for ICT capital, as shown in Figure 4.1). The economies with largest contribution of TFP included China, South Korea, Sri Lanka, and Taiwan, whereas the economies with smallest contribution of TFP included Bangladesh, Nepal, and Indonesia.

This finding suggests that, for most Developing Asia economies, the capital input was the main driver of GDP growth and that the second highest driver of GDP growth is TFP growth. In addition, the labor input was an important source of growth, but its role was less important compared with the capital input and TFP.

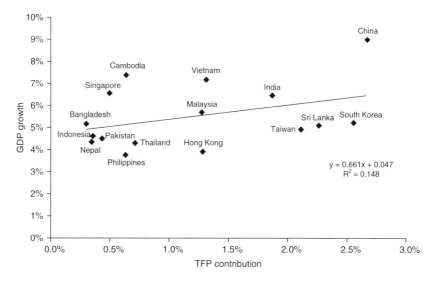

Source: Author's calculations.

*Figure 4.3   Correlation between TFP and GDP growth in Developing
              Asia, 1990–2010*

4.3   SOURCES OF ALP GROWTH IN DEVELOPING ASIA

4.3.1   Empirical Results

The empirical results of the sources of ALP growth for the 16 Developing
Asia economies, which are based on the decomposition framework
(A4.1.3) presented in Appendix 4.1, are reported in Table 4.2. Panel A of
the table reflects the period 1990–2010, whereas panels B and C reflect the
sub-periods 1990–2000 and 2000–2010, respectively.

China–India
Both China and India recorded strong ALP growth over the period 1990–
2010, although China outperformed India by a margin of 3.7 percentage
points (8.1 versus 4.4 per cent). For both countries, capital deepening was
the leading source of ALP growth, and this source accounted for 65.4
per cent and 53.9 per cent of ALP growth exhibited by China and India,
respectively. The contribution of TFP to the two economies' ALP growth
over 1990–2010 was also sizable: 32.8 per cent for China and 42.6 per cent

Table 4.2 Sources of ALP growth: 1990–2010, 1990–2000, and 2000–2010

(A) Period 1990–2010

Economy	ALP Growth (%)	Contribution to Growth (% ppa)					ALP Growth	Share in Growth (%)				
		Capital Deepening			Labor Quality	TFP		Capital Deepening			Labor Quality	TFP
		All	ICT	Non-ICT				All	ICT	Non-ICT		
China–India												
China	8.1	5.3	1.0	4.4	0.2	2.7	100.0	65.4	11.8	53.6	1.8	32.8
India	4.4	2.4	0.5	1.9	0.2	1.9	100.0	53.9	10.9	43.0	3.5	42.6
Tigers-4												
Hong Kong	2.5	1.1	0.3	0.9	0.1	1.3	100.0	44.4	10.7	33.7	5.0	50.5
Singapore	3.2	2.2	0.6	1.6	0.5	0.5	100.0	67.8	18.9	48.9	16.5	15.7
South Korea	4.8	1.5	0.5	1.1	0.7	2.6	100.0	32.1	10.1	22.0	14.8	53.1
Taiwan	4.2	1.7	0.4	1.3	0.3	2.1	100.0	42.0	10.8	31.3	7.1	50.8
ASEAN-6												
Cambodia	4.0	3.2	0.3	2.9	0.1	0.6	100.0	81.5	7.0	74.5	2.4	16.1
Indonesia	2.8	2.3	0.4	1.9	0.2	0.4	100.0	81.4	12.7	68.7	5.9	12.7
Malaysia	3.1	1.6	0.3	1.3	0.2	1.3	100.0	52.0	11.1	40.9	7.3	40.7
Philippines	1.3	0.5	0.3	0.2	0.2	0.6	100.0	34.9	19.1	15.7	17.7	47.4
Thailand	3.1	2.1	0.2	1.8	0.3	0.7	100.0	66.8	7.8	59.0	10.2	23.0
Vietnam	4.6	3.2	0.6	2.6	0.1	1.3	100.0	69.4	12.9	56.5	2.0	28.5
SAC-4												
Bangladesh	3.1	2.7	0.1	2.6	0.1	0.3	100.0	87.8	4.5	83.2	2.4	9.8
Nepal	1.4	0.9	0.2	0.7	0.1	0.3	100.0	67.6	15.0	52.6	6.6	25.8
Pakistan	1.7	1.2	0.4	0.8	0.1	0.4	100.0	71.0	21.9	49.1	3.2	25.8
Sri Lanka	3.3	0.9	0.3	0.6	0.1	2.3	100.0	27.7	10.6	17.2	3.3	68.9

161

Table 4.2 (continued)

(B) Period 1990–2000

Economy	ALP Growth (%)	Contribution to Growth (% ppa)					ALP Growth	Share in Growth (%)				
		Capital Deepening			Labor Quality	TFP		Capital Deepening			Labor Quality	TFP
		All	ICT	Non-ICT				All	ICT	Non-ICT		
China–India												
China	6.0	4.6	0.8	3.9	0.2	1.2	100.0	77.7	13.1	64.6	2.6	19.8
India	3.6	1.9	0.2	1.7	0.2	1.5	100.0	53.6	6.9	46.7	4.5	41.9
Tigers-4												
Hong Kong	1.9	1.5	0.3	1.2	0.1	0.3	100.0	80.8	16.8	64.0	4.5	14.7
Singapore	4.2	3.4	0.6	2.8	0.6	0.1	100.0	82.0	15.2	66.8	15.1	2.9
South Korea	5.4	1.6	0.6	1.0	0.9	2.9	100.0	30.2	10.8	19.3	15.9	53.9
Taiwan	5.0	2.4	0.6	1.9	0.3	2.3	100.0	48.3	11.3	37.0	5.6	46.0
ASEAN-6												
Cambodia	3.2	2.1	0.3	1.7	0.1	1.0	100.0	65.7	10.7	54.9	1.9	32.5
Indonesia	2.4	2.7	0.2	2.5	0.2	-0.4	100.0	109.6	7.2	102.4	6.8	-16.4
Malaysia	3.6	2.4	0.2	2.2	0.3	0.9	100.0	66.8	6.4	60.4	8.1	25.1
Philippines	0.7	0.7	0.1	0.5	0.2	-0.1	100.0	90.9	17.7	73.3	20.6	-11.6
Thailand	3.9	3.6	0.2	3.4	0.2	0.1	100.0	91.2	4.4	86.8	5.5	3.4
Vietnam	4.8	2.3	0.3	2.0	0.1	2.5	100.0	47.6	7.1	40.6	1.6	50.8
SAC-4												
Bangladesh	3.4	3.0	0.1	2.9	0.1	0.3	100.0	89.5	3.5	86.1	2.3	8.1
Nepal	1.9	1.2	0.2	1.0	0.1	0.6	100.0	65.2	12.6	52.6	3.2	31.6
Pakistan	2.3	1.5	0.3	1.2	-0.1	0.9	100.0	63.0	12.9	50.1	-2.4	39.4
Sri Lanka	2.9	0.3	0.2	0.1	0.1	2.5	100.0	11.8	7.3	4.5	3.0	85.2

(C) Period 2000–2010

Economy	ALP Growth (%)	Contribution to Growth (% ppa)					ALP Growth	Share in Growth (%)				
		Capital Deepening			Labor Quality	TFP		Capital Deepening			Labor Quality	TFP
		All	ICT	Non-ICT				All	ICT	Non-ICT		
China–India												
China	10.3	6.0	1.1	4.9	0.1	4.2	100.0	58.2	11.0	47.2	1.4	40.4
India	5.2	2.8	0.7	2.1	0.1	2.2	100.0	54.2	13.7	40.4	2.8	43.0
Tigers-4												
Hong Kong	3.2	0.8	0.2	0.5	0.2	2.3	100.0	23.6	7.2	16.4	5.3	71.0
Singapore	2.2	0.9	0.6	0.3	0.4	0.9	100.0	40.9	25.9	14.9	19.2	39.9
South Korea	4.2	1.5	0.4	1.1	0.6	2.2	100.0	34.6	9.2	25.4	13.3	52.1
Taiwan	3.3	1.1	0.3	0.7	0.3	1.9	100.0	32.3	9.9	22.4	9.4	58.3
ASEAN-6												
Cambodia	4.7	4.4	0.2	4.2	0.1	0.2	100.0	92.0	4.6	87.5	2.8	5.1
Indonesia	3.2	1.9	0.5	1.4	0.2	1.1	100.0	60.1	16.9	43.2	5.2	34.8
Malaysia	2.7	0.9	0.5	0.4	0.2	1.7	100.0	32.2	17.4	14.8	6.3	61.6
Philippines	1.9	0.3	0.4	-0.1	0.3	1.3	100.0	13.5	19.7	-6.2	16.6	69.9
Thailand	2.3	0.6	0.3	0.3	0.4	1.3	100.0	24.9	13.7	11.3	18.4	56.7
Vietnam	4.4	4.1	0.8	3.2	0.1	0.2	100.0	93.7	19.3	74.3	2.6	3.8
SAC-4												
Bangladesh	2.8	2.4	0.2	2.2	0.1	0.3	100.0	85.6	5.7	79.9	2.5	11.9
Nepal	0.8	0.6	0.2	0.4	0.1	0.1	100.0	73.2	20.6	52.6	14.7	12.1
Pakistan	1.0	0.9	0.4	0.5	0.2	-0.1	100.0	89.1	42.3	46.8	15.9	-5.0
Sri Lanka	3.7	1.5	0.5	1.0	0.1	2.1	100.0	40.2	13.1	27.1	3.6	56.2

Source: Author's calculations.

163

for India (Table 4.2, Panel A). The contribution of labor quality to ALP growth was low at 1.8 per cent for China and 3.5 per cent for India.

Both China and India experienced a notable acceleration in their ALP growth between the two sub-periods: from 6.0 per cent in 1990–2000 to 10.3 per cent in 2000–2010 for China and from 3.6 to 5.2 per cent for India. Furthermore, for both countries, capital deepening and TFP growth played significant roles in driving their ALP acceleration. The contribution of capital deepening increased from 4.6 percentage points in 1990–2000 to 6.0 percentage points in 2000–2010 for China, and from 1.9 to 2.8 percentage points for India. The contribution of TFP growth increased from 1.2 to 4.2 percentage points for China and 1.5 to 2.2 percentage points for India (Table 4.2, Panels B and C).

Note that the contribution of the ICT capital deepening to ALP growth was significant and exhibited a rising trend for both China and India. However, the magnitude of this contribution was notably larger for China than for India: 1 percentage point for China compared to 0.5 percentage points for India during the period of 1990–2010. In addition, this pattern was consistent over the two sub-periods.

Tigers-4
The Tigers-4 economies showed strong ALP growth during the period of 1990–2010, with South Korea as the leader with an ALP growth of 4.8 per cent, followed by Taiwan (4.2 per cent), Singapore (3.2 per cent), and Hong Kong (2.5 per cent). For all Tigers-4 economies, capital deepening accounted for a sizable share in ALP growth during 1990–2010: 67.8 per cent for Singapore, 44.4 per cent for Hong Kong, 42 per cent for Taiwan, and 32.1 per cent for South Korea. However, with the exception of Singapore, capital deepening was less important than TFP in driving ALP growth of the Tigers-4 economies during this period. In fact, the contribution of TFP to ALP growth during 1990–2010 was 53.1 per cent for South Korea, 50.8 per cent for Taiwan, and 50.5 per cent for Hong Kong (Table 4.2, Panel A).

As shown in Panels B and C of Table 4.2, the dynamic change between the two sub-periods, 1990–2000 and 2000–2010, demonstrated several salient features. First, with the exception of Hong Kong, all of the Tigers-4 economies experienced a notable slowdown in ALP growth over the two sub-periods: from 4.2 per cent in 1990–2000 to 2.2 per cent in 2000–2010 for Singapore, from 5.4 to 4.2 per cent for South Korea, and from 5.0 to 3.3 per cent for Taiwan. In contrast, Hong Kong's ALP increased from 1.9 per cent in the first sub-period to 3.2 per cent in the second. Second, the contribution of capital deepening decreased substantially for all Tigers-4 economies over the two sub-periods: from 1.5 to 0.8 percentage points for

Hong Kong, from 3.4 to 0.9 percentage points for Singapore, from 1.6 to 1.5 percentage points for South Korea, and from 2.4 to 1.1 percentage points for Taiwan. Third, the contribution share of TFP in ALP growth substantially increased over the two sub-periods for Hong Kong (from 14.7 per cent in 1990–2000 to 71 per cent in 2000–2010) and Singapore (from 2.9 to 39.9 per cent) and remained large (approximately 50 per cent) for South Korea and Taiwan during both sub-periods. These findings imply that, since the Asian financial crisis of 1997–1998, the Tigers-4 economies have experienced significant economic transformations, which have shifted the focus from the promoting of growth via capital accumulation to technological progress and efficiency improvements.

ASEAN-6
ALP growth over the period of 1990–2010 was highest for Vietnam (4.6 per cent) and lowest for the Philippines (1.3 per cent), whereas this growth was 4 per cent for Cambodia, 2.8 per cent for Indonesia, and 3.1 per cent for both Malaysia and Thailand. With the exception of the Philippines, capital deepening was the major driver of ALP growth in this period with a contribution share of 81.5 per cent for Cambodia, 81.4 per cent for Indonesia, 52 per cent for Malaysia, 66.8 per cent for Thailand, and 69.4 per cent for Vietnam. In contrast, TFP growth played a more varied role in driving ALP growth during this period. The share of TFP in ALP growth during 1990–2010 was lowest for Indonesia (12.7 per cent) and Cambodia (16.1 per cent), largest for the Philippines (47.4 per cent) and Malaysia (40.7 per cent); while it was 23 per cent for Thailand and 28.5 per cent for Vietnam (Table 4.2, Panel A).

As shown in Panels B and C of Table 4.2, the dynamic changes in the sources of ALP growth of the ASEAN-6 economies between the two sub-periods show several striking features. On the one hand, the two leading performers in terms of ALP growth (Vietnam and Cambodia) sustained strong ALP growth in both sub-periods: 3.2 per cent in 1990–2000 and 4.7 per cent in 2000–2010 for Cambodia and 4.8 per cent and 4.4 per cent for Vietnam. However, the changes in the composition of these countries' sources of ALP growth showed a significant deterioration of their growth efficiency. The contribution share of capital deepening increased from 65.7 per cent in 1990–2000 to 92 per cent 2000–2010 for Cambodia and from 47.6 to 93.7 per cent for Vietnam; while the contribution share of TFP decreased from 32.5 per cent to 5.1 per cent for Cambodia and from 50.8 to 3.8 per cent for Vietnam. On the other hand, capital deepening became much less important in ALP growth of the remaining four ASEAN-6 economies, whereas the role of TFP in driving their ALP growth was substantially enhanced. The contribution share of capital deepening in

ALP growth decreased from 109.6 per cent in 1990–2000 to 60.1 per cent in 2000–2010 for Indonesia, from 66.8 to 32.2 per cent for Malaysia, from 90.9 to 13.5 per cent for the Philippines, and from 91.2 to 24.9 per cent for Thailand, whereas the contribution share of TFP increased from −16.4 per cent to 34.8 per cent for Indonesia, from 25.1 to 61.6 per cent for Malaysia, from −11.6 to 69.9 per cent for the Philippines, and from 3.4 to 56.7 per cent for Thailand. These findings suggest that the economies that were most affected by the Asian financial crisis that erupted in 1997–1998 have since undergone significant transformations that have boosted the efficiency of their growth.

SAC-4

Among the economies of this group, ALP growth over the period of 1990–2010 was highest for Sri Lanka at 3.3 per cent, followed by 3.1 per cent for Bangladesh, 1.7 per cent for Pakistan, and 1.4 per cent for Nepal. With the exception of Sri Lanka, ALP growth of the SAC-4 economies during this period was largely driven by capital deepening, which contributed a share of 87.8 per cent for Sri Lanka, 67.6 per cent for Nepal, and 71 per cent for Pakistan. At the same time, the contribution share of TFP was minor: 9.8 per cent for Bangladesh and 25.8 per cent for both Nepal and Pakistan. In contrast, capital deepening accounted for only 27.7 per cent of Sri Lanka's ALP growth during this period, whereas TFP claimed a dominant share of approximately 70 per cent (Table 4.2, Panel A).

Sri Lanka and the other three SAC-4 economies exhibited different dynamic changes between the two sub-periods of 1990–2000 and 2000–2010. Sri Lanka's ALP growth increased from 2.9 per cent in 1990–2000 to 3.7 per cent in 2000–2010; however, it decreased from 3.4 to 2.8 per cent for Bangladesh, from 1.9 to 0.8 per cent for Nepal, and from 2.3 to 1 per cent for Pakistan. Capital deepening was the main driver of the con-trast in these dynamics: the contribution of capital deepening increased from 0.3 to 1.5 percentage points for Sri Lanka and decreased from 3.0 to 2.4 percentage points for Bangladesh, from 1.2 to 0.6 percentage points for Nepal, and from 1.5 to 0.9 percentage points for Pakistan. In contrast, Sri Lanka sustained a robust TFP growth that exceeded 2 per-centage points in both sub-periods, whereas TFP growth was meager in both sub-periods for Bangladesh and decreased for Nepal and Pakistan from the first to the second sub-period (Table 4.2, Panels B and C).

4.3.2   Sources of ALP Growth in Developing Asia: A Regional Picture

This subsection analyses the sources of ALP growth of the economies of Developing Asia during 1990–2010 as part of a regional picture. The findings are consistent with those found from the comparative examination of the sources of GDP growth presented in subsection 4.2.2.

Capital deepening
Figure 4.4A shows a strong positive correlation between the contribution of the total capital deepening and ALP growth ($R^2 = 0.706$). China, Cambodia, and Vietnam exhibited the highest contribution of total capital deepening, whereas the Philippines, Nepal, and Sri Lanka had lower contribution of total capital deepening. A similar pattern was observed for the relationship between the contribution of non-ICT capital deepening and ALP growth (Figure 4.4B). The contribution of ICT capital deepening and ALP growth also had a strong positive correlation ($R^2 = 0.674$), but the distribution of the economies was somewhat changed (Figure 4.4C). China, Singapore, and Vietnam exhibited the highest contributions of ICT capital deepening, whereas Cambodia exhibited a modest contribution, and Bangladesh, Nepal, and Thailand exhibited the lowest contributions.

Labor quality
As shown in Figure 4.5, the correlation between the contribution of labor quality and ALP growth was positive but not strong ($R^2 = 0.027$). South

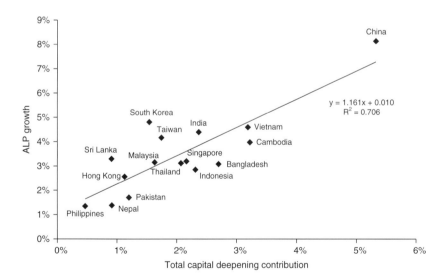

Source: Author's calculations.

Figure 4.4A   Correlation between total capital deepening and ALP growth in Developing Asia, 1990–2010

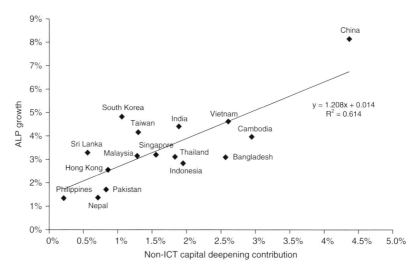

Source: Author's calculations.

*Figure 4.4B   Correlation between non-ICT capital deepening and ALP
            growth in Developing Asia, 1990–2010*

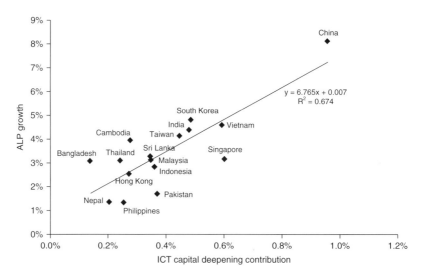

Source: Author's calculations.

*Figure 4.4C   Correlation between ICT capital deepening and ALP growth
            in Developing Asia, 1990–2010*

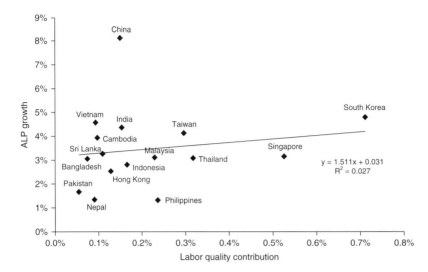

Source: Author's calculations.

Figure 4.5   Correlation between labor quality and ALP growth in Developing Asia, 1990–2010

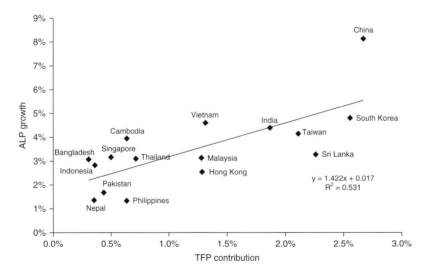

Source: Author's calculations.

Figure 4.6   Correlation between TFP and ALP growth in Developing Asia, 1990–2010

Korea, Singapore, and Thailand were the leading performers on the contribution of labor quality, whereas Pakistan and Bangladesh were the economies with the lowest values of this measure.

TFP growth
As shown in Figure 4.6, TFP growth and ALP growth had a strong positive correlation ($R^2 = 0.531$). China, South Korea, and Sri Lanka were the economies that exhibited the highest TFP growth, whereas Bangladesh, Nepal, and Indonesia exhibited the lowest values of this measure.

4.4 ALP AS A DRIVER OF GDP GROWTH IN DEVELOPING ASIA

To examine the role of ALP in driving GDP growth, one can decompose GDP growth into the contributions of two sources: ALP growth and employment expansion. The framework for this decomposition is presented in Appendix 4.3. This section investigates the role of ALP in driving GDP growth for the 16 Developing Asia economies over the period of 1990–2010. The results from this exercise are reported in Table 4.3.

4.4.1 The Contribution of ALP and Employment to GDP Growth

China–India
ALP was the major driver of GDP growth for both China and India. Its contribution share in GDP growth over the period of 1990–2010 was 90.7 per cent for China and 68.3 per cent for India. Moreover, the role of ALP in driving GDP growth was enhanced from the first to the second sub-period for both countries: the share of ALP in GDP growth increased from 84.3 per cent in 1990–2000 to 94.9 per cent in 2000–2010 for China and from 66.4 to 69.6 per cent for India. Note that more than 30 per cent of India's GDP growth was due to employment expansion, whereas this share was less than 10 per cent for China (Table 4.3).

Tigers-4
With the exception of Singapore, ALP was the major driver of GDP growth for the Tigers-4 economies, especially South Korea and Taiwan. The contribution share of ALP in GDP growth over the period 1990–2010 was 92.6 per cent for South Korea, 84.4 per cent for Taiwan, 65.2 per cent for Hong Kong, and 48.7 per cent for Singapore. In addition, the role of ALP in driving GDP growth was strengthened from the first to the second sub-period for South Korea, Taiwan, and Hong Kong. In fact, the share

Table 4.3 Contributions of ALP and employment to GDP growth, 1990–2010

Economy	1990–2010			1990–2000			2000–2010		
	GDP Growth (%)	Contribution to GDP Growth (%)		GDP Growth (%)	Contribution to GDP Growth (%)		GDP Growth (%)	Contribution to GDP Growth (%)	
		ALP	Employment		ALP	Employment		ALP	Employment
China–India									
China	9.0	90.7	9.3	7.1	84.3	15.7	10.9	94.9	5.1
India	6.4	68.3	31.7	5.4	66.4	33.6	7.4	69.6	30.4
Tigers-4									
Hong Kong	3.9	65.2	34.8	3.9	48.0	52.0	4.0	81.9	18.1
Singapore	6.5	48.7	51.3	7.3	57.1	42.9	5.8	38.1	61.9
South Korea	5.2	92.6	7.4	6.3	85.6	14.4	4.1	103.6	-3.6
Taiwan	4.9	84.4	15.6	6.0	83.4	16.6	3.8	86.2	13.8
ASEAN-6									
Cambodia	7.4	53.7	46.3	7.0	45.1	54.9	7.7	61.6	38.4
Indonesia	4.6	61.5	38.5	4.1	59.1	40.9	5.1	63.4	36.6
Malaysia	5.7	55.2	44.8	6.9	52.4	47.6	4.5	59.4	40.6
Philippines	3.8	35.5	64.5	2.9	25.8	74.2	4.7	41.5	58.5
Thailand	4.3	72.2	27.8	4.4	90.0	10.0	4.2	53.9	46.1
Vietnam	7.2	64.2	35.8	7.3	66.3	33.7	7.0	62.1	37.9
SAC-4									
Bangladesh	5.2	59.7	40.3	4.7	71.5	28.5	5.6	49.9	50.1
Nepal	4.3	31.3	68.7	4.9	39.0	61.0	3.8	21.4	78.6
Pakistan	4.5	37.7	62.3	4.3	54.5	45.5	4.7	22.2	77.8
Sri Lanka	5.1	64.6	35.4	5.1	56.3	43.7	5.1	72.9	27.1

Source: Author's calculations.

of ALP in GDP growth increased from 85.6 per cent in 1990–2000 to 103.6 per cent in 2000–2010 for South Korea, from 83.4 to 86.2 per cent for Taiwan, and from 48 to 81.9 per cent for Hong Kong. In contrast, although Singapore was the leading economy in the Tigers-4 group in terms of GDP growth, its growth was more driven by employment expansion, especially in the second sub-period of 2000–2010. The share of ALP in Singapore's GDP growth decreased from 57.1 per cent in 1990–2000 to 38.1 per cent in 2000–2010 (Table 4.3). These findings suggest that Singapore's GDP growth may slow down significantly in the next decade if its inflows of foreign workers are reduced.

ASEAN-6

With the exception of the Philippines, ALP was also the major driver of GDP growth during 1990–2010 for the ASEAN-6 economies. The share of ALP in GDP growth during this period was 53.7 per cent for Cambodia, 61.5 per cent for Indonesia, 55.2 per cent for Malaysia, 72.2 per cent for Thailand, 64.2 per cent for Vietnam, and 35.5 per cent for the Philippines.

Furthermore, for most of the ASEAN-6 economies, the share of ALP in GDP growth increased over the two sub-periods: from 45.1 per cent in 1990–2000 to 61.6 per cent in 2000–2010 for Cambodia, from 59.1 to 63.4 per cent for Indonesia, from 52.4 to 59.4 per cent for Malaysia, and from 25.8 to 41.5 per cent for the Philippines. However, the share of ALP in GDP growth decreased from 90 per cent to 53.9 per cent for Thailand and from 66.3 to 62.1 per cent for Vietnam (Table 4.3).

SAC-4

Among the economies in this group, Sri Lanka and Bangladesh were the leading performers in terms of GDP growth. Moreover, ALP was the main driver of their growth. In contrast, GDP growth experienced by Pakistan and Nepal was lower and more dependent on employment expansion. The share of ALP in GDP growth during the period of 1990–2010 was 64.6 per cent for Sri Lanka, 59.7 per cent for Bangladesh, 31.3 per cent for Nepal, and 37.7 per cent for Pakistan (Table 4.3).

With the exception of Sri Lanka, the role of ALP in driving growth in the SAC-4 economies tended to weaken from the first to the second sub-period. The share of ALP in GDP growth decreased from 71.5 to 49.9 per cent for Bangladesh, from 39 to 21.4 per cent for Nepal, and from 54.5 to 22.2 per cent for Pakistan. In contrast, Sri Lanka was the only economy in this group that exhibited an increase in the share of ALP in GDP growth (from 56.3 to 72.9 per cent).

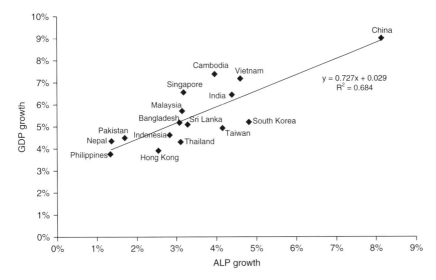

Source: Author's calculations.

*Figure 4.7   Correlation between ALP and GDP growth in Developing
Asia, 1990–2010*

4.4.2   ALP as a Driver of GDP Growth in Developing Asia: A Regional Picture

As shown in Figure 4.7, ALP growth and GDP growth exhibited a strong
positive correlation ($R^2 = 0.684$). China, South Korea, and Vietnam
were the leading performers in terms of the contribution of ALP to GDP
growth, whereas the Philippines, Nepal, and Pakistan exhibited the lowest
contribution of ALP to GDP growth.

4.5   THE DRIVING FORCES BEHIND DEVELOPING ASIA'S LEADING ECONOMIC PERFORMANCE

This section examines the drivers of the lead in economic performance
that Developing Asia commanded over other parts of the world during
the period of 1990–2010. Thus, this section examines the composition of
the gap in economic performance between Developing Asia and two other
groups: non-Asian developing economies and developed economies.

Confined to the sample of 119 economies introduced in Chapter 2,
the group of non-Asian developing economies, which are referred to as

the Rest of the World (ROW), consists of 79 developing economies, of which 20 are from Latin America, 21 are from Eastern Europe, 27 are from Sub-Saharan Africa, and 11 are from North Africa and Middle East. The group of developed economies, which is referred to as Developed Economies, includes 24 developed economies, of which seven are from G7 and 17 are from Non-G7.[5] The analysis in this section uses the unweighted means of economic growth rates and their sources for the economies in a given group to capture the characteristics of a typical economy of the group. It is worth noting that there are both high performers (such as China and India) and laggards (such as Nepal, Pakistan, and the Philippines) in the Developing Asia group. The same is true for the Rest of World (ROW) and the Developed Economies groups. The results of the analysis, however, are robust to sample outliers.[6]

4.5.1 The Sources of Developing Asia's Lead in GDP Growth

This subsection analyses the sources responsible for the lead in GDP growth exhibited by Developing Asia compared with the two comparison groups (the Industrialized Economies and the ROW, which includes all of the developing economies that do not belong to Developing Asia). This analysis used unweighted means by group as reported in Table 4.4 to capture the growth pattern of each group's typical economy.[7]

GDP growth gap between Developing Asia and Industrialized Economies was large at 3.2 percentage points. This GDP growth lead exhibited by Developing Asia was the result of all sources of GDP growth, but capital input was the major contributor to this gap with a share of 54 per cent (Table 4.4). It is important to note, however, that the contribution of capital input to the gap was totally driven by non-ICT capital, whereas the ICT capital had a negative share in this gap. The labor input accounted for 16.1 per cent of the gap, of which 18.7 per cent was due to the hours worked, whereas the labor quality had a negative

[5] Details on the sample of 119 economies and its seven groups are presented in Section 2.1 of Chapter 2.

[6] The analysis yields similar results if the outliers (upper 10 per cent and lower 10 per cent based on GDP or ALP growth) are removed from each of the groups. This finding indicates that the potential distorting effect of the sample outliers is not a cause of concern.

[7] Note that simple means instead of weighted means are used for this analysis because the use of the latter can cause a bias toward large economies. For example, the weighted means for Developing Asia represent the growth pattern of China more than the group's average economy. Appendix 4.4 provides results based on weighted means. Although these results show more vivid evidence on the importance of capital formation in Developing Asia's growth, they are heavily influenced by the growth pattern of China.

Table 4.4 Sources of Developing Asia's lead in GDP growth, 1990–2010

		Sources of GDP Growth, 1990–2010 (% points per annum)			The Gap between Developing Asia and			
		Developing Asia	Industrialized Economies	Rest of World (ROW)	Industrialized Economies		Rest of World (ROW)	
		(1)	(2)	(3)	(4) = (1)–(2)	Structure	(5) = (1)–(3)	Structure
GDP Growth		5.5	2.3	3.2	3.2	100	2.3	100
Capital Input	All	3.0	1.3	1.6	1.7	54.0	1.4	61.7
	ICT	0.5	0.5	0.3	–0.02	–0.8	0.1	6.0
	Non-ICT	2.6	0.8	1.3	1.8	54.7	1.3	55.7
Labor Input	All	1.3	0.7	1.0	0.5	16.1	0.2	10.7
	Quality	0.2	0.3	0.1	–0.1	–2.5	0.1	3.3
	Hours	1.0	0.4	0.9	0.6	18.7	0.2	7.3
TFP		1.2	0.2	0.6	1.0	29.9	0.6	27.6

Note: The measures for a given group are its unweighted means.

Source: Author's calculations.

share of −2.5 per cent. TFP was a strong driver of the growth gap with a share of approximately 30 per cent. This analysis suggests that the non-ICT capital, TFP, and hours worked, in this order, were important sources of the lead in GDP growth exhibited by Developing Asia over the Industrialized Economies. However, Developing Asia exhibited a lower contribution of ICT capital and labor quality to the growth compared with the Industrialized Economies.

As shown in Table 4.4, Developing Asia outperformed the ROW on GDP growth during 1990–2010 by a gap of 2.3 percentage points, and all of the sources of GDP growth contributed to this gap. However, capital input was the main determinant of the gap with a contribution of 61.7 per cent, of which 55.7 per cent was due to non-ICT capital and 6 per cent was due to ICT capital. In contrast, labor input accounted for approximately 10 per cent of GDP growth gap, of which 7 per cent was due to hours worked and 3 per cent was due to the labor quality, whereas the share contributed by TFP was 27.6 per cent. The comparison of GDP growth between Developing Asia and the ROW indicates that capital accumulation, especially in non-ICT capital, was the major driver of GDP growth gap that Developing Asia commanded over other developing economies. TFP was the second most important source of this lead, whereas labor input, including hours worked and labor quality, had a positive but quite modest contribution share.

4.5.2   The Sources of Developing Asia's Lead in ALP Growth

Table 4.5 elaborates the gaps in ALP growth between Developing Asia and the two comparison groups: Industrialized Economies and the ROW. Similar to Table 4.4, the rate of ALP growth for a group and its components were measured as group means.

Developing Asia commanded an ALP growth gap of 1.9 percentage points over Industrialized Economies. Capital deepening and TFP growth contributed almost equally to this gap: capital deepening accounted for 53.5 per cent of the gap, and the share of TFP was 50.9 per cent. The contribution of capital deepening to the gap was completely driven by non-ICT capital, whereas the contribution of ICT capital deepening was negative (−3.5 per cent). Furthermore, the labor quality had a negative contribution to this gap with a share of −4.3 per cent. This finding suggests that non-ICT capital accumulation was the major driver, and TFP was an important source of Developing Asia's catching-up with the developed nations on labor productivity. Developing Asia, however, can accelerate its catching-up speed by fostering investment in ICT capital and boosting improvements in labor quality.

Table 4.5 Sources of Developing Asia's lead in ALP growth, 1990–2010

		Sources of ALP Growth, 1990–2010 (% points per annum)			The Gap between Developing Asia and			
		Developing Asia	Industrialized Economies	Rest of World (ROW)	Industrialized Economies		Rest of World (ROW)	
		(1)	(2)	(3)	(4) = (1)–(2)	Structure	(5) = (1)–(3)	Structure
ALP Growth		3.5	1.6	1.4	1.9	100	2.0	100
Capital Deepening	All	2.1	1.0	0.7	1.0	53.5	1.3	65.5
	ICT	0.4	0.5	0.3	–0.1	–3.5	0.1	5.8
	Non-ICT	1.7	0.6	0.4	1.1	57.0	1.2	59.7
Labor Quality		0.2	0.3	0.1	–0.1	–4.3	0.1	3.7
TFP		1.2	0.2	0.6	1.0	50.9	0.6	30.8

Note: The measures for a given group are its unweighted means.

Source: Author's calculations.

Table 4.5 shows that Developing Asia outperformed the ROW on ALP growth during 1990–2010 by a gap of 2 percentage points, and all of the sources of ALP growth contributed positively to this gap. Among these sources, capital deepening was the largest driver of the gap with a share of nearly 66 per cent, of which almost 60 per cent was due to non-ICT capital deepening and 6 per cent was due to ICT capital deepening. This finding indicates that capital deepening, especially non-ICT capital, was the major driver of the lead in ALP growth of Developing Asia over the ROW. TFP, which was responsible for 30.8 per cent of the gap, was the second most important source of Developing Asia's ALP growth. The labor quality, however, accounted for less than 5 per cent of the gap.

4.5.3 ALP as a Driver of Developing Asia's Lead in GDP Growth

As presented in Section 4.4, GDP growth can be split into the contributions of ALP growth and employment (hours worked) expansion. GDP growth gaps between Developing Asia and the two compared groups, therefore, can be decomposed into the contributions of ALP and employment, as shown in Table 4.6.

ALP was also the leading driver of GDP growth gap of 3.2 percentage points between Developing Asia and the Industrialized Economies with a share of nearly 60 per cent of the gap. Employment claimed the remaining share of approximately 40 per cent. This finding indicates that both the pace of catching-up represented by ALP growth and the employment expansion were important sources of Developing Asia's GDP growth lead over the Industrialized Economies.

GDP growth gap of 2.3 percentage points between Developing Asia and the ROW was largely determined by ALP, which contributed nearly 90 per cent. ALP growth was the overriding driver of the difference in GDP growth between Developing Asia and other developing economies.

4.6 SOURCES OF ECONOMIC GROWTH, 1990–2010: A GLOBAL PICTURE

The findings from the previous sections, particularly the major role of capital accumulation and TFP in the economic growth of Developing Asia, can be generalized to the world and other groups of economies. Similar to the analysis presented in Section 4.5, this section analyses the unweighted means of economic growth rates and their sources for each of the groups of interest. The section uses the sample of 119 economies to represent the world. The sample is divided into two groups: Industrialized Economies

Table 4.6 ALP as a driver of Developing Asia's lead in GDP growth, 1990–2010

	Sources of GDP Growth, 1990–2010 (% points per annum)			The Gap between Developing Asia and			
	Developing Asia	Industrialized Economies	Rest of World (ROW)	Industrialized Economies		Rest of World (ROW)	
	(1)	(2)	(3)	(4) = (1)–(2)	Structure	(5) = (1)–(3)	Structure
GDP Growth	5.5	2.3	3.2	3.2	100	2.3	100
ALP Growth	3.5	1.6	1.4	1.9	58.8	2.0	89.6
Employment Growth	2.0	0.7	1.8	1.3	41.2	0.2	10.4

Note: The measures for a given group are its unweighted means.

Source: Author's calculations.

and Developing Economies. The Industrialized Economies consists of 24 economies representing developed economies, and the group of Developing Economies, which represent the developing economies, consists of two developing groups: Developing Asia (16 economies) and the remaining 79 developing economies, which are referred to as the Rest of World (ROW) in this chapter. Similar to the approach employed in Section 4.5, the results of the analysis in this section are robust to sample outliers.[8]

Sources of GDP growth
The sources and structure of the unweighted average GDP growth during 1990–2010 obtained for the world and the sub-samples are reported in Table 4.7. The worldwide GDP growth rate was 3.3 per cent, higher at 3.6 per cent for the Developing Economies, and lower at 2.3 per cent for the Industrialized Economies. At the same time, Developing Asia far outperformed the ROW on GDP growth (5.5 versus 3.2 per cent). The following features stand out from the inspection of the structure of GDP growth of the world and its sub-samples:

● The main driver of GDP growth was capital formation. The share of capital input in GDP growth was 52.5 per cent for the world (represented by 119 economies) and exceeded 50 per cent for all of its sub-samples. The major role of capital accumulation in the growth is consistent with the analysis performed by Lin (2009), who found that development is a transition toward more capital-intensive forms of growth.
   ● It is interesting to note that the share of capital input in GDP growth was larger for Industrialized Economies (56.9 per cent) compared with the developing groups: 51.8 per cent for the Developing Economies, 55.2 per cent for Developing Asia, and 50.6 per cent for the ROW. A large part of the contribution of capital input to the growth of Industrialized Economies was due to ICT capital input, which accounted for 21.8 per cent of the group's growth, whereas the corresponding share was only 11.6 per cent for the world, 10 per cent for the Developing Economies, 8.6 per cent for Developing Asia, and 10.5 per cent for the ROW.
   ● The share of non-ICT capital input in growth was 40.9 per cent for the world and substantial for all of the sub-samples.

---

[8]   The analysis yields similar results if the outliers (upper 10 per cent and lower 10 per cent based on GDP or ALP growth) are removed from each of the groups. This finding indicates that the potential distorting effects of outliers should not be a cause of concern.

Table 4.7   Sources of GDP growth, 1990–2010: a global picture

		World	Industrialized Economies	Developing Economies		
				All	Developing Asia	Rest of World (ROW)
Sources of Growth (% points per annum)						
GDP Growth		3.3	2.3	3.6	5.5	3.2
Capital Input	All	1.7	1.3	1.9	3.0	1.6
	ICT	0.4	0.5	0.4	0.5	0.3
	Non-ICT	1.4	0.8	1.5	2.6	1.3
Labor Input	All	1.0	0.7	1.1	1.3	1.0
	Quality	0.2	0.3	0.2	0.2	0.1
	Hours	0.8	0.4	0.9	1.0	0.9
TFP		0.6	0.2	0.7	1.2	0.6
Structure (GDP Growth = 100)						
Capital Input	All	52.5	56.9	51.8	55.2	50.6
	ICT	11.6	21.8	10.0	8.6	10.5
	Non-ICT	40.9	35.1	41.8	46.6	40.1
Labor Input	All	29.7	32.4	29.3	22.9	31.5
	Quality	5.4	13.0	4.2	3.9	4.3
	Hours	24.3	19.4	25.1	19.0	27.2
TFP		17.8	10.7	18.9	21.9	17.9

Note: The measures for a given group are its unweighted means.

Source: Author's calculations.

This share was largest for Developing Asia (46.6 per cent), followed by the ROW (40.1 per cent), while it was lowest for the Industrialized Economies (35.1 per cent).

- The ratio between the contributions of non-ICT to ICT capital toward GDP growth was approximately 4:1 for Developing Economies and approximately 3:2 for Industrialized Economies.

- The second most important contribution to GDP growth is labor input. The share of the total labor input in growth was 29.7 per cent for the world, 32.4 per cent for Industrialized Economies, 29.3 per cent for Developing Economies, 22.9 per cent for Developing Asia, and 31.5 per cent for the ROW.

- It is interesting to note that the share of labor input was larger for Industrialized Economies compared with those obtained for the world and the other analysed groups. This is because the labor quality had a notably larger share in the growth for Industrialized Economies (13 per cent) compared to the world (5.4 per cent) and other groups: Developing Economies (4.2 per cent), Developing Asia (3.9 per cent), and the ROW (4.3 per cent). The small contribution of labor quality to growth, which is proxied by education, implies an important policy issue. Education alone may not have a solid effect on growth if the business environment and economic conditions are not favorable to capital accumulation that requires high-skilled labor. This observation is consistent with the findings from various studies, which have shown that education alone does not exhibit a robust significant effect on growth.
- In contrast, the share of hours worked on GDP growth was 24.3 per cent for the world. This share was largest for the ROW (27.2 per cent) and lowest for Developing Asia (19 per cent) and was as low as 19.4 per cent for Industrialized Economies.

- TFP is the third most important contribution to GDP growth. The share of TFP in GDP growth was 17.8 per cent for the world. This share was higher for the developing groups: 18.9 per cent for Developing Economies, 21.9 per cent for Developing Asia, and 17.9 per cent for the ROW. In contrast, it was lower at 10.7 per cent for the Industrialized Economies. Three conclusions can be drawn from this observation. First, the large share of TFP in economic growth of the developing groups suggests, to some extent, the advantage of 'backwardness': a country distant to the technological frontier can boost its productivity growth by importing ideas and innovation from more advanced countries. Second, the share of TFP in growth is larger for Developing Asia than for the ROW because the former was more effective in technology imitation and knowledge diffusion, as presented in Chapter 3. Third, the contributions of the labor quality and the ICT input capture a significant part of the residual in GDP growth decomposition, which is defined as TFP growth. Therefore, the large contributions of the labor quality and the ICT input toward GDP growth of the Industrialized Economies group reduce the residual, which implies a smaller TFP growth.

It is important to emphasize that, although TFP played an important role, 80–90 per cent of the world's GDP growth was driven by capital

accumulation and labor input. This finding implies the crucial role of
the policies that foster capital investment and job creation in the promotion of economic growth. These findings suggest that the creation
of an enabling environment that encourages robust capital investment and vibrant job creation plays a crucial role in the promotion
and sustainment of high economic performance in a country.

Sources of ALP growth
The sources and structure of the unweighted average ALP growth during
1990–2010 for the world and its sub-samples are reported in Table 4.8.
ALP growth rate was 1.7 per cent for the world; in contrast, it was higher
at 1.8 per cent for Developing Economies and lower at 1.6 per cent for
Industrialized Economies. Developing Asia, on average, far outperformed
the ROW on ALP growth (3.5 versus 1.4 per cent). With regard to the
structure of ALP growth of the world and its sub-samples, the following
findings are salient.

Table 4.8   Sources of ALP growth, 1990–2010: a global picture

		World	Industrialized Economies	Developing Economies		
				All	Developing Asia	Rest of World (ROW)
Sources of Growth (% points per annum)						
ALP Growth		1.7	1.6	1.8	3.5	1.4
Capital Deepening	All	1.0	1.0	0.9	2.1	0.7
	ICT	0.3	0.5	0.3	0.4	0.3
	Non-ICT	0.6	0.6	0.6	1.7	0.4
Labor Quality		0.2	0.3	0.2	0.2	0.1
TFP		0.6	0.2	0.7	1.2	0.6
Structure (ALP Growth = 100)						
Capital Deepening	All	55.5	65.9	53.2	59.2	50.2
	ICT	19.2	29.3	16.9	11.5	19.6
	Non-ICT	36.3	36.6	36.2	47.7	30.6
Labor Quality		10.4	18.7	8.5	6.2	9.7
TFP		34.1	15.4	38.3	34.7	40.1

Note: The measures for a given group are its unweighted means.

Source: Author's calculations.

- The main driver of ALP growth was capital deepening. The share of capital deepening in ALP growth was 55.5 per cent for the world and exceeded 50 per cent for all of its sub-samples. Among the sub-samples, this share was largest for Industrialized Economies (65.9 per cent), moderate for Developing Asia (59.2 per cent), and smallest for the ROW (50.2 per cent).
- The structure of capital deepening differed notably between the sub-samples:
  - The share of ICT capital deepening in ALP growth was 29.3 per cent for Industrialized Economies compared with 16.9 per cent for Developing Economies. This finding indicates that developed countries were more heavily reliant on ICT capital deepening than developing economies in boosting ALP growth.
  - The share of non-ICT capital deepening in ALP growth was 47.7 per cent for Developing Asia, and this share was far larger than the shares of 30.6 per cent for the ROW and 36.6 per cent for Industrialized Economies. This finding suggests that Developing Asia relied more heavily on non-ICT capital deepening than other groups in fostering its ALP growth.
- The second most important contribution to ALP growth is TFP growth. The share of TFP in ALP growth was 34.1 per cent for the world. This share was lower for Industrialized Economies (15.4 per cent) and higher for the developing groups: 38.3 per cent for Developing Economies, 34.7 per cent for Developing Asia, and 40.1 per cent for the ROW.
- The share of labor quality in ALP growth was 10.4 per cent for the world. This share was much larger for the developed group (18.7 per cent) and lower for the developing group (8.5 per cent). This result suggests that the developing countries can increase their ALP growth by making more efforts toward the improvement of their labor quality.

ALP as a driver of GDP growth
Details on the breakdown of GDP growth during 1990–2010, that is, the contribution of ALP and employment, for the world and its sub-samples are reported in Table 4.9. The following features stand out:

- On average, ALP growth was the major driver of GDP growth for the world, and this pattern was much more pronounced for Industrialized Economies and Developing Asia. The share of ALP in GDP growth was 52.2 per cent for the world, 69.6 per cent for Industrialized Economies, and 63.3 per cent for Developing Asia.

Table 4.9   *ALP as a driver of GDP growth, 1990–2010: a global picture*

	World	Industrialized Economies	Developing Economies		
			All	Developing Asia	Rest of World (ROW)
GDP Growth	3.3	2.3	3.6	5.5	3.2
ALP Growth	1.7	1.6	1.8	3.5	1.4
Employment Growth	1.6	0.7	1.8	2.0	1.8
	Structure (GDP Growth=100)				
ALP Growth	52.2	69.6	49.4	63.3	44.6
Employment Growth	47.8	30.4	50.6	36.7	55.4

Note: The measures for a given group are its unweighted means.

Source: Author's calculations.

- For the ROW, however, ALP was less important than the hours worked in the driving of GDP growth. The share of ALP in GDP growth of this group was only 44.6 per cent, whereas the share of employment was 55.4 per cent.

4.7   SUMMARY OF KEY RESULTS

This chapter examines the sources of GDP growth and ALP growth experienced by the 16 Developing Asia economies to gain insights from regional and global comparisons. The findings of the chapter can be divided into three groups. One group of findings includes the sources responsible for the growth of GDP and ALP of the individual economies compared with their peers and to the overall pattern of the group. The second set of findings is the drivers of the lead in economic performance experienced by Developing Asia over the rest of the world. The third group of findings consists of the global pattern of the sources of economic growth.

4.7.1   Sources of Economic Growth of Individual Economies

Capital accumulation was the largest source of GDP growth over the period of 1990–2010 for most of the 16 Developing Asia economies. ICT capital was a significant source of GDP and ALP growth for all of the 16 Developing Asia economies. Its contribution to GDP growth during 1990–2010 was notably larger for China, Singapore, Vietnam, Malaysia,

India, South Korea, Taiwan, and Pakistan compared with the remaining economies of the group. In addition, the contribution to growth was larger in the second sub-period, 2000–2010, in comparison to the first sub-period, 1990–2000. This observation for Developing Asia supports the conclusion of Kretschmer (2012) based on his survey of a large number of studies that the effect of investment in ICT on growth is not only significant and positive, but also increasing over time.

The share of TFP in GDP growth was notably enhanced from the first sub-period, 1990–2000, to the second sub-period, 2000–2010, for most of the 16 Developing Asia economies. This trend was most pronounced for the economies that suffered the most from the 1997–1998 Asian financial crises, which includes all four Asian Tiger economies and four of the ASEAN-6 countries: Indonesia, Malaysia, the Philippines, and Thailand. This finding suggests that the crisis stimulated some significant structural transformations in these economies that boosted their growth efficiency. In contrast, the share of TFP in GDP growth decreased sharply over the two sub-periods to alarmingly low levels (below 10 per cent) for several economies: Cambodia, Vietnam, Nepal, and Pakistan.

ALP was the main driver of GDP growth over the period of 1990–2010 for the Developing Asia economies, with the exception of Singapore (for which ALP accounted for 48.7 per cent of GDP growth), Pakistan (37.7 per cent), the Philippines (35.5 per cent), and Nepal (31.3 per cent). This low contribution of ALP to GDP growth was most evident for Nepal and Pakistan in the second sub-period, 2000–2010, during which approximately 80 per cent of GDP growth was due to employment expansion.

4.7.2 Sources of Developing Asia's Lead in Economic Performance

Developing Asia outperformed the Industrialized Economies by a gap of 3.2 percentage points and the Rest of World (ROW) by a gap of 2.3 percentage points on GDP growth during the period of 1990–2010. Capital accumulation, especially non-ICT capital, was the main driver of the lead exhibited by Developing Asia and accounted for more than 50 per cent of the gap. TFP growth was also an important source of Developing Asia's superior GDP growth and accounted for nearly 30 per cent of the gap that Developing Asia commanded over the other groups.

With regard to ALP growth during 1990–2010, Developing Asia commanded a lead of 1.9 percentage points over the Industrialized Economies and 2.0 percentage points over the ROW. The principal driver of Developing Asia's lead was non-ICT capital deepening. Its share in ALP growth gap was approximately 60 per cent. TFP was the second most important source of Developing Asia's lead in ALP growth. In particular, the share of TFP in ALP growth gap between Developing Asia and Industrialized Economies was 50.9 per cent, which indicates that TFP growth played a very important role in the catch-up exhibited by Developing Asia toward the developed nations. Developing Asia, however, exhibited lower contributions of ICT capital deepening and labor quality toward ALP growth compared with the developed countries.

ALP growth was the major driver of the outperformance in GDP growth during 1990–2010 exhibited by Developing Asia over the other two groups. In fact, ALP accounted for approximately 90 per cent of GDP growth gap between Developing Asia and the ROW, whereas the corresponding share in the gap between Developing Asia and Industrialized Economies was approximately 60 per cent.

4.7.3 Global Patterns of the Sources of Economic Growth

The examination of the global patterns of the sources of economic growth revealed results that were similar to those found for Developing Asia. Capital accumulation played a crucial role in driving economic growth. The share of capital input in GDP growth exceeded 50 per cent for the world and its sub-samples. The share of ICT capital input in GDP growth, however, was far larger for developed countries than for developing ones. TFP was an important source of GDP growth with share close to 20 per cent for the world and the developing groups.

Similar results were found for the sources of ALP growth. Capital deepening was the major source of ALP growth with shares that exceeded 50 per cent for the world and its sub-samples. TFP growth was the second most important source of ALP growth with shares that exceeded one third for the world and its developing groups.

ALP and employment contributed rather equally to GDP growth in the world sample: the share in GDP growth was approximately 52 per cent for ALP and 48 per cent for hours worked. The role of ALP in GDP growth, however, was far more important for Industrialized Economies and Developing Asia. The share of ALP in GDP growth was approximately 70 per cent for Industrialized Economies and 63 per cent for Developing Asia.

APPENDIX 4.1:   THE ACCOUNTING FRAMEWORKS FOR DECOMPOSING THE SOURCES OF ECONOMIC GROWTH

Jorgenson et al. (2003) provided a framework for decomposing economic growth into the contribution of capital and labor inputs and total factor productivity (TFP) growth. In the general production function below, output (Y) is produced by an input bundle X of capital services and labor services. Capital services can be decomposed into ICT capital (K_{ICT}) and non-ICT capital (K_{NICT}). Labor services is the product of hours worked (H) and labor quality (L_Q). Input (X) is augmented by Hicks-neutral total factor productivity (A).

$$Y = A.X(K_{ICT}, K_{NICT}, H, L_Q) \qquad (A4.1.1)$$

Under the assumption of perfect competitive factor markets where the marginal product of each input equals its price and constant returns to scale, Equation (A4.1.1) can be transformed into the following growth accounting framework:

$$\Delta \ln Y = \bar{v}_K \Delta \ln K + \bar{v}_L \Delta L + \Delta \ln A = \bar{v}_{K_{ICT}} \Delta \ln K_{ICT} + \bar{v}_{K_{NICT}} \Delta \ln K_{NICT} + $$
$$\bar{v}_L \Delta \ln H + \bar{v}_L \Delta \ln L_Q + \Delta \ln A \qquad (A4.1.2)$$

where $\bar{v}$ denotes the two-period average shares of total factor income, and Δln in front of a variable denotes its real growth rate over the period of interest. The assumption of constant returns to scale of the aggregate input function implies that $\bar{v}_K + \bar{v}_L = 1$ ($\bar{v}_K = \bar{v}_{K_{ICT}} + \bar{v}_{K_{NICT}}$).

Equation (A4.1.2) means that GDP growth can be decomposed into three main sources:

- Contribution of capital inputs, which consists of the contributions of ICT and non-ICT capital: $\bar{v}_K \Delta \ln K = \bar{v}_{K_{ICT}} \Delta \ln K_{ICT} + \bar{v}_{K_{NICT}} \Delta \ln K_{NICT}$,
- Contribution of labor input, which comprises the contributions of hours worked and labor quality: $\bar{v}_L \Delta \ln L = \bar{v}_L \Delta \ln H + \bar{v}_L \Delta \ln L_Q$, and
- Contribution of TFP growth: $\Delta \ln A$

The framework (A4.1.2) can be rearranged to decompose the growth of the average labor productivity (ALP), y ($y = Y/H$), as follows:

$$\Delta \ln y = \Delta \ln Y - \Delta \ln H$$

$$\Delta \ln y = \bar{v}_{K_{ICT}} \Delta \ln k_{ICT} + \bar{v}_{K_{NICT}} \Delta \ln k_{NICT} + \bar{v}_L \Delta \ln L_Q + \Delta \ln A \quad (A4.1.3)$$

where $k_{ICT} = K_{ICT}/H$ and $k_{NICT} = K_{NICT}/H$ are referred to as ICT capital deepening and non-ICT capital deepening, respectively.

Equation (A4.1.3) indicates that ALP growth comes from three sources:

- Contribution of capital deepening, which consists of the contributions of ICT capital deepening and non-ICT capital deepening: $\bar{v}_K \Delta \ln k = \bar{v}_{K_{ICT}} \Delta \ln k_{ICT} + \bar{v}_{K_{NICT}} \Delta \ln k_{NICT}$,
- Contribution of labor quality: $\bar{v}_L \Delta \ln L_Q$, and
- TFP growth: $\Delta \ln A$.

APPENDIX 4.2:   DATASET FOR THE GROWTH DECOMPOSITION EXERCISE

The dataset used for the growth decomposition exercise is from Jorgenson and Vu (2011), which is constructed based on the two datasets: the Conference Board's Total Economy Database (TED)[9] and the World Bank's World Development Indicators (WDI) database.[10] The TED dataset is used because it provides complete data needed for the growth decomposition exercise for a large sample of economies for the period 1990–2010, to which all the large economies belong. The WDI dataset is used as a supplementary source of data for the economies for which the TED data are missing. Among the 16 Developing Asia economies, the complete TED data for the period 1990–2010 is not available for four economies: Cambodia, Nepal, Singapore, and Vietnam.

The methods for estimating capital stocks, capital services, and labor services are elaborated in the Methodological Notes of the Conference Board's TED dataset, which is available on its website. The sections below provide a brief description of these estimation methods.

1.   Estimating Capital Stocks and Capital Services

Capital stocks
The quantity of capital stock for asset type i is determined using the 'perpetual inventory method' as follows:

$$S_{i,T} = S_{i,T-1}(1 - \delta_i) + I_{i,T} = \sum_{t=0}^{\infty}(1 - \delta_i)^t I_{i,T-t} \qquad (A4.2.1)$$

[9]   The TED is available on the Conference Board's website at URL: http://www. conference-board.org/data/economydatabase/.
[10]   The WDI database is available on the World Bank's website at URL: http://data. worldbank.org/data-catalog/world-development-indicators.

where $S_{i,T}$ is the capital stock in year T for asset type i which is one of the six asset types listed below, δ_i is its constant rate of geometric depreciation, and $I_{i,T-t}$ is the constant price investment flow in year $T-t$

The six asset types belong to two capital categories: ICT and non-ICT. The ICT capital category consists of Computer hardware ($\delta_i=30$ per cent), Telecom Equipment ($\delta_i=12$ per cent), and Computer software ($\delta_i=46$ per cent); while the non-ICT capital category include Construction ($\delta_i=3$ per cent), Transportation equipment ($\delta_i=20$ per cent), and Machinery ($\delta_i=13$ per cent).

Capital services

The procedure used to estimate the capital services rendered by a given type of capital asset was presented by Jorgenson et al. (2005). The procedure requires the estimation of the quantity of capital services, the rental price of those capital services, the contribution of the capital asset to income, and the ex-post nominal rate of return.

The quantity of capital services rendered by capital asset type i in year T is defined as the average capital stock between years T and T−1:

$$K_{i,T} = \frac{(S_{i,T} + S_{i,T-1})}{2} \qquad (A4.2.2)$$

The rental price $c_{i,T}$ of capital services from capital asset type i in period T is obtained using the assumption that the typical investor in period $T-1$ who invests in this capital asset at price $p_{i,T-1}$ will obtain a return rate that will justify the nominal rate of return r_T observed for the economy and the market price of the remaining value of the asset in year T. Under the market equilibrium condition, this assumption implies that

$$p_{i,T-1}(1+r_T) = c_{i,T} + (1-\delta_i)p_{i,T} \qquad (A4.2.3)$$

Equation (A4.2.3) suggests the formula for computing the rental price $c_{i,T}$

$$c_{i,T} = r_T p_{i,T-1} + \delta_i p_{i,T} - \pi_{i,T} p_{i,T-1} \qquad (A4.2.4)$$

where $\pi_{i,T} = (p_{i,T} - p_{i,T-1})/p_{i,T-1}$ is the asset's price change over the period.

The contribution to income $v_{i,T}$ of capital services rendered by capital good i in year T is computed as

$$v_{i,T} = \frac{K_{i,T}}{Y_T} c_{i,T} \qquad (A4.2.5)$$

where Y_T is the GDP in current prices in year T

The nominal rate of return r_T is determined as follows. The contribution to income of aggregate capital input is the sum of the contributions of all capital asset types as follows:

$$v_K = \sum_i v_{i,T} \tag{A4.2.6}$$

Combining Equations (A4.2.4), (A4.2.5), and (A4.2.6) yields

$$v_K = \sum_i \frac{K_{i,T}}{Y_T}(r_T p_{i,T-1} + \delta_i p_{i,T} - \pi_{i,T} p_{i,T-1}) \tag{A4.2.7}$$

Therefore, the nominal rate of return r_T (based on the ex-post approach), can be estimated using Equation (A4.2.7) as follows:

$$r_T = \frac{\left\{ v_K Y_T + \sum_i K_{i,T} \pi_{i,T} p_{i,T-1} - \sum_i K_{i,T} \delta_i p_{i,T} \right\}}{\sum_i K_{i,T} p_{i,T-1}} \tag{A4.2.8}$$

The income share of capital input v_k is assumed one-third if it cannot be estimated from the country's national account. In this case, the income share of labor input is two-thirds.

2. Estimating Labor Services

Labor quantity
It is ideal to use total hours worked as the measure of labor quantity. However, data on total hours worked is available only for 51 economies from the TED dataset. For the remaining countries, labor quantity is captured by the number of full-time equivalent workers, which can be converted into total hours worked under the assumption that a full-time equivalent works on average 2,000 hours per year.

Labor quality
For the countries for which data on labor quality is not provided by the TED dataset, the labor quality index L_Q is constructed, following the approach employed by Barro and Lee (2010):[11]

$$L_Q = e^{\theta.s} \tag{A4.2.9}$$

---

[11] This formula for estimating human capital is used by Barro and Lee (2010).

where *s* is the mean of years of schooling for adults aged 25 years and older;[12] the return rate to schooling θ is assumed to be at a conservative rate of 3 per cent.[13]

APPENDIX 4.3:   THE SHARES OF ALP AND EMPLOYMENT IN GDP GROWTH

GDP generated by a given economy, denoted by *Y* can be expressed as:

$$Y = (Y/L) . L = y . L \qquad (A4.3.1)$$

where *L* is the economy's quantity of labor input, which can be measured as number of full-time equivalent workers or total hours worked; $y = Y/L$ is its average labor productivity (ALP).

Equation (A4.3.1) suggests that GDP growth can be split into two components–ALP growth and employment growth:

$$\Delta\ln Y = \Delta\ln y + \Delta\ln L \qquad (A4.3.2)$$

where Δln in front of a variable denotes its growth over the period of interest. Equation (A4.3.2) allows one to estimate the share of ALP in GDP growth as (Δln *y* / Δln *Y*) * 100% and the share of employment as (Δln *L* / Δln *Y*) * 100%.

APPENDIX 4.4:   SOURCES OF DEVELOPING ASIA'S LEAD IN GDP GROWTH (WEIGHTED MEANS), 1990–2010

Table A4.1 provides the sources of growth for groups, using weighted means instead of simple means as used in Table 4.4 presented in the chapter. GDP measured in purchasing power parity is used to compute the weight of a country in a given group.

---

[12]   The data is available on the United Nation Development Program (UNDP)'s Human Development Report website, http://hdr.undp.org, accessed March 10, 2013.
[13]   Psacharopoulos and Patrinos (2004), surveying the studies on returns to schooling for 98 countries, showed that the raw rate of returns to schooling varied largely, which ranged from 1.5 per cent (for Estonia) to 16.5 per cent (for Brazil).

Table A4.1 Sources of Developing Asia's lead in GDP growth (weighted means), 1990–2010

		Sources of GDP Growth, 1990–2010 (% points per annum)			The Gap between Developing Asia and			
		Developing Asia	Industrialized Economies	Rest of World (ROW)	Industrialized Economies	Structure	Rest of World (ROW)	Structure
		(1)	(2)	(3)	(4) = (1)–(2)		(5) = (1)–(3)	
GDP Growth		6.8	2.0	2.5	4.8	100	4.3	100
Capital Input	All	3.9	1.1	1.2	2.8	58.0	2.7	63.9
	ICT	0.7	0.5	0.3	0.2	3.5	0.3	7.5
	Non-ICT	3.2	0.6	0.8	2.6	54.5	2.4	56.3
Labor Input	All	0.9	0.5	0.7	0.4	8.9	0.2	5.0
	Quality	0.2	0.3	0.2	-0.1	-1.3	0.1	1.3
	Hours	0.7	0.2	0.5	0.5	10.2	0.2	3.8
TFP Growth		1.9	0.4	0.6	1.6	33.0	1.3	31.1

Notes: The measures for a given group are its weighted means.

Source: Author's calculations.

5. Sustaining high economic growth in Developing Asia: strategic insights and a catch-up policy framework

5.1 INTRODUCTION

Developing Asia has made remarkable achievements in economic growth over the past few decades. This success, however, is only an initial step. There remains a large gap to overcome before the countries in the region transform into prosperous nations. Using the income level relative to the US as an indicator of development, in 2010, this indicator was at 13 per cent for Developing Asia, 11 per cent for the ASEAN-6, 5 per cent for the SAC-4, 16 per cent for China, and 8 per cent for India (Figure 5.1).

In addition, Developing Asia as a whole remains a poor region relative to the world average. In 2010, the region's share in the world population was 53.5 per cent, while its share in the world's GDP was only 27.8 per cent, which implies that the region's income level was only about one half of the world average (Table 1.1). With the exception of the four Asian Tiger economies and Malaysia, the developing Asian countries, especially the South Asian nations, are notably below the world's average income level. In particular, the income level relative to the world average in 2010 was only 67 per cent for China, 30 per cent for India, and 11 per cent for Nepal, the poorest country in the group. Therefore, for most developing Asian economies to reach the world average level of per capital income over the next few decades, it is essential that they achieve sustained high economic growth in many decades to come.

This chapter aims to gain insights into the policy mechanisms that have allowed successful Asian economies to achieve sustained outstanding economic growth through intensive capital accumulation over extended periods. For this purpose, Section 5.2 summarizes the results from the previous chapters, which show that Developing Asia's growth over 1990–2010 was heavily driven by capital accumulation and that there was a strong link between the high-performing economies and high rates of savings and investment. Section 5.3 investigates the strategic policy framework underlying the success of the Asian growth model. This framework consists of

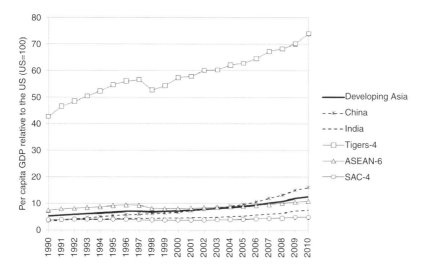

Note: Per capita GDP is measured using purchasing power parity.

Source: Author's calculations; data from WDI and ADB.

Figure 5.1   *Developing Asia's catch-up with the US on per capita income,*
1990–2010

three components: exploiting the 'backwardness' advantage, upgrading the absorptive capability, and creating favorable conditions for investment, structural change, and efficiency improvements. Section 5.4 provides illustrative evidence from China and India—the two economic giants of the group—regarding their efforts to foster growth during 1990–2010 using the three strategic components of the Catch-up Policy framework. Section 5.5 summarizes and provides the concluding remarks.

5.2   THE PATTERN OF DEVELOPING ASIA'S ECONOMIC GROWTH AND POLICY INSIGHTS

One key finding of this book is the crucial role that capital accumulation has played in driving outstanding economic growth in Developing Asia over the past two decades, 1990–2010. As presented in Chapter 3, the expansion of Developing Asia's share in the world's GDP was driven by a far larger expansion of its share in the world's fixed investment. In fact, the share of the region in the world's GDP increased by 14.9 percentage points during 1990–2010, while its share in the world's fixed investment

rose by 29.1 percentage points over the same period (Figure 3.29). China
and India drove this pattern. Over the period, China's share in the world's
GDP increased by 10.1 percentage points, while its share in the world's
fixed investment raised by 24.7 percentage points. For India, these two
respective figures were 2.6 percentage points (for GDP) and 4.3 percentage
points (for fixed investment).

The role of fixed investment in driving growth in Developing Asia over
1990–2010 is more clearly depicted in Figure 5.2A (for Developing Asia),
Figure 5.2B (for China), and Figure 5.2C (for India). Figure 5.2A shows
that fixed investment, which played the major role in driving GDP growth,
grew far more rapidly than GDP in Developing Asia during 1990–2010.
The share of the region in the world's fixed investment fell sharply in 1998
due to the Asian financial crisis, but it rebounded quickly with a robust
expanding trend over 1999–2010. The pattern showing the stronger expansion of fixed investment relative to GDP was even more notable for China,
which was the most rapidly growing economy in the region during 1990–
2010. For India, this pattern was observed for the second sub-period (from
2003 onward). This observation explains why India's GDP growth surged
by 2 percentage points, from 5.4 per cent in the first sub-period, 1990–2000,
to 7.4 per cent in the second sub-period, 2000–2010 (Table 4.1).

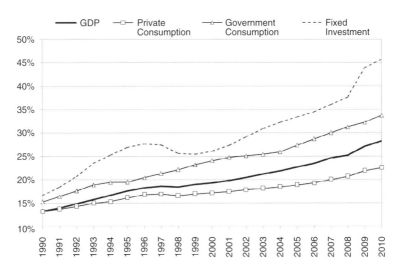

Source: Author's calculations.

*Figure 5.2A   Developing Asia's shares in the world's GDP, private
consumption, government consumption, and fixed investment,
1990–2010*

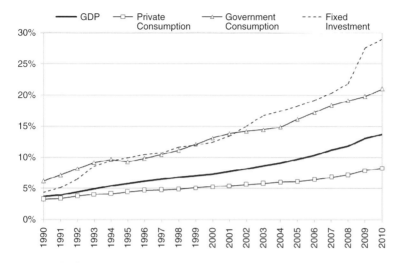

Source: Author's calculations.

Figure 5.2B   China's shares in the world's GDP, private consumption, government consumption, and fixed investment, 1990–2010

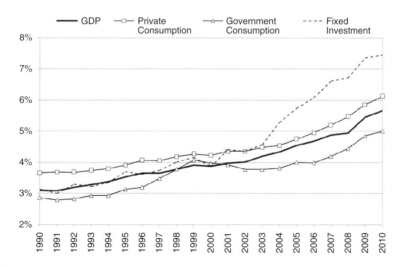

Source: Author's calculations.

Figure 5.2C   India's shares in the world's GDP, private consumption, government consumption, and fixed investment, 1990–2010

Chapter 4 provides more detailed evidence on the role of capital input in driving economic growth in Developing Asia economies by examining their sources of growth. This chapter shows that the contribution of capital input to GDP growth over 1990–2010 was 64.2 per cent for China and 52.7 per cent for India (Table 4.1), while the region's average was 55.2 per cent (Table 4.7). Similarly, the contribution of capital deepening to labor productivity growth was 65.4 per cent for China and 53.9 per cent for India (Table 4.2), while the region's average was 59.2 per cent (Table 4.8).

Furthermore, capital accumulation was also the primary driver of Developing Asia's lead over other parts of the world in terms of economic growth. In fact, capital input contributed 54 per cent to the gap between Developing Asia and the industrialized group in GDP growth over 1990–2010 and contributed even larger at 61.7 per cent to the gap between Developing Asia and the other developing economies (Table 4.4). Similarly, the capital deepening contributed 53.5 per cent to Developing Asia's lead in labor productivity growth over the industrialized group, while it contributed 65.5 per cent to the lead of Developing Asia over other developing economies (Table 4.5).

This finding regarding the role of capital accumulation as the primary driver of the rapid growth of Developing Asia echoes the prominent work by Young (1995), which concluded that the miraculous growth achieved by the four Asian Tiger economies (during 1965–1990) was primarily due to factor accumulation. The pattern of rapid growth driven by intensive capital investment, therefore, is consistent over time and robust to different types of economies in terms of size, location (North-East Asia, South-East Asia, and South Asia), and level of development.

However, the importance of capital accumulation as the driving force of economic growth is not unique to Asia but pervasive worldwide. For example, Jorgenson and Stiroh (2000), Oliner and Sichel (2000), Jorgenson (2003), and Jorgenson and Vu (2005, 2010) found that capital input is the most important source of growth in most economies. This source of growth is important not only for developing countries, in which the capital stock per capita is low, but also for developed nations, in which the capital stock per capita is relatively high. For example, Jorgenson (2003) found that even for the G7 economies, investment in tangible assets was the most important source of economic growth and the contribution of capital input exceeded that of total factor productivity (TFP) for all countries for all periods examined. This finding is supported by the result presented in Table 4.7 in Chapter 4, which shows that, on average, capital input accounted for approximately 57 per cent of GDP growth in the industrialized group.

The important role of capital investment in economic growth was taken seriously by leading economists long before the East Asian miracle occurred. Arthur Lewis (a Nobel laureate in economics and a prominent economist on economic growth in developing countries) in his book *Theory of Economic Growth* (1955), observed that the communities with sluggish growth in their per capita income invest 5 per cent of their national income per annum or less, while progressive economies invest 12 per cent of their national income per annum or more. This finding led him to stress the importance of understanding the factors underlying the shift of a developing country toward higher rates of saving and investment:

> The central problem in the theory of economic development is to understand the process by which a community is converted from being a 5 percent to a 12 percent saver – with all the changes in attitudes, in institutions and in techniques which accompany this conversion. (Lewis, 1955, pp. 225–226)

In this spirit, Developing Asia is a fascinating case. The countries in the regions evidenced a strong link between the rates for saving and investment and economic growth. As shown in Figure 5.3, the rates for savings and investment were higher for the economies with high performance in terms of their ability to catch up over the 1990–2010 period (as presented

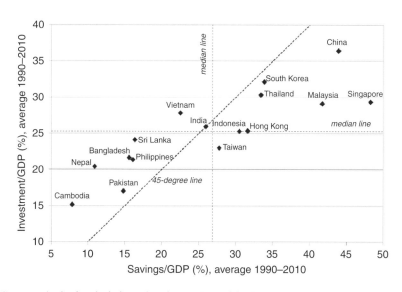

Source: Author's calculations; data from WDI and ADB.

Figure 5.3   Developing Asia: Savings and investment as percentage of GDP

in Chapter 2), including China, South Korea, Singapore, Malaysia, Thailand, Vietnam, India, Hong Kong, Indonesia, and Taiwan.[1]

However, it is important to note that the level of capital stock per capita for developing Asian economies, with the exception of the four Asian Tigers, is still far below the US level. In 2010, the level of capital stock per capita relative to the US (the US level=100) was 8.4 for India and 29.6 for China; it ranged from 3.0 (Cambodia) to 42.6 (Malaysia) for the ASEAN-6 and from 3.4 (Nepal) to 12.5 (Sri Lanka) for the SAC-4 (Table 5.1). At the same time, all of the Developing Asia economies significantly narrowed their gaps with the US on the level of capital stock per capita during 1990–2010. This pattern was most pronounced for the countries with rapid growth over the period. In particular, the level of capital stock per capita increased by 8.4 times for China during 1990–2010, from 3.5 in 1990 to 29.6 in 2010, while it doubled from 4.2 to 8.4 over the same period for India. It should be noted that for these two countries, this change accelerated between the two sub-periods, from 2.3 in 1990–2000 to 3.7 in 2000–2010 for China and from 0.9 to 2.3 for India (Table 5.1).

At the same time, the four Asian Tiger economies also recorded a notable increase in their level of capital stock per capita relative to the US during 1990–2010. However, the pattern of this change differed strikingly between the two sub-periods, 1990–2000 and 2000–2010. Over the first sub-period, 1990–2000, the level of capital stock per capita relative to the US increased by 1.7 times for Singapore, 1.6 times for South Korea and Hong Kong, and 1.5 times for Taiwan; in the second sub-period, it declined by a factor of 0.7 for Hong Kong and stagnated for Singapore and Taiwan. South Korea was the only country among the four Asian Tigers that managed to increase its level of capital stock per capita relative to the US. In addition, it is worth noting that since 2000, the levels of capital stock per capita of the four Tiger economies have been comparable or higher relative to the US level. The pattern of the change in the relative level of capital stock per capita observed for the four Asian

[1]   One may note that Cambodia recorded strong growth during 1990–2010, although its average rates of savings and investment for the period were relatively low. This growth can be explained by several of the country's characteristics during this period. First, Cambodia was almost destroyed by the Khmer Rouge, and it did not start its recovery until the early 1990s. With a very low level of capital stock in 1990, a moderate rate of investment could result in the high growth of capital input. Second, the savings and investment rates of Cambodia were on a rapidly increasing trend during 1990–2010. For example, the average savings rate was below 3 per cent in the first five years of this period (1990–1994), while it was above 15 per cent in the last five years (2006–2010). Similarly, the average investment rate was below 10 per cent for 1990–1994, while it was close to 20 per cent in 2006–2010. Third and finally, Cambodia received large inflows of foreign aid, and hence its rate of investment was notably larger than its savings rate.

Table 5.1 *Capital stock per capita relative to the US (US = 100): 2010 versus 1990*

Economy	Level Relative to the US (US = 100)			Change over Period (Sub-period) (Times)		
	1990	2000	2010	1990–2010	1990–2000	2000–2010
China–India						
China	3.5	8.0	29.6	8.4	2.3	3.7
India	4.2	3.6	8.4	2.0	0.9	2.3
Tigers-4						
Hong Kong	102.5	164.9	122.8	1.2	1.6	0.7
Singapore	104.6	174.0	176.7	1.7	1.7	1.0
South Korea	41.1	67.3	89.5	2.2	1.6	1.3
Taiwan	53.5	78.6	78.1	1.5	1.5	1.0
ASEAN-6						
Cambodia	0.5	1.5	3.0	6.0	3.0	2.0
Indonesia	6.3	5.9	18.3	2.9	0.9	3.1
Malaysia	29.3	37.2	42.6	1.5	1.3	1.1
Philippines	8.8	9.2	10.5	1.2	1.0	1.1
Thailand	20.1	25.8	34.1	1.7	1.3	1.3
Vietnam	1.3	4.0	9.7	7.7	3.1	2.4
SAC-4						
Bangladesh	2.6	2.7	3.6	1.4	1.0	1.4
Nepal	2.3	2.0	3.4	1.5	0.9	1.7
Pakistan	3.1	3.5	4.1	1.3	1.1	1.2
Sri Lanka	5.5	7.6	12.5	2.3	1.4	1.6

Note: The capital stock is measured in purchasing power parity, using the PPP conversion factor from the World Bank 2005 ICP report.

Source: Author's estimation (see Appendix 4.2 in Chapter 4 for the estimation method). This aggregate capital stock is estimated from the gross fixed capital formation, using a geometric depreciation rate of 7 per cent per year.

Tiger economies implies that once an economy has reached a relatively high level of capital stock per capita, it become much more difficult, if not impossible, for it to mobilize intensive capital formation to foster growth.

The discussions concerning capital stock per capita presented above suggest that the economies with low capital stock per capita should actually consider this disadvantage as an important strength. This strength allows them to intensively foster capital formation to achieve high growth. A policy framework for this strategic approach is investigated in Section 5.3 below.

5.3   A CATCH-UP POLICY FRAMEWORK

5.3.1   Enhancing the Marginal Product of Capital as an Effective Method for Sustaining High Rates of Capital Formation

The distinctive features that have enabled successful Asian economies to achieve sustained high growth through intensive capital accumulation can be identified using an analytical approach. In a market economy, investment can be sustained only if the investors are willing to invest. Therefore, high investment growth for extended periods implies that the economy continues to enhance its attractiveness to investors as its capital stock rapidly increases. The attractiveness of an economy to investors depends on its marginal product of capital and the factors enabling their investments. As presented in Box 5.1, a country can enhance its attractiveness to investors to sustain a high rate of capital accumulation over extended periods using the following three primary channels:

1.   Boosting total factor productivity;
2.   Fostering human capital development, which increases labor quality; and
3.   Reducing the costs of investment.

The paragraphs below elaborate the details of the policy issues for promoting capital investment through these three channels.

1.   Boosting total factor productivity growth

Total factor productivity (TFP) growth is essential for sustained long-term growth. However, TFP does not have to account for the lion's share of the economic growth, especially in the countries with intensive factor accumulation. The case of successful Asian economies indicates that TFP may not account for a large share of the growth, but sustaining TFP growth is important for a market economy to remain attractive to investors as they intensively mobilize factor inputs to achieve rapid growth. In fact, Young (1995) noted that the TFP growth rates observed for the four Asian Tiger economies were on par with the historical performance of many of the OECD countries, although their growth rates for capital and labor inputs were much higher. The secret of successful Asian economies, therefore, lies not in achieving high TFP growth but in sustaining reasonable TFP growth despite the intensive mobilization of factor inputs over extended periods.

The Asian growth model is fundamentally different from the investment-driven model that was previously adopted by the former socialist countries, which can be referred to as the Soviet model, in three aspects: openness,

BOX 5.1   THE FACTORS UNDERLYING THE INTENSITY OF CAPITAL INVESTMENT

Let us start with the Cobb–Douglas aggregate production function, introduced in Weil (2009, p. 174):

$$Y = AK^{\alpha} (hL)^{1-\alpha} \tag{1}$$

where Y, the gross domestic product GDP, is a function of the total factor productivity A, the capital input K, the number of workers L and labor quality h. Parameter α $(0 < \alpha < 1)$ is the share of capital income in national output.

The marginal product of capital (MPK), therefore, can be expressed as

$$MPK = \frac{\partial Y}{\partial K} = A\alpha k^{\alpha-1}(hL)^{1-\alpha} = \alpha . A. \left(\frac{h}{(K/L)}\right)^{1-\alpha} \tag{2}$$

Under perfect competitive conditions, the MPK is equal to the gross return rate of capital. Therefore, increasing MPK is an effective way to make capital investment more attractive. As indicated in Equation (2), a country can increase its MPK through two primary channels:

- Boosting the total factor productivity A and
- Improving labor quality h by fostering human capital development.

In addition, Equation (2) indicates that an economy with a lower capital stock per worker (K/L) has a higher MPK, all else being equal. This relationship suggests that a lower-income country tends to be more attractive to investors if it is on par with other economies in the region on other key factors. In fact, Caselli and Feyrer (2007), examining a large sample of economies, showed that the MPK is much higher on average in poor countries. However, they also pointed out that the net return rate on investment in these economies may not be attractive because their costs of investment are too high. Therefore, reducing the cost of investment is an effective method, especially in developing economies, to foster productive capital investment.

market mechanisms, and private sector. The Asian growth model embraced openness using export-led growth strategies while heavily relying on market forces and the non-government sectors for the efficient allocation of resources and the stimulation of structural change. In contrast, the Soviet model follows import-substitution strategies, while resource allocations totally depend on the government's decisions and the state-owned sector.

TFP growth, which is the part of output growth that is unexplained by the growth in inputs (Hornstein and Krusell, 1996), can come from various sources. These sources can be grouped into three categories: technological progress (Romer, 1990; Grossman and Helpman, 1991; Aghion and Howitt, 1992, 1998), externalities (Romer, 1986; Lucas, 1988; Grossman and Helpman, 1994), and other efficiency improvements.

Technological progress is driven by the application of new technology that allows the producer to produce more output per unit of combined inputs. Technological progress depends on innovation and the adoption of new technology. Developing economies, which are distant from the world technology frontier, possess the 'backwardness' advantage (Gerschenkron, 1962). This advantage allows the developing countries to benefit from the technologies, methods of production, and management techniques that have been developed by advanced countries. There are a number of factors that determine how much a developing country can benefit from its 'backwardness' advantage, which include, among others, human capital, infrastructure, openness, governance quality, innovation capacity, and the distance from the world technology frontier.[2] In addition, Coe and Helpman (1995) found that a country's TFP growth also benefits from R&D of its key trade partners.

Externalities imply that when individuals and firms make a new investment, which could be in physical capital, human capital, or R&D, they inadvertently make the similar investments by others more profitable (Grossman and Helpman, 1994). Such spillovers can help boost and sustain high rates of investment for extended periods. This relationship suggests the important role of the government in encouraging investors to make pioneering investments, not only in physical capital, but also in learning and in the production of knowledge.

The other sources of efficiency improvements, which are not directly driven by technology progress or externalities, include the reduction of transaction costs,[3] better decisions in resource allocation, the shift of

---

[2] For example, see Verspagen (1991), Coe and Helpman (1995), Edwards (1998), and Kneller (2005).

[3] Examples of these costs include bribery, red tape, and the deficient supply of public goods.

resources from less efficient to more efficient users (firms, sectors, and locations), an increase in economies of scale, better management at the firm level, and the more vigorous formation of clusters. For an economy to achieve these efficiency improvements, a number of key factors need to be in place. Among these factors, an effective government and human capital play critical roles.

2. Fostering human capital formation

Fostering human capital formation, which increases labor quality, is also an effective way to raise the marginal product of capital and hence to encourage investors to invest. This strategy requires a special effort to establish a high quality educational system that ultimately links to scientific and technological development in the world economy. These efforts range from achieving universal literacy to producing a skilled labor force by upgrading the secondary and vocational educational systems to enhancing the country's innovation capacity by building a strong network of universities and research institutes.

In addition, it is worth noting that the business sector and labor market reforms also play an important role in improving labor quality. Businesses can help workers to improve their skills through on-the-job training and by cooperating with vocational schools and universities to make their training programs more effective at meeting the demand of the job market. Workers also need an efficient labor market so that they can find jobs that match their skills, which is important to allowing them to realize their 'labor quality' potential.

3. Reducing the costs of investment

As presented in Box 5.1, the marginal product of capital in developing countries is high, but the return rates in many of these economies are unattractive because of their high cost of investment (Caselli and Feyrer, 2007). Therefore, reducing the cost of investment is a highly effective way for a developing economy to foster capital investment. The costs of investment not only include finance-related factors such as financing costs or the price of capital goods but also include the obstacles that affect the feasibility and profitability of investment projects such as poor infrastructure conditions, red tape, and macroeconomic instability.

5.3.2 A Strategic Policy Framework for Sustaining High Rates of Capital Formation

The aforementioned discussion suggests a strategic policy framework to allow a low-income country to achieve sustained high economic growth through intensive capital formation. The core concept of this framework is to maintain simultaneously an attractive marginal product of capital and a high rate of capital mobilization. This framework allows lower income countries to foster their growth by effectively exploiting their 'backwardness' and low capital stock per capita advantages. This framework consists of a number of policy measures along three strategic directions:

- Exploiting the 'backwardness' advantage;
- Upgrading the absorptive capability; and
- Creating favorable conditions for investment, structural change, and efficiency improvements with a special focus on reducing the costs of investment and boosting efficiency.

The framework for achieving sustained high economic growth through intensive capital formation is summarized in Table 5.2.

Exploiting the 'backwardness' advantage
'Backwardness' is a significant advantage possessed by developing countries. The countries with greater distance to the world technology frontier have a stronger potential for boosting productivity growth; that is, a country tends to catch up faster if it is initially more behind (Abramovitz, 1986).

A developing country can exploit its 'backwardness' advantage by 'fast following' and/or 'leapfrogging.' With the 'fast following' strategy, the country can quickly learn and adopt ideas, technologies, and methods that are already available in advanced countries, without bearing the costs of the initial development and experimentation. With the 'leapfrogging' strategy, the country can leapfrog into the latest generation of technologies while avoiding the 'legacy' problem of having too many assets locked up in earlier generations of obsolete technologies (Wong, 2002).

Exploiting the 'backwardness advantage' allows the country to reap the full benefit of its distance from the world technology frontier to speed up its technological progress and, hence sustain a high marginal product of capital. In this strategic direction, the country needs to proactively liberalize its economy and embrace openness, which exposes the country's businesses to international competition, global markets, and world technologies. With this policy approach, the government encourages, forces, and enables businesses to learn, adapt, and upgrade to enhance their competitiveness. The policy measures in this direction focus on market liberalization, strengthening market forces, and embracing globalization, to promote exports, attract FDI, and foster technology and know-how transfer.

Table 5.2   *Achieving high economic growth through rapid capital*
accumulation: a strategic policy framework

Strategic direction	Policy focus
1. *Exploiting the* *'backwardness'* *advantage*	• Opening the economy up to the world and embracing globalization • Attracting FDI and deepening the linkages of the FDI sector with domestic businesses • Importing technologies and diffusing knowledge

2. *Upgrading the* *absorptive* *capability*	• Fostering human capital formation
	  ○ Educational system
	  ○ Health
	  ○ Attracting talent
	• Building innovation capacity
	  ○ R&D expenditure
	  ○ R&D labor force
	  ○ Innovation productivity
	• Strengthening national learning capabilities
	  ○ Competencies acquisition
	  ○ Experimentation
	  ○ Benchmarking against the best and peers
	  ○ Continuous improvement

3. *Creating favorable* *conditions for* *investment,* *structural change* *and efficiency* *improvements*	• Building good governance
	  ○ Macroeconomic stability
	  ○ Government effectiveness and regulatory quality
	  ○ Control of corruption
	• Improving the business environment
	  ○ The facilitation of business start-ups
	  ○ Infrastructure modernization
	  ○ The development of the banking system and the financial markets
	• Fostering structural change and efficiency improvements
	  ○ Reforms that foster structural change
	  ○ Effective urbanization strategy
	  ○ Scale economies and cluster formation

Upgrading the absorptive capability

Abramovitz (1986) argued that the backwardness of a developing country is not usually a mere accident; rather, it is due to some structural deficiencies in the country's social capability. The vast disparity among countries in their adoption of improved technology, the import of new ideas, and the diffusion of knowledge as observed by Prescott (1998) implies the large variation in their absorptive capability. The absorptive capability of a country can be seen as its commitment and competence in searching for, learning, and internalizing new ideas, knowledge, and technologies to generate new value and to strengthen its competitiveness.[4] Upgrading the absorptive capability, therefore, is a fundamental way for a developing country to more effectively exploit its 'backwardness' advantage and hence foster its growth.

A country can strategically upgrade its absorptive capability through three policy approaches: promoting human capital formation, building innovation capacity, and strengthening national learning capabilities. These efforts should particularly focus on two locomotives of growth: companies and cities.. Promoting human capital formation focuses on establishing a high quality educational system with strong links to the scientific and technological developments in the world economy. In addition, attracting global talent, especially those from the national diaspora, can help speed up the country's human capital formation.

Building innovation capacity requires the following measures, among others:[5]

- Deepening the familiarity of the domestic research institutes and businesses with the world knowledge frontier and technology trends and developing the links between them;
- Strengthening the quantity and quality of the pool of technicians, engineers, and scientists;
- Increasing expenditures on research and development (R&D);
- Enhancing the linkages between research institutes, universities, and the business sector; and
- Fostering competition to force business to succeed through innovation.

Strengthening the national learning capabilities allows a country to leverage its human capital to absorb new knowledge more effectively and vigorously. This endeavor can be conducted by every organization (be it a government agency, a business, or a research institute) through four channels:[6]

---

[4]   Rogers (2004, p. 579) considered the absorptive capability to have three components: 'accessibility to overseas technology, learning ability, and the incentives or barriers to implementing new technologies.'

[5]   For a comprehensive discussion on the determinants of national innovative capacity, see Stern et al. (2000). Fagerberg and Srholec (2008) found strong links between improvements in the national innovation system and governance quality and a country's catch-up performance.

[6]   See Yeung et al. (1999) for a rich discussion on learning capability.

- Competencies acquisition: the organization acquires new competencies, especially through recruitment and investment in training and development.
- Experimentation: through this channel, the organization learns by trying pilot policies and conducting experiments to test whether a significant change in policy or in the way of doing things works.
- Benchmarking: through this channel, the organization identifies the best practices around the world to upgrade its competence and enhance its performance.
- Continuous improvement: through this channel, the organization focuses on learning from review, reflection, and its own mistakes and failures, with a strong commitment to excellence.

Creating favorable conditions for investment, structural change, and efficiency improvements

These policy measures focus on reducing the costs of investment and creating business conditions that increase the country's profitability. These policy measures can be classified into three approaches: building good governance, improving the business environment, and enhancing the economy's efficiency.

Good governance plays a crucial role in inducing productive behavior of businesses and people. The quality of governance determines whether businesses and people invest or speculate, innovate or cheat, strive for efficiency improvements or opt for rent seeking; and how far they can go in each of these two opposite directions. In particular, building good governance helps to minimize the government-induced uncertainty and corrupt practices that discourage businesses from making long-term investments. The policy priorities along this approach include maintaining macroeconomic stability, enhancing government effectiveness and regulatory quality, and strengthening the control of corruption.

The success of the government in these endeavors critically depends on its commitment to its market principles, vision of the future, and learning capabilities.

Improving the business environment helps businesses to reduce the costs of doing business and to enhance competitiveness. The priorities along this policy approach include facilitating business start-ups, upgrading infrastructure, and strengthening the banking system and financial markets.

The third policy approach—fostering structural change and efficiency improvements—is involved with policy initiatives and reforms that enable and push for continual and vigorous structural change and efficiency

improvements.[7] In this approach, fostering competition, implementat-
ing effective urbanization strategies, and promoting scale economies
and cluster formation should be among the top priorities.[8] The reforms
that foster structural change enable, stimulate, and facilitate resources
to shift from lower- to higher-value activities and from lower- to higher-
productivity users. This approach is consistent with the new structural
economics argued by Lin (2012), which considers driving structural change
as a strategic priority for policy to promote long-term economic development. Implementing effective urbanization strategies plays an important
role in ensuring that the country's rapid pace of urbanization strengthens,
not weakens, the efficiency and vibrancy of its cities—the driving force of
economic growth and structural change.[9] Promoting scale economies and
cluster formation[10] involves encouraging specialization, deepening the
integration of markets (domestically, regionally, and globally), fostering
the agglomeration of production, and stimulating business collaboration.

It is important to note that this strategic policy framework must be
designed and implemented by the government as a core component of its
development strategy, of which the effectiveness depends on three crucial
factors: concept, commitment, and competence. The concept factor implies
the soundness in the belief of the government in the prevailing power of
market forces in driving economic efficiency, the critical role of government
in overcoming market failure and enabling the achievement of synergistic
values through coordination, the fundamental function of good governance
in encouraging productive behaviors of all players in the society, and the
great benefits a country can reap from embracing globalization with a wise
strategic positioning in the world economy. The commitment factor is associated with the vision and devotion of the country's leaders in creating its
future. The competence factor is determined not only by the competence of
government officials in terms of human resources, but also by the organizational structure and institutional settings, which enable government officials
and government agencies to achieve their highest possible performance.

[7] Hausmann et al. (2005), analysing the growth acceleration patterns of 110 countries over 36 years (1957–1992), found that sustained acceleration in economic growth is stimulated by a major reform in the government's economic policy.

[8] Fagerberg (2000) showed that countries that managed to reallocate their resources towards most technologically progressive industry in a given period experienced higher productivity growth than other countries.

[9] Gill and Kharas (2007) mentioned that the cities in East Asia generate approximately three-quarters of the annual output, and much of this is concentrated in major cities. However, rapid but poorly managed urbanization in a country can weaken the vibrancy and efficiency of its cities, which in East Asia are plagued by pollution, traffic congestion, and the inefficient use of land.

[10] For an in-depth discussion on government policy to promote cluster formation, see Porter (1998, 2007) and Roelandt and Hertog (1999).

5.4 THE CATCH-UP POLICY FRAMEWORK IN ACTION: ILLUSTRATIVE EVIDENCE FROM CHINA AND INDIA DURING 1990–2010

This section examines the experience of China and India, the two fastest-growing economies of Developing Asia, during 1990–2010 to see how the Catch-up Policy framework presented in Section 5.3 can be used to explain the reform efforts and achievements of these two giant economies. This exercise will also help us better understand the challenges that these two countries as well as other fast-growing economies must effectively address to sustain their outstanding performance in the decade to come.

5.4.1 Exploiting the 'Backwardness' Advantage

The period of 1990–2010 witnessed notable efforts by China and India to exploit their 'backwardness' advantage. Liberalizing trade, embracing openness, and importing technologies and know-how are salient indicators of these efforts.

Trade liberalization and openness

Economic reforms were launched in China in 1978 and in India in 1991. One of the main features of the reforms in the two countries is their fundamental shift in economic strategy, from import substitution to an outward orientation. Below are selected pieces of evidence on the two countries' efforts in this direction, which include liberalizing the economy, embracing international trade, and attracting foreign direct investment.

China initiated its open-door policy in 1979 from a closed economic system characterized by three strict restrictions (Wei, 1995): (1) international trade was conducted only by monopolized state-owned companies; (2) the domestic prices of goods (including tradable goods) were determined by the government without links to world prices; and (3) foreign exchange was strictly controlled by the government, which retained all foreign exchange revenues from exports. Furthermore, foreign investment was not allowed, while foreign technology imports were strictly controlled in favor of accumulating indigenous experience (Jaggi et al., 1996).

Since its open-door policy launched in 1979, China has addressed these restrictions with decisive and innovative measures that have paved the way for the economy to surge in international trade and attracting foreign investment. In particular, a series of special economic zones, opened regions, opened cities, and Economic and Technological Development Zones (ETDZs) were established to stimulate exports and attract FDI

(Table 5.3).[11] In particular, the ETDZs were designated to focus on attracting foreign capital and technologies to promote high-tech industries and exports.

In the 1990s, China's openness was further boosted,[12] marked by the tour of Deng Xiaoping to Southern China in January 1992. The effect of China's greater openness in the 1990s was apparent. The level of FDI flows to China surged to US$156 billion for the period 1991–1996 compared to US$23.3 billion for 1978–1991 (Wong, 2001, Table 1, p. 44).

India's economic reforms, initiated in 1991, addressed the four elements of India's highly regulated economic policy, known as the 'license-permit-quota raj,' which are as follows: restrictions on international trade in the form of tariff and non-tariff barriers on imports; restrictions on both the domestic and foreign private sector; state control of banking and insurance; and public sector monopolies (Das, 2007). India's decisive efforts toward trade liberalization can be seen through its sharp reduction in tariff and non-tariff barriers on the imports of manufactured goods shown in Figure 5.4. The effective rate of protection for manufactured goods decreased notably between 1986–1990 and 1991–1995 and continued to decline from 1991–1995 to 1996–2000 (upper panel). This declining trend was most pronounced for intermediate goods (from 149 per cent in 1986–1990 to 88 per cent in 1991–1995 to 40 per cent in 1996–2000) and capital goods (from 112 to 81 to 49 per cent, respectively). At the same time, the non-tariff barriers on manufactured goods were substantially lowered for consumer goods as well as for intermediate and capital goods (lower panel).

China and India's solid progress on trade liberation and openness during 1990–2010 can also be seen from cross-country comparable measures. On trade liberalization, the two countries substantially improved their trade freedom scores over time as tracked by the World Heritage Foundation[13] (Figure 5.5). In 2010, the trade freedom scores of the two countries were approximately 70, a high level of trade freedom from a global perspective.

---

[11]   These zones, regions, provinces, and cities received favorable development policies from the central government in terms of tax incentives, simplified administrative procedures, and infrastructure investment support (Chen et al., 2008).

[12]   In August 1992, 15 more hinterland cities were opened, and then all the major cities across China followed suit (Galbraith and Lu, 2000).

[13]   The trade freedom score, which is among the 10 economic freedom benchmarks, has been constructed on an annual basis by *The Wall Street Journal* and The Heritage Foundation since 1995 for 185 economies around the world. Trade freedom is a composite measure. The trade freedom score of a given economy is computed from its trade-weighted average tariff rate and its non-tariff barriers and is standardized to make it comparable across economies. The score can range from 0 to 100, being higher for an economy with more trade freedom. More details are available at The Heritage Foundation's webpage: http://www.heritage.org/index/.

Table 5.3   Chronology of China's open-door policy initiatives

Year of Establishment	Number and type of opened zones	Location
1979/1980	Four Special Economic Zones	Shenzhen, Zhuhai, Shantou, and Xiamen
1982	Five Open Regions	The Yangtze River Delta, Zhu River Delta, Fujian, Liaoning, and Shandong
1984	14 Open Coastal Cities	Liaoning, Hebei, Tianjin, Shandong, Jiangsu, Shanghai, Zhejiang, Fujian, Guangdong and Guangxi
	10 Economic and Technological Development Zones (ETDZs)	Liaoning, Hebei, Tianjin, Shandong, Jiangsu, Zhejiang and Guangdong
1985	1 ETDZ	Fujian
	3 Coastal Open Economic Zones in Pearl river delta, Yangtze river delta and Fujian	Pearl river delta, Yangtze river delta and Fujian
1986	2 ETDZs	Shanghai
1988	Open Coastal Belt	Liaoning, Shandong, Guangxi and Hebei
	Hainan Special Economic Zone	Hainan
	1 ETDZ	Shanghai
1990	Pudong New Area	Shanghai
1992	13 bonded areas in major coastal port cities	Tianjin, Guangdong, Liaoning, Shandong, Jiangsu, Zhejiang, Fujian and Hainan
	10 major cities along the Yangtze river	Jiangsu, Anhui, Jiangxi, Hunan, Hubei and Sichuan
	13 Border Economic Cooperation Zones	Jilin, Heilongjiang, Inner Mongolia, Xinjiang, Yunnan and Guangxi
	All capital cities of inland provinces and autonomous regions	Fujian, Liaoning, Jiangsu, Shandong and Zhejiang
	5 ETDZs	
1993	12 ETDZs	Anhui, Guangdong, Heilongjiang, Hubei, Liaoning, Sichuan, Fujian, Jilin and Zhejiang
1994	2 ETDZs	Beijing and Xinjiang

Sources: Galbraith and Lu (2000); Bajpai (2004, Appendix 1).

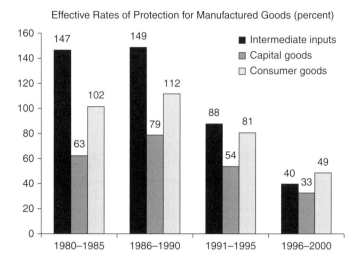

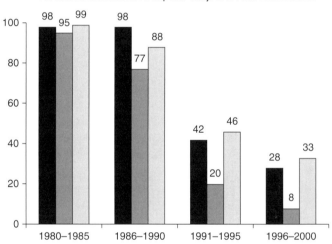

Source: Das (2007).

Figure 5.4   India's trade liberalization in the 1990s: trends on tariff and non-tariff barriers on manufactured goods

On international trade, both China and India recorded remarkable growth. As presented in Chapter 3, the exports of goods and services grew at 17.3 per cent for China and 14.1 per cent for India over 1990–2010, compared to 7.5 per cent for the world average (Table 3.5). At the same

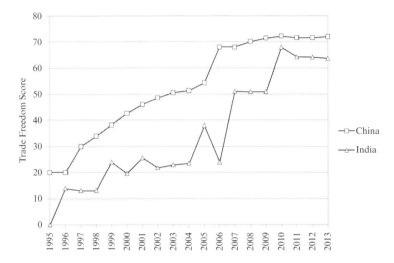

Note: Data for the years prior to 1995 is not available.

Source: World Heritage Foundation.

Figure 5.5   China and India's progress on trade freedom, 1995–2010

time, the imports of goods and services grew at 17.6 per cent for China and 14.1 per cent for India, compared to 7.3 per cent for the world average (Table 3.6). Furthermore, the two countries exhibited a solid upward trend on openness[14] during 1990–2010 (Figure 5.6), which recognizes the notable deepening of their integration into the world economy over the period.

Both China and India made outstanding achievements in attracting foreign direct investment (FDI). As presented in Chapter 3, India's FDI stock grew at 27 per cent over 1990–2010, while this rate was 18.1 per cent for China. As a result, from 1990 to 2010, the FDI stock increased almost 120 times for India and 28 times for China, compared to six times for the US (Figure 5.7, upper panel). It is also worth noting that the FDI capital stocks of India and China relative to the US increased significantly over 1990–2010, with a notable acceleration in the late 2000s. Compared to the US level, the FDI capital stock rose from 4 per cent in 1990 to 16.8 per cent in 2010 for China and from a negligible fraction to almost 6 per cent over the same period for India (Figure 5.7, lower panel).

---

[14]   The total trade (exports plus imports) to GDP ratio is a widely used measure of openness.

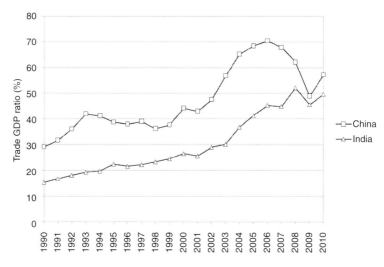

Source: WDI.

Figure 5.6   *Openness to international trade: China and India, 1990–2010*

The import of technology and know-how
The import of technology and know-how is an important channel through which developing countries can exploit their 'backwardness' advantage and make their rapid capital accumulation more productive and sustainable. Grossman and Helpman (1991), Edwards (1992, 1998), Romer (1992, 1993), and Barro and Sala-i-Martin (1995) showed that the countries with more openness to the world have a greater ability to achieve higher growth by absorbing technological advances from developed nations. A country that encourages international knowledge diffusion and the adoption of new technologies and promotes the trade of goods and FDI reaps greater benefits from its outward orientation strategy.

The efforts of China and India, especially those of China, on the import of technology and know-how during 1990–2010 were substantial. As shown in Figure 5.8, their payments on royalty and license fees as a percentage of GDP display a robust upward trend. In particular, China surpassed the US on this measure in most years during the 2000s.

The stronger performance of China relative to India in exploiting the 'backwardness' advantage can be explained in part by China's deeper business and social linkages with the more advanced economies in East Asia, especially Hong Kong and Taiwan. Rogers (2004) argued that these linkages greatly enhance China's access to advanced technologies and know-how. The remarkable success of Shenzhen, one of China's major

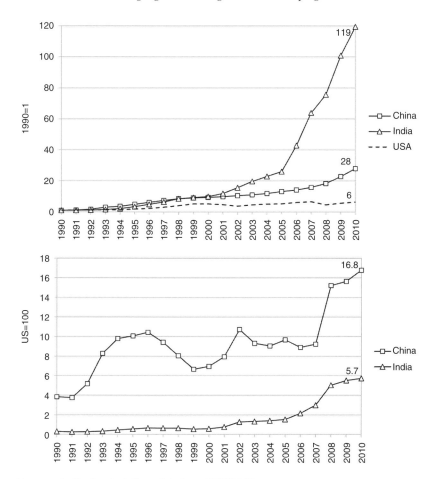

Source: Author's calculations; data from UNCTAD.

Figure 5.7   Inward FDI stock, 1990–2010: China and India versus the US

special economic zones, can serve as a vivid example of the benefits China has realized from these linkages in exploiting its 'backwardness' advantage. Shenzhen was transformed in 1980 from a fishing village of 30,000 people into a special economic zone. Shenzhen's only strategic advantage is its location across a narrow river from Hong Kong. After 30 years since its establishment, Shenzhen has transformed itself into one of China's major economic hubs with a population of over 10 million.[15] The city,

---

[15]   As pointed out by Wei (2000), Shenzhen can serve as an excellent example that, with

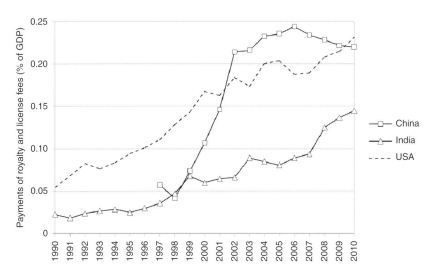

Source: WDI.

*Figure 5.8   Import of technology and know-how, 1990–2010: China and
                India versus the US*

with export revenues exceeding US$200 billion in 2010, accounts for over
10 per cent of China's total exports; Shenzhen was also ranked first in
Forbes' 2011 list of China's innovative cities.[16]

5.4.2 Upgrading the Absorptive Capability

As shown in Table 5.2, the policy efforts to upgrade absorptive capability
can be seen in three areas: fostering human capital formation, building
innovation capacity, and strengthening learning capabilities. This subsection examines the progress of China and India in these three areas.

Fostering human capital formation
China and India significantly improved the quality of their human
capital during 1990–2010, which can be captured in two key areas: education and health. As shown in Figure 5.9, the education index (upper
panel) and the health index (lower panel) of the two countries show a

---

deliberate policies and a pro-competition approach, the government can speed up the acquisition of technology, foster learning, and promote structural transformation.
[16] From the official website of the Shenzhen government: http://english.sz.gov.cn/
economy/, accessed March 20, 2013.

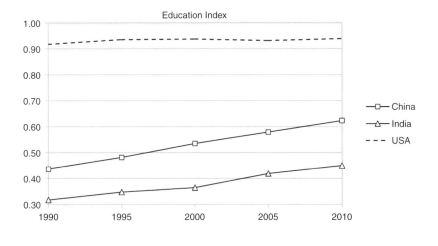

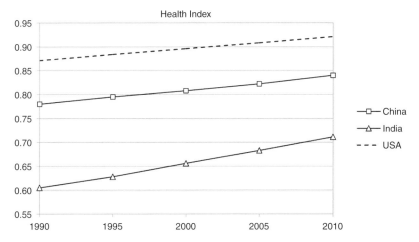

Source: UNDP.

Figure 5.9   *Human capital development, 1990–2010: China and India*
            versus the US

solid upwards trend. Moreover, the two countries noticeably narrowed their gap with the US on these two measures during 1990–2010. China sustained its lead over India on both the education and the health indexes throughout 1990–2010. This lead implies that China was in a more competitive position than India in leveraging its absorptive capacity for growth.

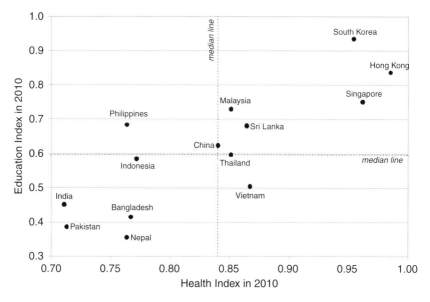

Source: UNDP.

Figure 5.10   Developing Asia economies and human capital, 2010

In addition, it should be noted that the position of India remained very moderate in 2010 on human capital in comparison to other Developing Asia economies. As shown in Figure 5.10, India was below all of the East Asian economies on both education and health measures. This result suggests that India will need to make more vigorous efforts to foster its human capital development to upgrade its absorptive capability and sustain its high economic growth in the decades to come.

Attracting global talent, especially from the diaspora, is one highly effective measure to speed human capital formation. China has embraced this approach through major initiatives (see Box 5.2), which can be characterized by the following features:

- Strategic approach: clear purpose; good knowledge of targeted candidates; and concerted efforts (between governments, businesses, and universities).
- Competition and competitive offerings: The hunt for global talent is vibrant across all levels of government (national, provincial, and country), types of organization (universities, research institutes, industrial parks), and sectors (state, private). In particular, the local

BOX 5.2   CHINA'S INITIATIVES TO ATTRACT OVERSEAS TALENTS

China has been actively recruiting global talents since the 1990s, particularly targeting overseas Chinese. Earlier programs, such as the Chinese Academy of Sciences' '100-Talents Scheme' and the Ministry of Education's 'Yangtze River Scholar Scheme,' have attracted more than 4,000 researchers in the past 15 years.

The Chinese government, in particular, considers the new migrants, who were born and educated in China and maintain strong cultural, social and family ties with China, as valuable assets for economic development. China has a great advantage in attracting global talents thanks to its large pool of talent formed over the years as more than 1.2 million Chinese had studied abroad by 2007. It is estimated that more than 200,000 Chinese have been working in the developed countries after receiving education there, including 67,000 who have titles equivalent to assistant professor, and 15,000 equivalents to associate or full professor.

Local governments have been very effective in promoting returnee entrepreneurship in high-tech industries such as Internet, IT, communication, media and new energy. By February 2009, China had established more than 110 overseas returnee entrepreneurship incubation centers, with more than 8,000 enterprises and 20,000 returnees.

The success of China in attracting increasingly large flows of return migration has been driven by several key factors. Among them, central government policies and competition among cities, universities, research institutes, and enterprises have provided not only a positive atmosphere but also excellent incentives and competitive schemes for attracting return migration.

The central government policies and initiatives to encourage return migration include the following:

- Organization efforts: the government set up 52 educational bureaus in embassies and consulates in 38 countries with highest concentrations of overseas students, which helped establish over 2,000 Overseas Students Associations and over 300 professional associations for overseas scholars.

These organizational efforts deepen the link between overseas scholars and the opportunities at home.

- Financial policies: the government introduced numer-
ous programs to give returnees financial support if they
return. Among the examples are the 'Seed Fund for
Returned Overseas Scholars' (1990), the 'Cross-Century
Outstanding Personnel Training Program' (1991), the
'National Science Fund for Distinguished Young Scholars'
(1994), and 'The One Hundred, One Thousand, and Ten
Thousand Program' (1995). The government also provided
additional funding for leading universities and the Chinese
Academy of Science to attract global talents.
- Other efforts: they range from improving information flow
(through magazines, websites, and conferences) to easing
the process of returning.

China launched the 'One Thousand Talents Scheme' in
December 2008 to accelerate its transition from a manufacturing
hub to a world leader in innovation. The scheme plans to recruit
2,000 top talents in the next 5–10 years and will consider any
nationality. This scheme has the following salient features:

1. Compared to the previous programs, the new scheme not
only sets the bar higher, but also casts the net wider. It
targets three types of talent: (1) scholars with an academic
title equivalent to professor in world-class universities; (2)
senior managing staff in well-known multinational corpora-
tions and banks; and (3) those who have developed technologies and patents or established their own business
abroad.
2. National innovation projects and key scientific sub-
jects and laboratories will benefit from this scheme, as
they did from earlier talent schemes. However, central
government-owned enterprises, banks, and high-tech
parks will join them for the first time in the global hunt for
top talents.
3. By April 2009, the scheme had shown early signs of
success, attracting the first batch of 96 scientists and 26
entrepreneurs to China, with more than 80 holding foreign
passports, and 4 of non-Chinese origin.

4. While the central government has stepped up efforts to lure top-notch talents, local governments are actively following suit. They are more interested in attracting entrepreneurs, especially those in high-tech industries such as Internet, IT, communication, media and new energy.
5. There are also inter-government efforts to create trans-local networks for returnee entrepreneurship. Through the initiative of different city governments, the Association of China Returnee Entrepreneurship Parks was formed to serve high-tech parks in Beijing, Nanjing, Shanghai, Shenzhen, and some other cities.
6. China's effort to attract global top talents is helped by a number of factors. China is now able to offer globally competitive salaries and promising career prospects, and its research and social environment has improved considerably over the years. Working and living in cities like Beijing and Shanghai has become a less daunting challenge for foreign talents and their families.
7. The large number of new migrants, who left China in the reform era for the purpose of studying and working in other countries and totaled over 6 million by 2008, form a tremendous pool for China's talent schemes. These well-educated new migrants maintain strong cultural, social and family ties with China.
8. Apart from the pull factors, some push factors also work to the advantage of China. The current global financial crisis has resulted in a cut back in research programs in some developed countries whereas China continues to increase spending on science and technology.
9. So far talents of ethnic Chinese origin have been recruited to Chinese universities, research institutions, state-owned enterprises and banks, and high-tech parks. However, foreign talents of non-Chinese origin have begun to show greater interest in working in China. While starting late, large cities such as Beijing and Shanghai are taking bold steps to compete with more internationalized Singapore and Hong Kong for global top talents.

Sources: Zhao and Zhu (2009) and Zweig (2006).

governments have been very effective at attracting talents by using innovative support schemes.
• Importing talents: the overseas Chinese have been the main source of talents recruited into China, but the recruitment of non-Chinese foreign talents has shown signs of increasing.

Building innovation capacity

The innovation efforts of a country can be revealed by its R&D expenditure, the number of its researchers, and the research productivity as captured by the number of patents granted. On these three indicators, China showed a strong catching-up performance, while India also made notable progress.

R&D expenditure as a percentage of GDP increased substantially for China and slightly for India over the past 20 years. During 1996–2009, the years for which data is available, R&D expenditure as a percentage of GDP nearly tripled from 0.57 per cent in 1996 to 1.7 per cent in 2009 for China, while it increased from 0.63 per cent in 1996 to almost 0.8 per cent in 2007 for India[17] (Figure 5.11). It should be noted that China

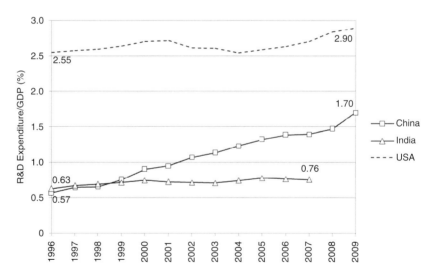

Source: UNESCO Institute for Statistics.

Figure 5.11   R&D expenditure as percentage of GDP, 1996–2009: China and India versus the US

[17]   Data for India in 2008 and 2009 is not available.

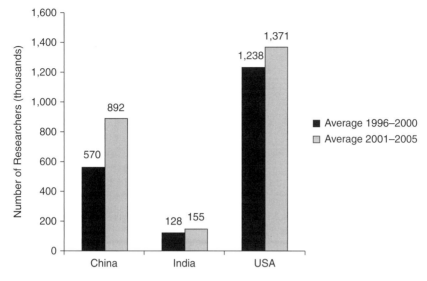

Source: UNESCO Institute for Statistics.

Figure 5.12   Increase in the number of researchers: China and India versus the US

surpassed India on this measure in 1999 and widened its lead rapidly in the 2000s, while it markedly narrowed its gap with the US over this period.

The number of researchers, to some extent, can be used as a proxy for the R&D labor force, which is the core of the research capacity of a nation. This number increased rapidly for China and moderately for India during their reform periods. Between the two periods for which data is available, 1996–2000 and 2001–2005, the average number of researchers increased by over 50 per cent for China from 570,000 in 1996–2000 to 892,000 in 2001–2005, and by approximately 20 per cent for India from 128,000 to 155,000 (Figure 5.12). It is worth noting that the number of researchers in China was not too far below that of the US (approximately 65 per cent in 2001–2005). Moreover, at its current rapid growth rate, China could well exceed the US on this measure soon. This finding means that if China can raise the quality of its researcher pool accordingly, it will possess a mighty innovation capacity and absorptive capability that few nations can match, which will allow China to continue to achieve robust economic growth for many years ahead.

The number of patents can be used as a measure for the productivity of a country's innovation capacity. There are two statistics on this

Table 5.4   Patents granted: China and India versus the world

	Patents Granted in the US			Patents Granted Locally		
	Growth	Share in World		Growth	Share in World	
	1995–2010	1995	2010	1995–2010	1995	2010
World	**5.3%**	**100**	**100**	**5.3%**	**100**	**100**
Developing Asia*	16.3%	1.7	7.6	15.9%	6.4	26.8
China	28.5%	0.1	1.2	27.8%	0.9	16.0
India	25.4%	0.04	0.5	10.4%	0.4	0.8
Industrialized Economies	4.6%	96.4	88.0	3.9%	78.8	64.3
Rest of Word (ROW)	11.5%	1.9	4.4	1.8%	14.8	8.9

Note: * Data is not available for Bangladesh, Cambodia, Indonesia, Nepal, Pakistan, Sri Lanka, Taiwan, and Vietnam for patents granted in the US; and for Cambodia, Indonesia, Nepal and Taiwan for patents granted locally. Growth is CAGR.

Source: Author's calculations; data from WIPO statistics database.

measure. One is the number of patents granted in the US, which is internationally comparable and indicates the strength of a country's innovation system. Another statistic is the number of patents granted locally, which, to some extent, reveals the vibrancy of innovation activities within a country. As shown in Table 5.4, China and India far outperformed the world average on the growth of the number of patents granted in the US as well as locally. With regard to the number of patents granted in the US, the average growth rate over 1995–2010, the period for which data is available, was 28.5 per cent for China and 25.4 per cent for India, while it was only 5.3 per cent for the world average and 4.6 per cent for the industrialized group. For the number of patents granted locally, the average growth rate over 1995–2010 was 27.8 per cent for China and 10.4 per cent for India, compared to 5.3 per cent for the world and 3.9 per cent for the industrialized group (Table 5.4). The outstanding growth of China and India on patents granted, although from low bases, suggests that the two countries have made unprecedented efforts to promote innovation activities. It should be noted, however, that China outperformed India on the vibrancy of ordinary innovation activities as indicated by its superior growth in the number of patents granted locally.

Strengthening national learning capabilities
China's efforts to strengthen its national learning capabilities were apparent. The dynamism of China in these efforts, to some degree, was driven by

its national ambition to catch up with the most advanced nations and by the intense competition among its local governments to boost their status and performance.[18] Among the four channels for building national learning capabilities (competencies acquisition, experimentation, benchmarking, and continuous improvement), China's initiatives in competencies acquisition and experimentation were distinctive. While the hunt for global talents as presented in Box 5.2 evidences China's efforts toward competencies acquisition, policy experimentation is a special learning approach embraced by China's government at both the central and the local levels. Heilmann (2008, p. 3), in his study of China's policy experimentation, defined this approach as 'a purposeful and coordinated activity geared to producing novel policy options that are injected into official policymaking and then replicated on a larger scale, or even formally incorporated into national law.' According to his study, this approach, which helps to ensure that the application of a policy concept works well in a given circumstance, enables and encourages the government to innovate to speed up and promote breakthroughs in economic, institutional, and social transformation, while minimizing the financial and political costs. China's policy experimentation ranged from the establishment of special economic zones to the introduction of experimental regulations. During the first two decades of China's economic reforms, over 30 per cent of the government's new regulations were conducted using experimental status (Heilmann, 2008).

5.4.3 Creating Favorable Conditions for Investment, Structural Change, and Efficiency Improvements

The efforts of China and India to create favorable conditions for investment during 1990–2010 can be seen first by their robust performance in fixed investments and domestic savings. As shown in Figure 5.13, fixed investment as a share of GDP soared from 26 per cent in 1990 to 38 per cent in 1993 and then rose to 41 per cent in 2004 and 46 per cent in 2010 for China, while for India, this share showed an improving trend within the 20–25 per cent range during 1990–2005 before jumping to 30 per cent or

---

[18] Attracting FDI, to some extent, reveals a country's effectiveness at strengthening its national learning capabilities. In this endeavor, China exhibits a distinctive performance through its clear national strategy, intense competition among provinces, which enjoy an increasingly high degree of autonomy, and the entrepreneurial spirit of local governments (Taube and Ogutcu, 2002). For India, Bajpai (2004) points out that the lack of decision-making authority at the state government level and the central government's ambiguity in objectives and strategy are among the factors underlying India's lag behind China in attracting FDI.

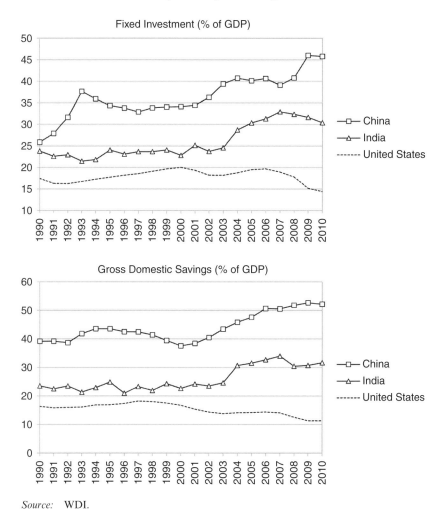

Source: WDI.

*Figure 5.13   Gross domestic savings and fixed investment, 1990–2010:
China and India versus the US*

above since 2005 (upper panel). At the same time, the domestic savings of
the two countries followed their investment patterns. For China, savings
as a share of GDP was as high as 40 per cent during the 1990s and steadily
increased from 40 per cent to 50 per cent during the 2000s, while for India,
this share gradually increased from 20 per cent in 1990 to 30 per cent in
2004 and has been sustained above 30 per cent since then. The notably
higher rates of fixed investment and savings of China relative to India

was probably a factor underlying the stronger performance of China over India during 1990 2010.[19]

It should be noted that China and India were above the US on both fixed investment and savings rates during 1990–2010. Moreover, in the 2000s, these rates were on declining trends for the US,[20] while they were on solid increasing trends for China and India. This result signifies that boosting fixed investment and domestic savings is an important strategy that both China and India have embraced in their catching-up endeavors.

This subsection examines the evidence regarding the efforts of China and India to improve their investment conditions during 1990–2010. As suggested by the strategic policy framework presented in the previous section, this examination exercise will address three policy approaches: building good governance, improving the business environment, and enhancing the economy's efficiency.

Building good governance

China and India have made significant efforts to maintain their macroeconomic stability and improve their government performance during 1990–2010. Using the inflation rate as an indicator of macroeconomic stability, one can see that both countries curbed their average inflation rate below 10 per cent in both the 1990–2000 and 2000–2010 sub-periods (Figure 5.14). Furthermore, for both China and India, the inflation rate was notably lower in the second sub-period, 2000–2010, than in the first sub-period, 1990–2000 (this is indicated by the positions of the two countries well below the 45-degree line in Figure 5.14). China appeared to better manage its macroeconomic stability than India, especially in the second sub-period.

Both China and India also made notable progress in improving their government performance during 1990–2010. This improvement can be captured by two World Bank governance indicators: Government Effectiveness (GE) and Regulatory Quality (RQ).[21] As shown in

---

[19] Srinivasan (2011) noted that thanks to its current notably higher rate of fixed investment, China has far more room than India in boosting economic growth through stimulating domestic consumption.

[20] It is worth noting that Sachs (2012) argued that the US needs a consistent, planned, decade-long boost in public investments in people, technology, and infrastructure to overcome its current economic challenges and prosper in the twenty-first century.

[21] According to Kaufmann et al. (2010), the GE and RQ indicators together reflect the capacity of the government to effectively formulate and implement sound policies. The GE indicator captures perceptions regarding the quality of public services, the quality of the civil service and the degree of its independence from political pressures, the quality of policy formulation and implementation, and the credibility of the government's commitment to

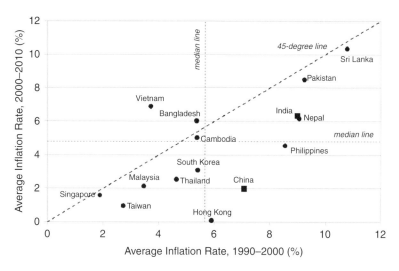

Source: WDI; ADB for Taiwan.

Figure 5.14   *Inflation as an indicator of macroeconomic stability: China and India in 1990–2000 and 2000–2010*

Figure 5.15, the two countries were on a clear upward trend in increasing their performance in both government effectiveness (upper panel) and regulatory quality (lower panel). Note that the measure for these two indicators was the percentile rank, which means that for a given indicator, a country increases its rank only if it improves its performance faster than its peers do. Between the two countries, China was stronger than India in enhancing its government effectiveness and regulatory quality during 1990–2010. It is worth noting that China's progress in enhancing government effectiveness and regulatory quality has been driven by its commitment to transform its economy through market-based mechanisms. For example, Perkins (2001) noted that the mergers and acquisitions process in China has taken on the characteristics of similar processes in market economies.

Although China and India's progress toward improving their government performance was notable, there was also a sign indicating that the two countries' efforts have slowed down in recent years. In fact, the three-year moving averages of the percentile ranks of the two countries on

such policies; the RQ indicator reflects the perceptions of the government's ability to formulate and implement sound policies and regulations that permit and promote private sector development.

Government Effectiveness: Percentile Rank

Regulatory Quality: Percentile Rank

Note: The figure uses the three-year moving average of the annual data to better reveal their trends. The data on the two indicators are available for 1996, 1998, 2000, and on an annual basis from 2002 onward.

Source: World Bank's World Governance Indicators.

Figure 5.15   *China and India and efforts to improve government performance*

government performance and regulatory quality declined in recent years (Figure 5.15).

Regarding the efforts to control corruption, however, there was a sign for concern for both China and India. Their global ranks on this measure were on declining trends in the 2000s (Figure 5.16). The corruption problem and its declining trend were more severe for China than India.

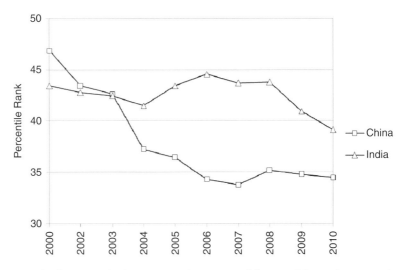

Note: The figure uses the three-year moving average of the annual data to better reveal their trends. The data on the two indicators are available for 1996, 1998, 2000, and on an annual basis from 2002 onward.

Source: World Bank's World Governance Indicators.

Figure 5.16   Control of corruption: China and India in the 2000s

Improving the business environment
The facilitation of business start-ups, which is captured by the time and cost it takes to start up a business, can be used as an indicator of a country's efforts to improve its business environment. China and India have made solid progress on this measure. As shown in Figure 5.17, the time (upper panel) and cost (lower panel) required to start a business in both countries sharply declined during the examined period (from 2004 onwards, the period for which data are available).

Upgrading the infrastructure is one important aspect of improving the business environment. It is difficult, however, to obtain comparable cross-country data to measure this progress. Fortunately, the pattern of information and communication technology (ICT) penetration can elucidate this process. This approach examines three ICT penetration indicators, mobile phone, Internet usage, and broadband, during 1990–2010 to capture, to some extent, the efforts of China and India to modernize their infrastructure during this period.

For mobile phone penetration, China and India rapidly increased their penetration rate from zero in 1990 to 65 per cent in 2010 (Figure 5.18, upper panel). The acceleration of India on the pace of penetration during

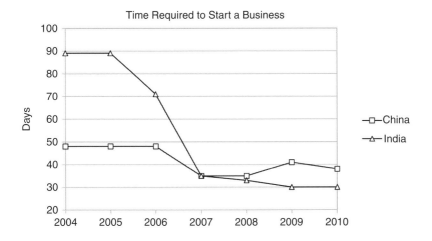

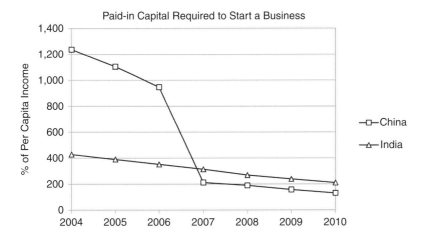

Source: World Bank's Doing Business database.

Figure 5.17   China's and India's performance on facilitating business start-ups

2005–2010 was phenomenal, and it allowed India to catch up with China on this measure in 2010.

Regarding Internet penetration, the penetration rate for China soared from zero in 1990 to 35 per cent in 2010 and increased from nil to 8 per cent for India (Figure 5.18, middle panel). Similarly, the rate of broadband penetration rose for China from nil in 2000 to over 9 per cent in

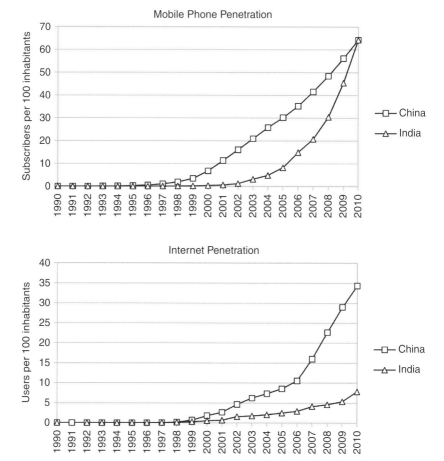

Source: WDI.

Figure 5.18   Infrastructure modernization: ICT penetration, 1990–2010

2010 and increased from nil to 1 per cent for India over the same period
(Figure 5.18, lower panel).

The discussion above supports the view that both China and India have
made significant progress in upgrading their infrastructure during 1990–
2010. However, China appears to have made greater efforts and advanced
far more than India in this endeavor.

The development of the banking sector and the financial markets
plays an important role in improving the business environment to foster
investment and economic growth. The progress of a country on this

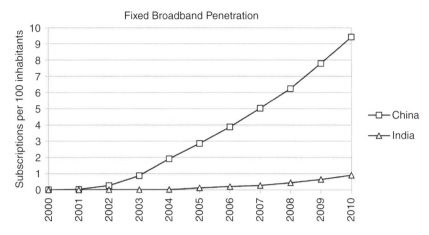

Figure 5.18   (continued)

dimension can be captured by two indicators provided by the World Bank: (1) domestic credit provided by the banking sector (as a percentage of GDP), which signifies the economy's financial depth; and (2) domestic credits to the private sector (as a percentage of GDP), which reflects the accessibility of the country's private sector to credits. As shown in Figure 5.19, both China and India made notable progress on these two indicators. Over 1990–2010, the domestic credit provided by the banking sector as a percentage of GDP rose by more than 50 percentage points, from 90 per cent in 1990 to over 140 per cent in 2010 for China; and by more than 20 percentage points, from 50 per cent to over 70 per cent, for India (Figure 5.19, upper panel). At the same time, domestic credits to the private sector as a percentage of GDP for China increased by over 40 percentage points, from below 90 per cent in 1990 to 130 per cent in 2010; and for India by approximately 30 percentage points, from 20 to 50 per cent (Figure 5.19, lower panel).

Fostering structural change and efficiency improvements
The outstanding economic growth of China and India during 1990–2010 was associated with their rapid structural change and efficiency improvements—the important dynamics that enhance their absorptive capability. One visible indicator of this process is the rapid reallocation of labor from agriculture to other sectors that have higher productivity, such as manufacturing and services.

Table 5.5 provides information on the employment shares and average labor productivity (ALP) of the key sectors of China and India during

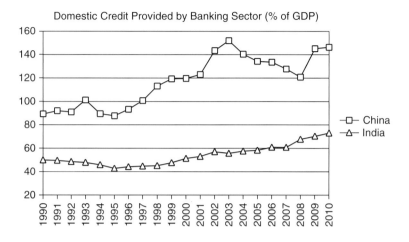

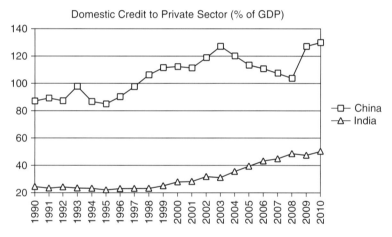

Source: WDI.

Figure 5.19   Development of the banking sector and the private sector's access to finance: China and India, 1990–2010

1990–2010. It shows that the employment share of the agriculture sector in the economy was reduced for China by 23.5 percentage points, from 60.1 per cent in 1990 to 36.6 per cent in 2010 for China; while it decreased for India over the same period by 14.8 percentage points, from 67.5 to 52.7 per cent (Table 5.5).

   It is interesting to note the sharp contrast between China and India in

Table 5.5   Reallocation of resources from agriculture to other sectors, 1990–2010

Sector	Employment Share in the Economy (Economy = 100)						Relative ALP (Economy = 100)	
	China			India			China	India
	1990	2010	Change 1990–2010	1990	2010	Change 1990–2010	Average 1990–2010	Average 1990–2010
	(1)	(2)	(3) = (2)–(1)	(4)	(5)	(6) = (5)–(4)	(7)	(8)
Economy	**100**	**100**	**0**	**100**	**100**	**0**	**100**	**100**
Agriculture	60.1	36.6	–23.5	67.5	52.7	–14.8	32.4	36.8
Manufacturing	15.1	17.9	2.8	10.2	21.8	11.5	154.3	95.0
Services	18.5	34.3	15.8	19.6	22.6	3.0	142.7	236.0
Others	6.3	11.2	4.9	2.6	2.9	0.3	142.1	426.2

Note: The 'Others' sector includes mining, construction, and utility sectors.

Source: Author's calculations; data from APO.

terms of the sectors that absorbed the labor reallocated from the agricultural sector during 1990–2010. For China, this sector was services, which increased its employment share by 15.8 percentage points, from 18.5 per cent in 1990 to 34.3 per cent in 2010. China's manufacturing sector, at the same time, absorbed only a small share of the reallocated labor, increasing its employment share by 2.8 percentage points, from 15.1 per cent in 1990 to 17.9 per cent in 2010.[22] In contrast, India's manufacturing sector absorbed most of the reallocated labor from agriculture, expanding its employment share by 11.5 percentage points over 1990–2010, from 10.2 per cent in 1990 to 21.8 per cent in 2010; while its services sector increased its employment share only moderately by 3 percentage points, from 19.6 per cent in 1990 to 22.6 per cent in 2010. The distinctive patterns of labor reallocation observed for the two countries during 1990–2010 suggest the depth of their structural change and economic transformation. For China, the services sector enlarged far more than the manufacturing sector, although the latter is its traditional strength. In fact, Nomura and Lau (2012) found that the engine of growth in China has started shifting more toward services in recent years. For India, the manufacturing sector expanded much faster than the services sector despite the fact that the services sector has always been its leading sector for driving economic growth. It is worth noting that China and India can rely more on their services sector to foster growth in the decade to come. This sector is capable of not only absorbing more labor migrating from other sectors but also boosting productivity growth through its within-sector structural change.[23]

Urbanization is associated with structural change. The urbanization process plays an important role in enhancing the efficiency of the economy. Over 1990–2010, China recorded a phenomenal pace of urbanization, expanding the share of its urban population in total by 18 percentage points, from 27 per cent in 1990 to 45 per cent in 2010. At the same time, rapid urbanization was also observed for India, which increased the share of its urban population in total over the period by 5 percentage points, from 25 per cent in 1990 to 30 per cent in 2010 (Figure 5.20).

---

[22] This observation for China supports the findings of van Ark and Timmer (2003), who investigated the pattern of growth of nine Asian economies in 1963–2001, that while reallocating resources from agriculture to industry is a powerful source of growth for low-income countries in the region, the shift of resources within the manufacturing sector from relatively labor-intensive and low-productivity industries toward high-productivity industries is also an important driver of growth.

[23] Jorgenson and Timmer (2011) found significant heterogeneity among different service subsectors in their study of productivity performance and employment expansion in the US, Japan, and Europe. This finding implies that the policies that effectively foster structural change within the services sector can boost growth in both the sector and the economy.

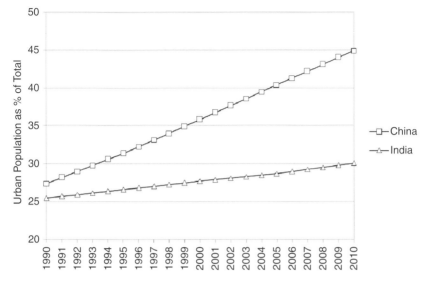

Source: WDI.

Figure 5.20   Urbanization: China and India, 1990–2010

China's urbanization process over the past three decades, which was phenomenal in both scale and speed, was successful according to Yusuf and Nabeshima (2008) (see Box 5.3 for details). China's urbanization has been driven by its effective urbanization strategies. These strategies have enabled the cities in China to mobilize a large proportion of GDP to invest in infrastructure and urban development to foster their economic vibrancy and efficiency. For example, in the 1990s, Shanghai spent 11–14 per cent of GDP to redevelop the city, while Beijing and Tianjin spend over 10 per cent of their GDP on urban infrastructure (Yusuf and Nabeshima, 2008). China's urbanization strategies, in fact, have been an integral part of their catching-up endeavor to achieve rapid growth using intensive capital accumulation and robust efficiency improvements.

China and India, especially China, have also benefited from economies of scale and cluster formation during 1990–2010. Thanks to their colossal domestic markets, these two countries have far more favorable conditions than other Asian economies for achieving economies of scale. At the same time, clusters have been taking roots in both countries in different locations and industries. This cluster formation has been particularly rapid and vibrant in China. In particular, multiple clusters, which range from toys, footwear and garments to computers, electronic components,

BOX 5.3   CHINA'S URBANIZATION STRATEGIES:
           INITIAL SUCCESS AND KEY SUCCESS
           FACTORS

China's urbanization in the three decades of its reform, 1980–
2010, was phenomenal in both speed and scale. China's urban
population increased by 110 million in the first decade, 1980–
1990, 150 million in the second decade, 1990–2000, and by over
200 million in the third decade, 2000–2010 (China's urban population increased from 190 million in 1980 to 300 million in 1990,
450 million in 2000 and 653 million in 2010). Urbanization, in fact,
has been a dominant economic force driving China's outstanding economic performance during its reform period. In 2007, the
urban economy generated 80 per cent of China's domestic output
(Yusuf and Nabeshima, 2008).

   Yusuf and Nabeshima (2008), among many studies, assessed
that China's urbanization process over the past three decades
had been relatively successful. Compared to cities in other
middle- and lower-middle-income countries:

● China's urban economy is more vibrant.
● Urban poverty and unemployment are relatively low in
  Chinese cities.
● China's cities are more effective at containing the spread of
  slums and crime.
● Chinese cities have effectively contained urban sprawl,
  with the frugal use of land space for urban development.

According to Yusuf and Nabeshima (2008), the following inter-
related factors have contributed to the effectiveness of China's
strategies to manage its rapid urbanization:

● Chinese cities enjoy a high degree of autonomy and
  assume more responsibilities, putting a particularly high
  premium on the planning and managerial skills of local
  authorities.
● Many cities in China are governed by able and energetic
  leaders. Intense competition among cities and provinces
  may be a factor that has enabled more competent people
  to rise to power.

- Cities in China have been more effective at mobilizing resources, upgrading infrastructure, and wooing industry than the cities in other middle- and lower-middle-income countries.

autos and software, have rapidly developed in three major urban industrial agglomerations: the Pearl River Delta region centered on Shenzhen, Dongguan, and Foshan; the Yangtze River region around the Shanghai–Suzhou axis; and the Bohai region in the vicinity of Beijing and Tianjin (McGee et al., 2007). As an example, the electronics cluster in the city of Dongguan can produce 95 per cent of the parts and components needed for the manufacture and processing of personal computers, and for several specific products, the factories located within the city account for over 40 per cent of global production (Gill and Kharas, 2007).

One of the key factors underlying the success of China's industrial clusters is the effective support of local governments (Zeng, 2010). According to Zeng (2010), the support of local governments in promoting cluster formation is focused on four areas: upgrading infrastructure; enhancing regulations, assuring quality, and setting standards; providing incentives for technological upgrades and innovation; and helping clusters to attract qualified enterprises.

Compared to China, the vibrancy of India's cluster formation is less apparent. However, the growth of its Bollywood filmed entertainment cluster in Mumbai and the software cluster in Bangalore over the past 20 years was remarkable (Lorenzen and Mudambi, 2013).

In summary, this section examines the efforts of China and India to promote their growth using a strategic policy framework that allows a developing country to achieve rapid growth through intensive capital accumulation while sustaining high rates of investment efficiency. The examination shows that both China and India made significant progress on most of the policy priorities, with the exception of the control of corruption, along the three strategic directions of the proposed catching-up framework: exploiting the 'backwardness' advantage, upgrading their absorptive capabilities, and creating favorable conditions for investment, structural change, and efficiency improvements. This investigation also reveals that during the 1990–2010 period, China notably outweighed India on all of the examined measures with the exception of the control of corruption. This finding, to a certain extent, explains why China outperformed India over this period.

5.5   CONCLUSION

This chapter aims to turn the insights gained from the analyses of the previous chapters into a strategic policy framework that allows low- and middle-income countries, both inside and outside of Asia, to achieve sustained high economic growth. The growth model of the successful Asian economies, in fact, is not outside of the realm of development economics. Rather, this model is the outcome of a strategic policy framework that focuses on fostering and sustaining the high marginal product of capital. In other words, this policy framework pays strategic attention to enhancing the attractive rates of capital investments. While the sequence and design of specific policies may differ across countries due to their idiosyncrasies, the concepts, strategic directions, and policy priorities underlying the strategic policy framework presented in this chapter can be replicated to all countries.

The results from the previous chapters confirm that Developing Asia far outperformed the groups of industrialized countries and other developing economies on economic growth over the past two decades, 1990–2010. As a result, many economies in the region have made substantial progress toward catching up on per capita income, while the group as a whole has become a major driver of the world's economic growth. Furthermore, the growth pattern of developing Asian economies in the past two decades is consistent with the growth model followed by the successful East Asian economies in the previous decades, which is characterized by sustained high growth driven by intensive capital accumulation. The remarkable performance of China and India during 1990–2010 indicates that this growth model works not only for small or mid-sized economies but also for very large countries, not only for the past but also for the present, and not only for East Asia but also for South Asia.

The results from the previous chapters of the book also reveal that the secret of the Asian economic growth model lies not in achieving high TFP growth but in sustaining reasonable TFP growth despite the intensive mobilization of factor inputs over extended periods. Although the Asian growth model may appear superficially similar to the Soviet growth model in their link between rapid growth and intensive capital accumulation, the two models are fundamentally different. Three distinctive features that distinguish these two models are related to openness, market mechanisms, and the role of the private sector. The Asian growth model embraces openness using export-led growth strategies and heavily relies on market forces and the private sector, including FDI enterprises, for the allocation of resources and the stimulation of structural change. In contrast, the Soviet model is characterized by an inward orientation and import-substitution strategies, while its resource allocations totally depend on the government's decisions and the state-owned sector.

The strategic policy framework that allowed successful Asian economies to sustain reasonable TFP growth despite their intensive capital mobilization focuses on relentless efforts to promote the marginal product of capital. This framework consists of three strategic directions: (1) exploiting the 'backwardness' advantage; (2) upgrading the absorptive capability; and (3) creating favorable conditions for investment, structural change, and efficiency improvements. The three strategic directions with their elaborated policy priorities can be used as a policy framework for a developing country to foster its catching-up endeavor. In this framework, exploiting the 'backwardness' advantage involves reform efforts to open up the economy, to attract FDI and deepen FDI's integration with the domestic economy, to promote exports, and to import ideas, technologies, and know-how. Upgrading the absorptive capability focuses on fostering human capital formation, building innovation capacity, and strengthening the national learning capabilities. The fundamental task in fostering human capital formation is to establish a high quality educational system that ultimately links to the scientific and technological development of the world economy. At the same time, attracting global talent, especially from the national diaspora, is an effective way to fast-track capital formation in the age of globalization—that is, globalization must be pursued in relation not only to capital but also to labor and the improvement of labor quality. Creating favorable conditions for investment, structural change, and efficiency improvements requires building good governance, improving the business environment, and effective development strategies, which foster structural change, rapid but efficient urbanization, and economic agglomeration.

Examining the efforts of China and India—two very large and rapidly growing economies during 1990–2010—along the key dimensions of the strategic policy framework summarized above confirms the predictive power of the framework and shows that the economic processes involved apply equally to large economies as well to the earlier rapidly growing but smaller 'Tiger' economies of Hong Kong, Singapore, South Korea and Taiwan. Both China and India made significant progress on almost all of the examined dimensions, which means that they have made serious efforts to promote growth through the Asian growth model. Furthermore, China notably outweighed India on almost all of the efforts suggested by the model, which means that the notable outperformance of China over India in terms of growth during 1990–2010 was determined by the degree of their success in embracing the Catch-up Policy framework.

The examination exercise, however, also reveals the notable risks and problems that China and India face in sustaining their outstanding growth in the years to come. While both countries share the same alarming concern about the deterioration in their corruption control and the slowdown in government performance enhancement, the two countries are facing different sets of urgent challenges.

For China, three urgent challenges are salient. First, China needs to maintain its image and true intention as a peaceful rising nation. China's economy and its growth model heavily rely on the world for markets, resources, and production networks; as a result, harmonious development not only at home but also in the entire Asia-Pacific region will be essential for China to sustain its momentum of success. Second, enhancing its effectiveness in intellectual property protection is becoming more critical for China to continue its successful exploitation of the 'backwardness' advantage as the country moves closer to the world technology frontier and also to allow China to protect its own innovative products.[24] Third, China needs to make more imperative efforts toward sustainable development, reducing environmental pollution and increasing energy efficiency. At its current levels of pollution generation and energy efficiency, it would be much more difficult for China to continue to expand its manufacturing production base as rapidly as it has over the past two decades.

The most urgent challenges facing India, however, are different. One challenge is to maintain macroeconomic stability because the country's performance in controlling inflation and its budget deficit is not strong compared to most of its Asian peers. Second, India needs to step up its efforts to upgrade its infrastructure and reduce the costs of investment because its progress has been too far behind China in this area. Third, India needs to strategically focus on the competitiveness of its manufacturing sector. As this sector rapidly expanded over the past two decades, its labor productivity fell below the economy average (Table 5.5), which means that the country needs to provide substantial support and stimulation for industrial restructuring and upgrading. In addition, India also needs to address the lack of dynamism in its states and cities in comparison to China. India may need institutional reforms to provide states and cities with more autonomy and incentives to spur competition between them and to foster bottom-up reforms, which are all critical to boosting the country's performance in its next phase of development.

---

[24] Gassmann et al. (2012) pointed out that the current state of intellectual property protection is a dark side to innovating in China. Intellectual property theft has risen exponentially. It is estimated that China's output of imitations accounted for 65–70 per cent of all fake goods globally.

References

Abramovitz, M. (1986). Catching up, forging ahead, and falling behind. *Journal of Economic History*, *46*(2), 385–406.

Acemoglu, D. and Ventura, J. (2002). The world income distribution. *Quarterly Journal of Economics*, *117*(2), 659–694.

Aghion, P. and Howitt, P.W. (1992). A model of growth through creative destruction. *Econometrica*, *60*(2), 323–351.

Aghion, P. and Howitt, P.W. (1998). *Endogenous growth theory*. Cambridge, MA: MIT Press.

Asian Development Bank (2011). *Asia 2050: Realizing the Asian century*. Manila: Asian Development Bank.

Bajpai, N. (2004). *Foreign direct investment in China's provinces: Lessons for the state of Gujarat*. CGSD Working Paper No. 13, Center on Globalization and Sustainable Development, The Earth Institute at Columbia University.

Barro, R. and Lee, J.-W. (2010). *A new data set of educational attainment in the world, 1950–2010*. NBER Working Paper No. 15902, National Bureau of Economic Research.

Barro, R.J. and Sala-i-Martin, X. (1995). *Economic growth*. New York: McGraw Hill.

Bosworth, B. and Collins, S.M. (2008). Accounting for growth: Comparing China and India. *Journal of Economic Perspectives*, *22*(1), 45–66.

Caselli, F. (2008). Growth accounting. In S.N. Durlauf and L.E. Blume, *The new Palgrave dictionary of economics*. New York: Palgrave Macmillan.

Caselli, F. and Feyrer, J. (2007). The marginal product of capital. *Quarterly Journal of Economics*, *122*(2), 535–568.

Chen, Z., Jin, Y., and Lu, M. (2008). Economic opening and industrial agglomeration in China. In M. Fujita, S. Kumagai, and K. Nishikimi, *Economic integration in East Asia: Perspectives from spatial and neo-classical economics* (pp. 276–315). Cheltenham, UK and Northampton, MA, USA: Edward Elgar Publishing.

Christensen, L.R. and Jorgenson, D.W. (1969). The measurement of U.S. real capital input, 1929–1967. *Review of Income and Wealth*, *15*(4), 293–320.

Christensen, L.R. and Jorgenson, D.W. (1970). U.S. real product and real factor input, 1929–1967. *Review of Income and Wealth*, *16*(1), 19–50.

Christensen, L.R., Jorgenson, D.W., and Lau, L.J. (1975). Transcendental logarithmic utility functions. *The American Economic Review*, *65*(3), 367–383.

Coe, D. and Helpman, E. (1995). International R&D spillovers. *European Economic Review*, *39*(5), 859–887.

Das, D.K. (2007). Trade barriers in manufacturing. In K. Basu, *Oxford companion to economics in India* (pp. 531–534). New Delhi: Oxford University Press.

Diewert, W.E. (1976). Exact and superlative index numbers. *Journal of Econometrics*, *4*(2), 115–145.

Easterly, W. (1995). Explaining miracles: Growth regressions meet the gang of four. In T. Ito and A.O. Krueger, *Growth theories in light of the East Asian experience* (pp. 267–299). Chicago, IL: University of Chicago Press.

Edwards, S. (1992). Trade orientation, distortions and growth in developing countries. *Journal of Development Economics*, *39*(1), 31–57.

Edwards, S. (1998). Openness, productivity and growth: What do we really know? *The Economic Journal*, *108*(447), 383–398.

Fagerberg, J. (2000). Technological progress, structural change and productivity growth: A comparative study. *Structural Change and Economic Dynamics*, *11*(4), 393–411.

Fagerberg, J. and Srholec, M. (2008). National innovation systems, capabilities and economic development. *Research Policy*, *37*(9), 1417–1435.

Fogel, R.W. (2011). The impact of the Asian miracle on the theory of economic growth. In D.L. Costa and N.R. Lamoreaux, *Understanding long run economic growth: Geography, institutions, and the knowledge economy*. Chicago, IL: University of Chicago Press.

Galbraith, J.K. and Lu, J. (2000). *Sustainable development and the open-door policy in China*. Council on Foreign Relations Press.

Gassmann, O., Beckenbauer, A., and Friesike, S. (2012). *Profiting from innovation in China*. Heidelberg: Springer.

Gerschenkron, A. (1962). *Economic backwardness in historical perspective*. Cambridge, MA: Belknap Press of Harvard University Press.

Gill, I. and Kharas, H. (2007). *An East Asia renaissance: Ideas for economic growth*. Washington, DC: World Bank Publications.

Grossman, G.M. and Helpman, E. (1991). *Innovation and growth in the global economy*. Cambridge, MA: MIT Press.

Grossman, G.M. and Helpman, E. (1994). Endogenous innovation in the theory of growth. *The Journal of Economic Perspectives*, *8*(1), 23–44.

Haraguchi, N. (2009). *Impact of the global economic crisis on the Thai automotive industry: From the perspective of the interplay between shocks and the industrial structure*. Working Paper 07/2009, Research and Statistics Branch, United Nations Industrial Development Organization.

Hausmann, R., Pritchett, L., and Rodrik, D. (2005). Growth accelerations. *Journal of Economic Growth*, *10*(4), 303–329.

Heilmann, S. (2008). Policy experimentation in China's economic rise. *Studies in Comparative International Development*, *43*(1), 1–26.

Hicks, G. (1989). The four little dragons: An enthusiast's reading guide. *Asian–Pacific Economic Literature*, *3*(2), 35–49.

Hornstein, A. and Krusell, P. (1996). Can technology improvements cause productivity slowdowns? In *NBER Macroeconomics Annual 11* (pp. 209–259). Cambridge, MA: MIT Press.

Jaggi, G., Rundle, M., Rosen, D.H., and Takahashi, Y. (1996). *China's economic reforms: Chronology and statistics*. Working Paper Series WP96–5, Peterson Institute for International Economics.

Jansen, M.B. (2000). *The making of modern Japan*. Cambridge, MA: Belknap Press of Harvard University Press.

Jones, C.I. (1997). On the evolution of the world income distribution. *Journal of Economic Perspectives*, *11*(3), 19–36.

Jorgenson, D.W. (2001). Information technology and the U.S. economy. *American Economic Review*, *91*(1), 1–32.

Jorgenson, D.W. (2003). Information technology and the G7 economies. *World Economics*, *4*(4), 139–169.

Jorgenson, D.W. and Griliches, Z. (1967). The explanation of productivity change. *The Review of Economic Studies*, *34*(3), 249–283.

Jorgenson, D.W. and Stiroh, K.J. (1999). Information technology and growth. *American Economic Review*, *89*(2), 109–115.

Jorgenson, D.W. and Stiroh, K.J. (2000). *Raising the speed limit: US economic growth in the information age*. OECD Economics Department Working Papers 261, OECD Publishing.

Jorgenson, D.W. and Timmer, M.P. (2011). Structural change in advanced nations: A new set of stylised facts. *Scandinavian Journal of Economics*, *113*(1), 1–29.

Jorgenson, D.W. and Vu, K.M. (2005). Information technology and the world economy. *Scandinavian Journal of Economics*, *107*(4), 631–650.

Jorgenson, D.W. and Vu, K.M. (2010). Potential growth of the world economy. *Journal of Policy Modeling*, *32*(5), 615–631.

Jorgenson, D.W. and Vu, K.M. (2011). The rise of developing Asia and the new economic order. *Journal of Policy Modeling*, *33*(5), 698–716.

Jorgenson, D.W., Gollop, F.M., and Fraumeni, B.M. (1987). *Productivity and U.S. economic growth*. Cambridge, MA: Harvard University Press.

Jorgenson, D.W., Ho, M.S., and Stiroh, K.J. (2003). Lessons from the US growth resurgence. *Journal of Policy Modeling*, *25*(5), 453–470.

Jorgenson, D.W., Ho, M.S., and Stiroh, K.J. (2005). *Productivity, volume 3: Information technology and the American growth resurgence.* Cambridge, MA: The MIT Press.

Kaufmann, D., Kraay, A., and Mastruzzi, M. (2010). *The worldwide governance indicators: Methodology and analytical issues.* Policy Research Working Paper No. 5430, World Bank.

Kawai, M. and Petri, P.A. (2010). *Asia's role in the global economic architecture.* ADBI Working Paper Series No. 235, Asian Development Bank.

Kim, E.M. and Park, G.-S. (2011). The Chaebol. In B.-K. Kim and E.F. Vogel, *The Park Chung Hee era: The transformation of South Korea.* Cambridge, MA: Harvard University Press.

Kim, J.I. and Lau, L. (1994). The sources of economic growth of the East Asian newly industrialized countries. *Journal of the Japanese and International Economies*, 8(3), 235–271.

Kneller, R. (2005). Frontier technology, absorptive capacity and distance. *Oxford Bulletin of Economics and Statistics*, 67(1), 1–23.

Kretschmer, T. (2012). *Information and communication technologies and productivity growth: A survey of the literature.* OECD Digital Economy Papers 195, OECD Publishing.

Krugman, P. (1994). The myth of Asia's miracle. *Foreign Affairs*, 73, 62–78.

Lee, K.Y. (2000). *From third world to first: The Singapore story 1965–2000: Memoirs of Lee Kuan Yew.* Singapore: Singapore Press Holdings.

Lewis, W.A. (1955). *The theory of economic growth.* Homewood, IL: Richard D. Irwin, Inc.

Leys, S. (1997). *The analects of Confucius.* New York: W.W. Norton & Company.

Lin, J.Y. (2009). *Economic development and transition: Thought, strategy, and viability.* Cambridge: Cambridge University Press.

Lin, J.Y. (2011). *Demystifying the Chinese economy.* Project Syndicate, December 22, 2011, available at http://www.project-syndicate.org/commentary/demystifying-the-chinese-economy.

Lin, J.Y. (2012). *New structural economics: A framework for rethinking development and policy.* Washington, DC: World Bank.

Lorenzen, M. and Mudambi, R. (2013). Clusters, connectivity and catch-up: Bollywood and Bangalore in the global economy. *Journal of Economic Geography*, 13(3), 501–534.

Lucas, R.E. (1988). On the mechanics of economic development. *Journal of Monetary Economics*, 22(1), 3–42.

Maddison, A. (1983). A comparison of levels of GDP per capita in developed and developing countries, 1700–1980. *The Journal of Economic History*, *43*(1), 27–41.

Maddison, A. (1987). Growth and slowdown in advanced capitalist economies: Techniques of quantitative assessment. *Journal of Economic Literature*, *25*(2), 649–698.

Maddison, A. (2001). *The world economy: A millennial perspective*. Paris: OECD Publishing.

Madhani, P.M. (2008). Indian software success story: A resource-based view of competitive advantage. *The Icfaian Journal of Management Research*, *7*(8), 61–83.

Mahbubani, K. (2008). *The new Asian hemisphere: The irresistible shift of global power to the East*. New York: Public Affairs.

Mahbubani, K. (2013). *The great convergence: Asia, the West, and the logic of one world*. New York: Public Affairs.

Marti, M.E. (2002). *China and the legacy of Deng Xiaoping: From communist revolution to capitalist evolution*. Dulles, VA: Potomac Books.

McGee, T., Lin, G.C., Wang, M., Marton, A., and Wu, J. (2007). *China's urban space: Development under market socialism*. London: Routledge.

Moon, C.-I. and Jun, B.-J. (2011). Modernization strategy: Ideas and influences. In B.-K. Kim and E.F. Vogel, *The Park Chung Hee era: The transformation of South Korea*. Cambridge, MA: Harvard University Press.

Naughton, B. (1995). Deng Xiaoping: The economist. In D. Shambaugh, *Deng Xiaoping: Portrait of a Chinese statesman*. Oxford: Oxford University Press.

Neo, B.S. and Chen, G. (2007). *Dynamic governance: Embedding culture, capabilities and change in Singapore*. Singapore: World Scientific Publishing Company.

Nomura, K. and Lau, E.Y. (2012). *APO productivity databook 2012*. Tokyo: Asian Productivity Organization.

O, W.-C. (2009). *The Korea story: President Park Jung-Hee's leadership and the Korean industrial revolution*. Seoul: Wisdom Tree.

OECD (2001). *Measuring Productivity – OECD Manual*. Paris: OECD Publishing.

Oliner, S.D. and Sichel, D.E. (2000). The resurgence of growth in the late 1990s: Is information technology the story? *Journal of Economic Perspectives*, *14*(4), 3–22.

Park, C.-H. (1971). *To build a nation*. Washington, DC: Acropolis Books (reprinted 2009).

Parsons, T. (1937). *The structure of social action*. New York: The Free Press.

Perkins, D. (2001). Industrial and financial policy in China and Vietnam.

In J.E. Stiglitz and S. Yusuf, *Rethinking the East Asian miracle.* Washington, DC: World Bank Publications.

Porter, M.E. (1998). Clusters and the new economics of competition. *Harvard Business Review, November–December*, 77–90.

Porter, M.E. (2007). *Clusters and economic policy: Aligning public policy with the new economics of competition.* White Paper, Institute for Strategy and Competitiveness, Harvard Business School.

Prescott, E.C. (1998). Needed: A theory of total factor productivity. *International Economic Review*, *39*(3), 525–551.

Psacharopoulos, G. and Patrinos, H. (2004). Returns to investment in education: A further update. *Education Economics*, *12*(2), 111–134.

Roelandt, T.J. and Hertog, P.D. (1999). Cluster analysis and cluster-based policy making: The state of the art. In OECD, *Boosting innovation: The cluster approach.* Paris: OECD Publishing.

Rogers, M. (2004). Absorptive capability and economic growth: How do countries catch-up? *Cambridge Journal of Economics*, *28*(4), 577–596.

Romer, P.M. (1986). Increasing returns and long-run growth. *Journal of Political Economy*, *94*(5), 1002–1037.

Romer, P.M. (1990). Endogenous technological change. *Journal of Political Economy*, *98*(5), 71–102.

Romer, P.M. (1992). *Two strategies for economic development: Using ideas and producing ideas.* World Bank Annual Conference on Economic Development. Washington, DC: World Bank.

Romer, P.M. (1993). Idea gaps and object gaps in economic development. *Journal of Monetary Economics*, *32*(3), 543–573.

Rosenstein-Rodan, P.N. (1961). International aid for underdeveloped countries. *Review of Economics and Statistics*, *43*(2), 107–148.

Sachs, J.D. (2012). *The price of civilization: Reawakening American virtue and prosperity.* New York: Random House Trade Paperbacks.

Sala-i-Martin, X. (2006). The world distribution of income: Falling poverty and . . . convergence, period. *Quarterly Journal of Economics*, *121*(2), 351–397.

Shin, B.S. (1970). *Major speeches by Korea's Park Chung Hee.* Seoul: Hollym Corporation.

Solow, R.M. (1957). Technical change and the aggregate production function. *Review of Economics and Statistics*, *39*(3), 312–320.

Srinivasan, T.N. (2011). *Growth, sustainability, and India's economic reforms.* New York: Oxford University Press.

Stern, S., Porter, M.E., and Furman, J.L. (2000). *The determinants of national innovative capacity.* NBER Working Paper 7876, National Bureau of Economic Research.

Subbotina, T.P. and Sheram, K.A. (2000). *Beyond economic growth: Meeting the challenges of global development.* Washington, DC: World Bank Publications.

Tai, H.-C. (1989). The oriental alternative: An hypothesis on culture and economy. In H.-C. Tai, *Confucianism and economic development: An oriental alternative* (pp. 6–37). Washington, DC: The Washington Institute Press.

Taube, M. and Ogutcu, M. (2002). Main issues on foreign investment in China's regional development: Prospects and policy challenges. In OECD, *Foreign direct investment in China: Challenges and prospects for regional development.* Paris: OECD Publishing.

Thomas, J.W. (2001). *Institutional Innovation and the Prospects for Transference, Part I: Transferring Singaporean Institutions to Suzhou, China.* John F. Kennedy School of Government Working Papers Series RWP02–001.

Tsunoda, R., De Bary, W., and Keene, D. (1958). *Sources of Japanese tradition.* New York: Columbia University Press.

United Nations (2002). *World economic and social survey 2002 – Trends and policies in the world economy.* New York: United Nations, Department of Economic and Social Affairs.

van Ark, B. and Timmer, M. (2003). *Asia's productivity performance and potential: The contribution of sectors and structural change.* Groningen Growth and Development Centre, University of Groningen.

Verspagen, B. (1991). A new empirical approach to catching up or falling behind. *Structural Change and Economic Dynamics, 2*(2), 359–380.

Weber, M. (1930). *The Protestant ethic and the spirit of capitalism.* Translated by T. Parsons. New York: Scribner's.

Wei, S.-J. (1995). The open door policy and China's rapid growth: Evidence from city-level data. In T. Ito and A.O. Krueger, *Growth theories in light of the East Asian experience, NBER–EASE, volume 4* (pp. 73–104). National Bureau of Economic Research.

Wei, X. (2000). Acquisition of technology capability through special economic zones (SEZs): The case of Shenzhen. *Industry and Innovation, 7*(2), 199–221.

Weil, D.N. (2009). *Economic growth, 2nd edition.* Boston: Pearson Addison Wesley.

Wong, J. (2001). The economics of the Naxun. In J. Wong and Y. Zheng, *The Nanxun legacy and China's development in the Post-Deng era.* Singapore: Singapore University Press.

Wong, P.-K. (2002). ICT production and diffusion in Asia digital dividends or digital divide? *Information Economics and Policy, 14*(2), 167–187.

World Bank (1993). *The East Asian miracle: Economic growth and public policy*. New York: Oxford University Press.

World Bank (2008). *The growth report: Strategies for sustained growth and inclusive development*. Washington, DC: World Bank.

World Bank (2013). *China 2030: Building a modern, harmonious, and creative society*. Washington, DC: World Bank.

Yeung, A.K., Ulrich, D.O., Nason, S.W., and Von Glinow, M.A. (1999). *Organizational learning capability*. New York: Oxford University Press.

Young, A. (1995). The tyranny of numbers: Confronting the statistical realities of the East Asian growth experience. *Quarterly Journal of Economics*, *110*(3), 641–680.

Yusuf, S. and Nabeshima, K. (2008). Optimizing urban development. In S. Yusuf and T. Saich, *China urbanizes: Consequences, strategies, and policies* (pp. 1–40). Washington, DC: World Bank Publications.

Zeng, D. (2010). *Building engines of growth and competitiveness in China: Experience with special economic zones and industrial clusters*. Washington, DC: World Bank Publications.

Zhao, L. and Zhu, J. (2009). China attracting global talent: Central and local initiatives. *China: An International Journal*, *7*(2), 323–335.

Zweig, D. (2006). Competing for talent: China's strategies to reverse brain drain. *International Labor Review*, *145*(1–2), 65–90.

Index